Learning OpenCV 3 Application Development

Build, create, and deploy your own computer vision applications with the power of OpenCV

Samyak Datta

BIRMINGHAM - MUMBAI

Learning OpenCV 3 Application Development

First published: December 2016

Production reference: 1131216

Published by Packt Publishing Ltd.

Livery Place

35 Livery Street

Birmingham B3 2PB, UK.

ISBN 978-1-78439-145-4

www.packtpub.com

Credits

Author

Samyak Datta

Reviewer

Nikolaus Gradwohl

Commissioning Editor

Kunal Parikh

Acquisition Editor

Sonali Vernekar

Content Development Editor

Nikhil Borkar

Technical Editor

Hussain Kanchwala

Copy Editor

Safis Editing

Project Coordinator

Sheejal Shah

Proofreader

Safis Editing

Indexer

Rekha Nair

Graphics

Abhinash Sahu

Production Coordinator

Shraddha Falebhai

About the Author

Samyak Datta has a bachelor's and a master's degree in Computer Science from the Indian Institute of Technology, Roorkee. He is a computer vision and machine learning enthusiast. His first contact with OpenCV was in 2013 when he was working on his master's thesis, and since then, there has been no looking back. He has contributed to OpenCV's GitHub repository. Over the course of his undergraduate and master's degrees, Samyak has had the opportunity to engage with both the industry and research. He worked with Google India and Media.net (Directi) as a software engineering intern, where he was involved with projects ranging from machine learning and natural language processing to computer vision. As of 2016, he is working at the Center for Visual Information Technology (CVIT) at the Indian Institute of Information Technology, Hyderabad.

About the Reviewer

Nikolaus Gradwohl was born 1976 in Vienna, Austria and always wanted to become an inventor like Gyro Gearloose. When he got his first Atari, he figured out that being a computer programmer is the closest he could get to that dream. He has written programs for nearly anything that can be programmed, ranging from 8-bit microcontrollers to mainframes, for a living. In his free time, he collects programming languages and operating systems.

He is the author of the book *Processing 2: Creative Coding Hotshot*. You can see some of his work on his blog at `http://www.local-guru.net/`.

www.PacktPub.com

For support files and downloads related to your book, please visit www.PacktPub.com.

Did you know that Packt offers eBook versions of every book published, with PDF and ePub files available? You can upgrade to the eBook version at www.PacktPub.com and as a print book customer, you are entitled to a discount on the eBook copy. Get in touch with us at service@packtpub.com for more details.

At www.PacktPub.com, you can also read a collection of free technical articles, sign up for a range of free newsletters and receive exclusive discounts and offers on Packt books and eBooks.

https://www.packtpub.com/mapt

Get the most in-demand software skills with Mapt. Mapt gives you full access to all Packt books and video courses, as well as industry-leading tools to help you plan your personal development and advance your career.

Why subscribe?

- Fully searchable across every book published by Packt
- Copy and paste, print, and bookmark content
- On demand and accessible via a web browser

Table of Contents

Preface   1

Chapter 1: Laying the Foundation   7

  Digital image basics   8
    Pixel intensities   9
    Color depth and color spaces   9
    Color channels   11
  Introduction to the Mat class   11
  Exploring the Mat class: loading images   13
  Exploring the Mat class – declaring Mat objects   15
    Spatial dimensions of an image   15
    Color space or color depth   16
    Color channels   16
    Image size   17
    Default initialization value   17
  Digging inside Mat objects   19
  Traversing Mat objects   22
    Continuity of the Mat data matrix   23
    Image traversals   24
  Image enhancement   28
  Lookup tables   30
  Linear transformations   31
    Identity transformation   32
    Negative transformation   33
  Logarithmic transformations   38
    Log transformation   38
    Exponential or inverse-log transformation   46
  Summary   50

Chapter 2: Image Filtering   51

  Neighborhood of a pixel   52
  Image averaging   54
  Image filters   55
  Image averaging in OpenCV   58
  Blurring an image in OpenCV   65
  Gaussian smoothing   66

Gaussian function and Gaussian filtering   68
Gaussian filtering in OpenCV   75
Using your own filters in OpenCV   77
Image noise   79
Vignetting   81
Implementing Vignetting in OpenCV   83
Summary   88

Chapter 3: Image Thresholding   91

Binary images   92
Image thresholding basics   94
Image thresholding in OpenCV   95
Types of simple image thresholding   97
   Binary threshold   98
   Inverted binary threshold   99
   Truncate   99
   Threshold-to-zero   100
   Inverted threshold-to-zero   102
Adaptive thresholding   103
Morphological operations   108
Erosion and dilation   110
Erosion and dilation in OpenCV   112
Summary   114

Chapter 4: Image Histograms   115

The basics of histograms   116
Histograms in OpenCV   120
Plotting histograms in OpenCV   121
Color histograms in OpenCV   126
Multidimensional histograms in OpenCV   131
Summary   134

Chapter 5: Image Derivatives and Edge Detection   137

Image derivatives   138
Image derivatives in two dimensions   143
Visualizing image derivatives with OpenCV   145
The Sobel derivative filter   149
From derivatives to edges   152
The Sobel detector – a basic framework for edge detection   153
The Canny edge detector   158
Image noise and edge detection   163

Laplacian – yet another edge detection technique 165
Blur detection using OpenCV 167
Summary 170

Chapter 6: Face Detection Using OpenCV 171

Image classification systems 172
Face detection 174
Haar features 175
Integral image 177
Integral image in OpenCV 184
AdaBoost learning 184
Cascaded classifiers 185
Face detection in OpenCV 186
Controlling the quality of detected faces 191
Gender classification 194
Working with real datasets 195
Summary 196

Chapter 7: Affine Transformations and Face Alignment 197

Exploring the dataset 198
Running face detection on the dataset 200
Face alignment – the first step in facial analysis 203
Rotating faces 205
Image cropping — basics 215
Image cropping for face alignment 220
Face alignment – the complete pipeline 223
Summary 226

Chapter 8: Feature Descriptors in OpenCV 229

Introduction to the local binary pattern 230
A basic implementation of LBP 232
Variants of LBP 234
What does LBP capture? 237
Applying LBP to aligned facial images 239
A complete implementation of LBP 241
Putting it all together – the main() function 242
Summary 244

Chapter 9: Machine Learning with OpenCV 245

What is machine learning 246
Supervised and unsupervised learning 248

Revisiting the image classification framework 249
k-means clustering – the basics 250
    k-means clustering – the algorithm 252
    k-means clustering in OpenCV 256
k-nearest neighbors classifier – introduction 258
    k-nearest neighbors classifier – algorithm 259
    What k to use 261
    k-nearest neighbors classifier in OpenCV 263
    Some problems with kNN 265
    Some enhancements to kNN 266
Support vector machines (SVMs) – introduction 267
    Intuition into the workings of SVMs 268
Non-linear SVMs 272
    SVM in OpenCV 273
Using an SVM as a gender classifier 275
Overfitting 277
Cross-validation 278
Common evaluation metrics 281
The P-R curve 283
Some qualitative results 284
Summary 286

Appendix: Command-line Arguments in C++ 289
Introduction to command-line arguments 289
    Parsing command-line arguments 292
Summary 293

Index 295

Preface

The mission of this book is to explain to a novice the steps involved in building and deploying an end-to-end application in the domain of computer vision using OpenCV/C++. The book will start with instructions about installing the library and end with the reader having developed an application that does something tangible and useful in computer vision/machine learning. All concepts included in the text have been selected because of their frequent use and relevance in practical computer vision-based projects. To avoid being too theoretical, the description of concepts is accompanied simultaneously by the development of some end-to-end applications. The projects will be explained and developed step-by-step during the entire course of the text, as and when relevant theoretical concepts will be introduced. This will help the readers grasp the practical applications of the concept under study while not losing sight of the big-picture.

What this book covers

Chapter 1, *Laying the Foundation*, will lay the foundation for the basic data structures and containers in OpenCV for example, the Mat, Rect, Point and Scalar objects . It also explains the need for each of them as a separate data types by offering an insight into the possible use cases. A major portion of the chapter focuses on how OpenCV uses the Mat object to store images so that your code can access them, basics of scanning images using the Mat object and the concept of R, G and B color channels. After the readers are comfortable with working with images, we introduce the concept of pixel-based image transformations and show examples of simple code that can achieve contrast/brightness modification using simple Mat object traversals.

Chapter 2, *Image Filtering*, progresses to slightly advanced pixel traversal algorithms. We introduce the concepts of masks and image filtering and talk about the standard filters such as box filter, median filter, and Gaussian blur in OpenCV. Also, we will mathematically explain the concepts of convolution and correlation and show how a generic filter can be written using OpenCV's filter2D method. As a practical use case, we implement a popular and interesting image manipulation technique called the Vignette filter.

Chapter 3, *Image Thresholding*, talks about image thresholding, which is yet another process that frequently comes up in the solution to most computer vision problems. In this chapter, the readers are made to understand that the algorithms that fall into this domain basically involve operations that produce a binary image from a grayscale one. The different variants such as binary and inverted binary, are available as part of the OpenCV imgproc module are explained in detail. The chapter will also briefly touch upon the concepts of erosion and dilation (morphological transformations) as steps that takes place after thresholding.

Chapter 4, *Image Histograms*, talks about aggregating pixel values by discussing image histograms and histogram-related operations on images such as calculating and displaying histograms, the concept of color and multi-dimensional histograms.

Chapter 5, *Image Derivatives and Edge Detection*, focuses on other types of information that can be extracted from the pixels in our image. The readers are introduced to the concept of image derivatives and the discussion then moves on to the application of image derivatives in edge detection algorithms. A demonstration of the edge detection methods in OpenCV for example Sobel, Canny and Laplacian is presented. As a small practical use-case of the Laplacian, we demonstrate how it can be used to detect the blurriness of images.

Chapter 6, *Face Detection Using OpenCV*, talks about one of the most popular and ubiquitous problems in the computer vision community--detecting objects, specifically faces in images. The main motivation of this chapter is to take a look at the Haar-cascade classifier algorithm, which is used to detect faces and then go on to show how the complex algorithm can be run using a single line of OpenCV code. At this point, we introduce our programming project of predicting gender of a person from a facial image. The reader is made to realize that any system involving analysis of facial images (be it face recognition or gender, age or ethnicity prediction) requires an accurate and robust face detection as its first step.

Chapter 7, *Affine Transformations and Face Alignment*, serves as a natural successor to the preceding chapter. After detecting faces from images, the readers will be taught about the post-processing steps that are undertaken--geometric (Affine) transformations such resizing, cropping and rotating images. The need for such transformations is explained. All images in the gender classification project have to go through this step before feature extraction.

Chapter 8, *Feature Descriptors in OpenCV*, introduces the notion of feature descriptors. The readers realize that in order to infer meaningful information from images, one must construct appropriate features from the pixel values. In other words, images have to be converted into feature vectors before feeding them into a machine learning algorithm. To that end, the chapter also goes on to introduce the concept of local binary pattern as a feature and also talks about the details of implementation. We demonstrate the process of calculating the LBP features from the cropped and aligned facial images that we obtained in the previous chapters.

Chapter 9, *Machine Learning with OpenCV*, teaches the readers different classifiers and machine learning algorithms available as part of the OpenCV library and how they can be used to make meaningful predictions from data. The readers will witness the learning algorithms accept the feature vectors that they had computed in the previous chapters as input and make intelligent predictions as outputs. All the steps involved with using a learning algorithm--training, testing, cross validation, selection of hyper-parameters and evaluation of results--will be covered in detail.

Appendix, *Command-line Arguments in C++*, talks about command line arguments in C++ and how to extract the best possible use of them while writing OpenCV programs.

Who this book is for

Learning OpenCV 3.0 Application Development is the perfect book for anyone who wants to dive into the exciting world of image processing and computer vision. This book is aimed at programmers having a working knowledge of C++. A prior knowledge of OpenCV is not required. The book also doesn't assume any prior understanding of computer vision/machine learning algorithms as all concepts are explained from basic principles. Although, familiarity with these concepts would help. By the end of this book, readers will get a first-hand experience of building and deploying computer vision applications using OpenCV and C++ by following the detailed, step-by-step tutorials. They will begin to appreciate the power of OpenCV in simplifying seemingly challenging and intensive tasks such as contrast enhancement in images, edge detection, face detection and classification.

What you need for this book

The book assumes a basic, working knowledge of C++. However, prior knowledge of computer vision, image processing or machine learning is not assumed. You will need an OpenCV 3.1 installation in your systems to run the sample programs spread across the various chapters in this book. The setup and installation details have already been shared.

Conventions

In this book, you will find a number of text styles that distinguish between different kinds of information. Here are some examples of these styles and an explanation of their meaning.

Code words in text, database table names, folder names, filenames, file extensions, pathnames, dummy URLs, user input, and Twitter handles are shown as follows: "We can include other contexts through the use of the `include` directive."

A block of code is set as follows:

```
typedef Size_<int> Size2i;
typedef Size2i Size;
```

New terms and **important words** are shown in bold. Words that you see on the screen, for example, in menus or dialog boxes, appear in the text like this: "Clicking the **Next** button moves you to the next screen."

Warnings or important notes appear in a box like this.

Tips and tricks appear like this.

Reader feedback

Feedback from our readers is always welcome. Let us know what you think about this book—what you liked or disliked. Reader feedback is important for us as it helps us develop titles that you will really get the most out of.

To send us general feedback, simply e-mail feedback@packtpub.com, and mention the book's title in the subject of your message.

If there is a topic that you have expertise in and you are interested in either writing or contributing to a book, see our author guide at www.packtpub.com/authors.

Customer support

Now that you are the proud owner of a Packt book, we have a number of things to help you to get the most from your purchase.

Downloading the example code

You can download the example code files for this book from your account at http://www.packtpub.com. If you purchased this book elsewhere, you can visit http://www.packtpub.com/support and register to have the files e-mailed directly to you.

You can download the code files by following these steps:

1. Log in or register to our website using your e-mail address and password.
2. Hover the mouse pointer on the **SUPPORT** tab at the top.
3. Click on **Code Downloads & Errata**.
4. Enter the name of the book in the **Search** box.
5. Select the book for which you're looking to download the code files.
6. Choose from the drop-down menu where you purchased this book from.
7. Click on **Code Download**.

Once the file is downloaded, please make sure that you unzip or extract the folder using the latest version of:

- WinRAR / 7-Zip for Windows
- Zipeg / iZip / UnRarX for Mac
- 7-Zip / PeaZip for Linux

The code bundle for the book is also hosted on GitHub at https://github.com/PacktPublishing/Learning-OpenCV-3-Application-Development We also have other code bundles from our rich catalog of books and videos available at https://github.com/PacktPublishing/. Check them out!

Downloading the color images of this book

We also provide you with a PDF file that has color images of the screenshots/diagrams used in this book. The color images will help you better understand the changes in the output. You can download this file from `https://www.packtpub.com/sites/default/files/down loads/LearningOpenCV3ApplicationDevelopment_ColorImages.pdf`.

Errata

Although we have taken every care to ensure the accuracy of our content, mistakes do happen. If you find a mistake in one of our books—maybe a mistake in the text or the code—we would be grateful if you could report this to us. By doing so, you can save other readers from frustration and help us improve subsequent versions of this book. If you find any errata, please report them by visiting `http://www.packtpub.com/submit-errata`, selecting your book, clicking on the **Errata Submission Form link**, and entering the details of your errata. Once your errata are verified, your submission will be accepted and the errata will be uploaded to our website or added to any list of existing errata under the Errata section of that title.

To view the previously submitted errata, go to `https://www.packtpub.com/books/conten t/support` and enter the name of the book in the search field. The required information will appear under the Errata section.

Piracy

Piracy of copyrighted material on the Internet is an ongoing problem across all media. At Packt, we take the protection of our copyright and licenses very seriously. If you come across any illegal copies of our works in any form on the Internet, please provide us with the location address or website name immediately so that we can pursue a remedy.

Please contact us at `copyright@packtpub.com` with a link to the suspected pirated material.

We appreciate your help in protecting our authors and our ability to bring you valuable content.

Questions

If you have a problem with any aspect of this book, you can contact us at `questions@packtpub.com`, and we will do our best to address the problem.

1
Laying the Foundation

Computer vision is a field of study that associates itself with processing, analyzing, and understanding images. It essentially tries to mimic what the human brain does with images captured by our retina. These tasks are easy for human beings but are not so trivial for a computer. In fact, some of them are computationally so challenging that they are open research problems in the computer vision community. This book is designed to help you learn how to develop applications in OpenCV/C++. So, what is an ideal place to start learning about computer vision? Well, images form an integral component in any vision-based application. Images are everywhere! Everything that we do in the realm of computer vision boils down to performing operations on images.

This chapter will teach you the basics of images. We will discuss some common jargons that come up frequently while we talk about images in the context of computer vision. You will learn about pixels that make up images, the difference between color spaces and color channels and between grayscale and color images. Knowing about images is fine, but how do we transfer our knowledge about images to the domain of a programming language? That's when we introduce OpenCV.

OpenCV is an open source computer vision and machine learning library. It provides software programmers an infrastructure to develop computer vision-based applications. The library has its own mechanisms for efficient storage, processing, and retrieval of these images. This will be a major topic of discussion in this chapter. We will learn about the different data structures that the OpenCV developers have made available to the users. We will try to get a glimpse of the possible use cases for each of the data structures that we discuss. Although we try to cover as many data structures as possible, for starters, this chapter will focus on one particular data structure of paramount importance, which lies at the core of everything that we can possibly do with the library: the Mat object.

At the most basic level, the Mat object is what actually stores the two-dimensional grid of pixel intensity values that represent an image in the digital realm. The aim of this chapter is to equip the readers with sufficient knowledge regarding the inner workings of the Mat object so that they are able to write their first OpenCV program that does some *processing* on images by manipulating the underlying Mat objects in the code. This chapter will teach you different ways to traverse your images by going over the pixels one by one and applying some basic modifications to the pixel values. The end result will be some cool and fascinating effects on your images that will remind you of filters in Instagram or any popular image manipulation app

We will be embarking on our journey to learn something new. The first steps are always exciting! Most of this chapter will be devoted to developing and strengthening your basics–the very same basics that will, in the near future, allow us to take up challenging tasks in computer vision, such as face detection, facial analysis, and facial gender recognition.

In this chapter, we will cover the following topics:

- Some basic concepts from the realm of digital images: pixels, pixel intensities, color depth, color spaces, and channels
- A basic introduction to the Mat class in OpenCV and how the preceding concepts are implemented in code using Mat objects
- A simple traversal of the Mat class objects, which will allow us to access as well as process the pixel intensity values of the image, one by one
- Finally, as a practical application of what we will learn during the chapter, we also present the implementations of some image enhancement techniques that use the pixel traversal concepts

Digital image basics

Digital images are composed of a two-dimensional grid of pixels. These pixels can be thought of as the most fundamental and basic building blocks of images. When you view an image, either in its printed form on paper or in its digital format on computer screens, televisions, and mobile phones, what you see is a dense cluster of pixels arranged in a two-dimensional grid of rows and columns. Our eyes are of course not able to differentiate one individual pixel from its neighbor, and hence, images appear continuous to us. But, in reality, every image is composed of thousands and sometimes millions of discrete pixels.

Every single one of these pixels carries some *information*, and the sum total of all this *information* makes up the entire image and helps us see the bigger picture. Some of the pixels are light, some are dark. Each of them is colored with a different hue. There are grayscale images, which are commonly known as *black and white* images. We will avoid the use of the latter phrase because in image processing jargon, *black and white* refers to something else all together. It does not take an expert to deduce that colored images hold a lot more visual detail than their grayscale counterparts.

So, what pieces of *information* do these individual, tiny pixels store that enable them to create the images that they are a part of? How does a grayscale image differ from a colored one? Where do the colors come from? How many of them are there? Let's answer all these questions one by one.

Pixel intensities

There are countless sophisticated instruments that aid us in the process of acquiring images from nature. At the most basic level, they work by capturing light rays as they enter through the aperture of the instrument's lens and fall on a photographic plate. Depending on the orientation, illumination, and other parameters of the photo-capturing device, the amount of light that falls on each spatial coordinate of the film differs. This variation in the intensity of light falling on the film is encoded as pixel values when the image is stored in a digital format. Therefore, the *information* stored by a pixel is nothing more than a quantitative measure of the intensity of light that illuminated that particular spatial coordinate while the image was being captured. What this essentially means is that any image that you see, when represented digitally, is reduced to a two-dimensional grid of values where each pixel in the image is assigned a numerical value that is directly proportional to the intensity of light falling on that pixel in the natural image.

Color depth and color spaces

Now we come to the issue of encoding light intensity in pixel values. If you have studied a programming language before, you might be aware that the range and the type of values that you can store in any data structure are closely linked to the data type. A single bit can represent two values: 0 and 1. Eight bits (also known as a byte) can accommodate $2^8 = 256$ different values. Going further along, an `int` (represented using 32 bits in most architectures) data type has the capacity to represent roughly 4.29 billion different entries. Extending the same logic to digital images, the range of values that can be used to represent the pixel intensities depends on the data type we select for storing the image. In the world of image processing, the term **color space** or **color depth** is used in place of data type.

The most common and simplest color space for representing images is using 8 bits to represent the value of each pixel. This means that each pixel can have any value between 0 and 255 (inclusive). Images made up of such color spaces are called grayscale images. By convention, 0 represents black, 255 represents white, and each of the other values between 0 and 255 stand for a different shade of gray. The following figure demonstrates such an 8-bit color space. As we move from left to right in the following figure, the grayscale values in the image gradually change from 0 to 255:

So, if we have a grayscale image, such as the following one, then to a digital medium, it is merely a matrix of values–where each element of the matrix is a grayscale value between 0 (black) to 255 (white). This grid of pixel intensity values is represented for a tiny sub-section of the image (a portion of one of the wing mirrors of the car).

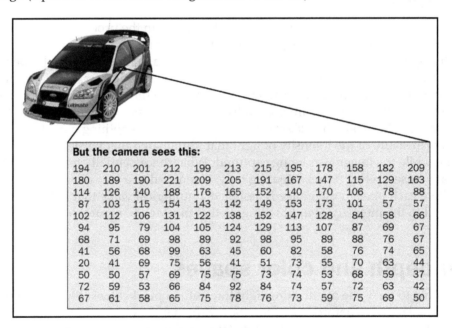

But the camera sees this:

194	210	201	212	199	213	215	195	178	158	182	209
180	189	190	221	209	205	191	167	147	115	129	163
114	126	140	188	176	165	152	140	170	106	78	88
87	103	115	154	143	142	149	153	173	101	57	57
102	112	106	131	122	138	152	147	128	84	58	66
94	95	79	104	105	124	129	113	107	87	69	67
68	71	69	98	89	92	98	95	89	88	76	67
41	56	68	99	63	45	60	82	58	76	74	65
20	41	69	75	56	41	51	73	55	70	63	44
50	50	57	69	75	75	73	74	53	68	59	37
72	59	53	66	84	92	84	74	57	72	63	42
67	61	58	65	75	78	76	73	59	75	69	50

Color channels

We have seen that using 8 bits is sufficient to represent grayscale images in digital media. But how do we represent colors? This brings us to the concept of color channels. A majority of the images that you come across are colored as opposed to grayscale. In the case of the image we just saw, each pixel is associated with a single intensity value (between 0 and 255). For color images, each pixel has three values or components: the *red* (*R*), *green* (*G*), and *blue* (*B*) components. It is a well-known fact that all possible colors can be represented as a combination of the *R*, *G*, and *B* components, and hence, the triplet of intensity values at each pixel are sufficient to represent the entire spectrum of colors in the image. Also, note that each of the three *R*, *G*, and *B* values at every pixel are stored using 8 bits, which makes it *8 x 3 = 24* bits per pixel. This means that the color space now increases to more than 16 million colors from a mere 256. This is the reason color images store much more information than their grayscale counterparts.

Conceptually, the color image is not treated as having a triplet of intensity values at each pixel. Rather, a more convenient form of representation is adopted. The image is said to possess three independent color channels: the *R*, *G*, and *B* channels. Now, since we are using 8 bits per pixel per channel, each of the three channels are grayscale images in themselves!

Introduction to the Mat class

We have discussed the formation and representation of digital images and the concept of color spaces and color channels at length. Having laid a firm foundation on the basic principles of image processing, we now turn to the OpenCV library and take a look at what it has got to offer us in terms of storing digital images! Just like pixels are the building blocks of digital images, the Mat class is the cornerstone of OpenCV programming. Any instantiation of the Mat class is called the Mat object.

Before we embark on a description of the Mat object, I would urge you to think, keeping in mind whatever we have discussed regarding the structure and representation of digital images, about how you would go about designing a data structure in C++ that could store images for efficient processing. One obvious solution that comes to mind is using a two-dimensional array or a vector of vectors. What about the data types? An unsigned char should be sufficient since we would rarely need to store values beyond the range of 0 to 255. How would you go about implementing channels? Perhaps we could have an array of two-dimensional grids to represent color images (getting a little complicated now, isn't it?).

The Mat object is capable of doing all of the preceding things that were described (and much more) in the most efficient manner possible! It lets you handle multiple color channels and different color spaces without you (the programmer) having to worry about the internal implementation details. Since the library is written in C++, it also lifts the burden of memory management from the hands of the user. So, all you've got to worry about is building your cool application and you can trust Mat (and OpenCV) to take care of the rest!

According to OpenCV's official documentation:

> *"The class Mat represents an n-dimensional dense numerical single-channel or multi-channel array."*

We have already witnessed that digital images are two-dimensional arrays of pixels, where each pixel is associated with a numerical value from a predefined color space. This makes the Mat object a very obvious choice for representing images inside the world of OpenCV. And indeed, it does enable you to load, process, and store images and image data in your program. Most of the computer vision applications that you will be developing (as part of this book or otherwise) would involve abundant usage of images. These images would typically enter your system from the outside (user input), your application would apply several image processing algorithms on them, and finally produce an output, which may be written to disk. All these operations involve storing images inside your program and passing them around different modules of your code. This is precisely where the Mat object lends its utility.

Mat objects have two parts: a header and the actual matrix of pixel values. The header contains information, such as the size of the matrix, the memory address where it is stored (a pointer), and other pieces of information pertaining to the internal workings of Mat and OpenCV. The other part of the Mat object is where the actual pixel values are stored. The header for every Mat object is constant in size, but the size of the matrix of pixel values depends on the size of your image.

As this book progresses, you will realize that a Mat object is not always synonymous with images. You will work with certain instantiations of the Mat class, which do not represent a meaningful image as such. In such cases, it is more convenient to think of the Mat object as a data structure that helps us to operate on (possibly multidimensional) numerical arrays (as the official document suggests). But irrespective of whether we use Mat as an image store or a generic multidimensional array, you will soon realize the immense power that the creators of the library have placed in your hands through the Mat class. As mentioned earlier, its scope goes beyond merely storing images. It can act as a data structure and can provide the users with tools to use the most common linear algebra routines–matrix multiplication, inverse, eigen-values, PCA, norms, SVD, and even DFT and DCT–the list goes on.

Exploring the Mat class: loading images

We have covered enough theory without writing any actual code. And this is precisely what we are going to do now–explore OpenCV and try to learn more about the Mat class! We just read about the utility of Mat object both as a structure for storing images and as a multidimensional array. We'll start by witnessing the former. To that end, we will be writing our first *Hello World* OpenCV program that will read an image from the disk, load the image data onto a Mat object, and then display the image. All of this will be done using OpenCV and C++. So, let's begin!

At the very outset, we include the relevant header files and namespace declarations:

```
#include <opencv2/highgui/highgui.hpp>
#include <opencv2/core/core.hpp>

using namespace std;
using namespace cv;
```

The highgui header contains declarations for the functions that do the following:

1. Read an image from disk and store it in a Mat object : imread().
2. Display the contents of a Mat object (the image) onto a window : imshow().

The core.hpp header file contains declarations for the Mat class. Now we come to the actual piece of code that performs the intended operations:

```
int main() {
    Mat image = imread("image.png", IMREAD_COLOR);
    imshow("Output", image);
    waitKey(0);

    return 0;
}
```

The first thing we encounter in the code snippet is the imread() function. It basically allows you to read an image from the disk and load its contents on to a Mat object. It accepts a couple of arguments.

The first argument is the full path name of the image file on disk. Here, we pass image.png as our path (make sure to give the complete path here; if you just pass the name of the image as we have done, ensure that the file lies in the same directory as your code).

The second argument is an OpenCV flag that tells us the format in which to load the image onto the Mat object. The different possible flags along with their descriptions are given in the following table. Out of all these flags, you will be using a couple of them quite frequently: IMREAD_UNCHANGED and IMREAD_GRAYSCALE. The former loads the image as is, whereas the latter always converts the image into a single channel grayscale image.

Flag	Description
IMREAD_UNCHANGED	If set, return the loaded image as is
IMREAD_GRAYSCALE	If set, always convert the image to the single channel grayscale image
IMREAD_COLOR	If set, always convert the image to the three channel BGR color image
IMREAD_ANYDEPTH	If set, return the 16-bit/32-bit image when the input has the corresponding depth, otherwise convert it to 8-bit
IMREAD_ANYCOLOR	If set, the image is read in any possible color format
IMREAD_LOAD_GDAL	If set, use the gdal driver for loading the image

Then comes imshow(). It does the opposite of what imread() accomplishes. It takes the contents of a Mat object and displays it on the screen inside a window. This function also accepts two arguments:

1. The first argument is the name that appears in the title of the window that displays the image. Here, we have named the window Output.
2. The second argument is, of course, the Mat object which stores the image.

The waitkey() method pauses the program for a specified amount of time, waiting for a keystroke. If, however, we pass 0 as an argument, it would wait indefinitely for us to press the key. Had we not included the waitKey(0) statement in our code, the OpenCV window with the image would have flashed on our screens and disappeared, following which our program would have terminated return 0. Having the waitKey(0) after imshow() displays the image and then waits for the user to press a key, and only then does the program terminate.

Exploring the Mat class – declaring Mat objects

We have just witnessed the creation of a Mat object by reading an image from disk. Is loading an existing image the only way to create Mat objects in code? Well, the answer is no. It would be prudent to assume that there are other ways to declare and initialize instances of the Mat class. In the subsequent sections, we will be discussing some of the methods in great detail. As we move along the discussions, we will touch upon the different aspects of digital images that we introduced at the beginning of this chapter. You will see how the concepts of spatial resolution (image dimensions), color spaces (bit depths or data types), and color channels are all elegantly handled by the Mat class.

Let's see a sample line of code that both declares and initializes a Mat object:

```
Mat M(20, 15, CV_8UC3, Scalar(0,0,255));
```

Spatial dimensions of an image

The first two arguments define the dimensions of the data matrix, that is, rows and columns, respectively. So the previous example will create a Mat object with a data matrix comprising 20 rows and 15 columns, which means a total of *20 x 15 = 300* elements. Often, you will see Mat declarations where both of these values are combined into a single argument: the Size object. The Size object, more specifically, the Size_ template class, is an OpenCV specific class that allows us to specify sizes for images and rectangles. It has two members: width and height. So, if you are using a Size object to specify the dimensions of a Mat, the height and width correspond to the number of rows and columns, respectively. The same Mat instantiation using a Size object is given as follows:

```
Mat M(Size(15, 20), CV_8UC3, Scalar(0,0,255));
```

There are a couple of things that are noteworthy regarding the preceding line of code. First, note that the number of rows and columns are in the reverse order with respect to the previous instantiation. This is because the constructor for the Size_ class accepts the arguments in this order–width and height. Second, note that although the class is templatized and named Size_, in the declaration, we simply use Size. This is due to the fact that OpenCV has defined some aliases as follows:

```
typedef Size_<int> Size2i;
typedef Size2i Size;
```

This basically means that writing `Size` is equivalent to saying `Size2i`, which in turn is the same as `Size_<int>`.

Color space or color depth

The next argument to the Mat declaration statement discussed earlier is for the type. This parameter defines the type of values that the data matrix of the Mat object would store. The choice of this parameter becomes important because it controls the amount of space needed to store the Mat object in memory. OpenCV has its own types defined. A mapping between the OpenCV types and C++ data types is given in the following table:

Serial No.	OpenCV type	Equivalent C++ type	Range
0	CV_8U	unsigned char	0 to 255
1	CV_8S	char	-128 to 127
2	CV_16U	unsigned short	0 to 65535
3	CV_16S	short	-32768 to 32767
4	CV_32S	int	-2147483648 to 2147483647
5	CV_32F	float	
6	CV_64F	double	

`16`, `32`, and `64` represent the number of bits used for storing a value of that data type. `U`, `S`, and `F` stand for `unsigned`, `short`, and `float`, respectively. Using these two pieces of information, we can easily deduce the range of values for each data type, as given in the right-most column of the table.

Color channels

You will notice a `C` followed by a number in the types used to declare our Mat objects (for example, `CV_8UC3`). The `C` here stands for channel, and the integer following it gives you the number of channels in the image. Given a multi-channel, RGB image, OpenCV provides you with a `split()` function that separates the three channels. Here is a short code snippet that demonstrates this:

```
Mat color_image = imread("lena.jpg", IMREAD_COLOR);
vector<Mat> channels;
split(color_image, channels);
```

```
imshow("Blue", channels[0]);
imshow("Green", channels[1]);
imshow("Red", channels[2]);
waitKey(0);
```

Image size

By looking at the complete OpenCV type (along with the number of channels) and the Mat object dimensions, we can actually calculate the number of bits that would be required to store all the pixel values in memory. For example, let's say we have a 100 x 100 Mat object of type CV_8UC3. Each pixel value will take 8 bits and there will be three such values for each pixel (three channels). That takes it to 24 bits per pixel. There are *100 x 100 = 10,000* pixels in total, which means a total space of (24 x 10,000) bits = 30 kilobytes. Keep in mind that this is the space used up by the grid of pixel values and does not include the header. The overall size of the Mat object will be higher, but not by a significant amount (the size of the data matrix is substantially larger than the size of a Mat header).

By looking at the range of data types available for declaring Mat objects, it's natural to think about the utility of all the different types. For storing and representing images, only CV_8UC1 and CV_8UC3 make sense, the former for grayscale images and the latter for images in the RGB color space. As stated earlier, in OpenCV, the Mat object is used for much more than an image store. For applications where Mat is best treated as a multidimensional numerical array, the other types make sense. However, irrespective of whether the Mat object serves as an image store or as a data structure, its importance and ubiquity inside the world of OpenCV is undeniable.

Default initialization value

The last argument is the default value for the data matrix of the Mat object. You will have noticed the use of yet another OpenCV specific data structure: Scalar. The Scalar_ class allows you to store a vector of at most four values. You might be wondering about the utility of restricting the size of a vector to just four. There are several use cases within OpenCV where we might require working with one, two, or three values (and not more than that). For example, we have just learnt that each pixel in an RGB image is represented using three values, one each for the *R*, *G*, and *B* channels. In such a scenario, the Scalar object provides a convenient method to pass the group of three values to the Mat object constructor, as has been done in the example under consideration. One important thing to note is that OpenCV reads the color channels in the reverse order–*B*, *G*, and *R*. This means that passing Scalar(255, 0, 0) would refer to blue, whereas Scalar(0, 0, 255) is red. Any combination of the three would then represent one of the 16 million+ colors. If, at this point of time, you are wondering about providing default values for a grayscale image, OpenCV allows what is intuitive. A simple `Scalar(0)` or `Scalar(255)` will color all pixels black or white, respectively, by default in a grayscale image. What I mean to say is that the constructor for the `Scalar` object is flexible enough to accept one, two, three, or even four values. If you are wondering about the discrepancy in the class names, `Scalar_` and `Scalar`, similar to the `Size_` class, OpenCV defines the following alias to make our code less verbose:

```
typedef Scalar_<double> Scalar;
```

The initialization method that we discussed here involved passing all the three pieces of information as arguments:

- Dimensions of the image
- The type of data stored at each pixel location
- The initial value to be filled in the data matrix

However, the `Mat` class allows greater flexibility in declaring objects. You do not have to specify all the three mentioned earlier. The `Mat` class has some overloaded constructors that allow you to declare objects even if you simply specify the following:

- Nothing at all
- The dimensions and the type
- The dimensions, the type, and the initial value

Here are some of the constructor declarations from the implementation of the `Mat` class:

```
Mat ()
Mat (int rows, int cols, int type)
Mat (Size size, int type)
Mat (int rows, int cols, int type, const Scalar &s)
Mat (Size size, int type, const Scalar &s)
```

Going by the preceding definitions, we present some sample valid Mat object declarations. You will get a chance to see them being used in the programs that we write as part of this book:

```
Mat I;
Mat I(100, 80, CV_8UC1);
Mat I(Size(80, 100), CV_8UC1);
```

Before we finish this section on declaring Mat objects, we will discuss one final technique, that is, creating Mat objects as a **region of interest** (**ROI**) from inside an existing Mat object. Often, situations arise where we are interested in a subset of the data from the data matrix of an existing Mat object. Putting it another way, we would like to initialize a new Mat object whose data matrix is a submatrix of the existing Mat object. The constructor for such an initialization is given as Mat (const Mat &m, const Rect &roi). A sample statement that invokes such a constructor is given as follows:

```
Mat roi_image(original_image, Rect(10, 10, 100, 100));
```

This will create a new Mat object named roi_image by taking the data from the matrix belonging to the existing Mat object, original_image. The submatrix will start from the pixel with coordinates (10, 10) as the upper-left corner and will have dimensions of 100 x 100. All the information pertaining to the size of the ROI has been passed via the Rect object, which is yet another OpenCV specific data structure.

Digging inside Mat objects

We have learnt how to create Mat objects and even populate them with data from an image read from the disk or with arbitrary numerical values. Now it's time to get a little more information regarding the internal workings of the Mat object. This will help you make some important design decisions while writing code for your applications.

As we have discussed earlier, Mat objects are composed of a header and the actual matrix of values with the size of the matrix being (usually) much greater than the size of the header. We have already seen that a modestly sized image with dimensions of 100 pixels by 100 pixels can take up as much as 30 kilobytes of space. Images are known to be much bigger in size than that. Moreover, when you are developing a computer vision-based application, your code is typically working with multiple images or multiple copies of images. These images (and their copies) are passed to-and-fro the various modules of your code. They may be the input to or store the result of some OpenCV function. The more sophisticated a system we are trying to build, the greater the complexity of these interactions.

If that is the case, with Mat being a memory-intensive data structure, how does OpenCV prevent its processes from running out of memory? The answer to the question lies in the manner in which the internal workings of the Mat objects are handled by the library. OpenCV is smart enough to avoid duplication of the Mat object data matrix wherever it possibly can. This is going to be the topic of our discussions in this section.

We have discussed several ways to declare and initialize Mat objects. One more method we will touch upon now is by initializing it with another Mat object (much like what a copy constructor does). So, we can do something like this:

```
Mat image = imread("lena.jpg");
Mat another_image(image);
Mat yet_another_image = image;
```

Now, your intuition might tell you that since there are three Mat objects, the data of the image read from the disk must have been duplicated three times in memory. Had that been the case, and had the original image, lena.jpg, contained a significant number of pixels, it would have meant using up a lot of memory. However, while using the copy constructor for Mat, OpenCV only creates a separate copy of the header and not the data matrix. Same is the case with using the equality operator. So, for all the three Mat objects, the header is different, but the data matrix is shared. The headers for each of the three objects point to the same data matrix in memory. In essence, we have three different aliases providing access to the same underlying data matrix. Modifying any of the three objects will change the same data and affect all three. It is very important to keep this in mind while writing code to avoid unnecessary complications and potential loss of data by overwriting!

Another place where such an issue might crop up is while passing images to functions in your code. Suppose you have a function in your application that looks something like this:

```
void processImage(Mat image) {
    // Does some processing on the Mat
}
```

When you invoke the preceding function, the processImage() method works on the same data matrix. Another way to put it is that Mat objects are always passed by reference (the actual data matrix is not copied). Therefore, modifying the image in the called function will modify it in the function from where it was called.

Let's test this using a concrete example that you can execute for your and check. We will start with the inclusion of the relevant header files and namespace declarations:

```
#include <iostream>
#include <opencv2/core/core.hpp>
#include <opencv2/highgui/highgui.hpp>

using namespace std;
using namespace cv;
```

We have an implementation of the `processImage()` method that turns all the pixels of the input image black:

```
void processImage(Mat input_image) {
    int channels = input_image.channels();
    int numRows = input_image.rows;
    int numCols = input_image.cols * channels;

    for (int i = 0; i < numRows; ++i) {
        uchar* image_row = input_image.ptr<uchar>(i);
        for (int j = 0; j < numCols; ++j)
            image_row[j] = 0;
    }
}
```

Don't worry if you aren't able to understand the meaning of these lines for now. Traversing Mat objects will be covered in the subsequent sections of this chapter. You can copy the code verbatim and it will execute just fine:

```
int main() {
    Mat image = imread("lena.png");
    processImage(image);
    imshow("Output", image);
    waitKey(0);

    return 0;
}
```

As you can see here in the `main()` function, we read an image from the disk (`lena.png`), loaded the image data into a Mat object named `image`, and then passed the same object to our `processImage()` method, which was defined previously. When we attempt to display the same Mat object using `imshow()`, we see that the image is now completely black (which is what the `processImage()` method was expected to do!). This means that the `processImage()` method has worked with the same data matrix as that of the input Mat object.

But what about the cases where you actually do want to copy the data matrix as well? OpenCV provides a couple of alternatives to achieve this. `copyTo()` and `clone()` are two methods belonging to the `Mat` class that allow you to create separate Mat objects by copying the data matrix along with the header. A typical use case for this might be when you want a copy of the original image to be preserved before sending the image through your processing pipeline:

```
Mat cloned_image = image.clone();
Mat another_cloned_image;
```

```
image.copyTo(another_cloned_image);
```

Let's test this on our previous example. The `processImage()` method remains unchanged. We will modify the `main()` function to look like this:

```
int main() {
    Mat image = imread("lena.png");
    Mat image_clone = image.clone();
    processImage(image);
    imshow("image", image);
    imshow("image_clone", image_clone);
    waitKey(0);

    return 0;
}
```

Notice that now, we create a copy of the input Mat object's data matrix by invoking the `clone()` method. If you run this, the `image_clone` parameter is Mat object would have remained unchanged, whereas the original data matrix has undergone the modifications of the `processImage` method.

This finishes our discussion of the Mat object. We have been through all the topics that you might need to begin working with images in your code. In the next section, we take a dive in and start by iterating through these images and playing around with their pixel values. Having learnt about the *image*, we now move on to some *processing*.

Traversing Mat objects

So far, you have learnt in detail about the `Mat` class, what it represents, how to initialize instances of the `Mat` class, and the different ways to create Mat objects. Along the way, we have also looked at some other OpenCV classes, such as `Size`, `Scalar`, and `Rect`. We have also successfully run our very first OpenCV *Hello World* program. Our sample program was fairly simplistic. It read an image from disk and loaded the contents into a Mat object. The real fun begins after this. In any application that you develop, you would typically be reading an image or images from a storage disk into your code and then apply image processing or computer vision algorithms to them. In this section, we will take our first steps towards starting with the *processing* aspect of things.

As we stated at the outset, an image is the sum total of its pixels. So, to understand any sort of processing that gets applied to images, we need to know how the pixel values would be modified as a result of the operations. This gives rise to the necessity of iterating over each and every pixel of a digital image. Now, since images are synonymous with Mat objects within the realm of OpenCV, we need a mechanism that allows us to iterate over all the values stored in the data matrix of a Mat. This section will discuss some techniques to do the same. We will present a couple of different ways to achieve such a traversal along with the pros and cons of using each approach. Once again, you will come to appreciate the utility of the Mat class when you encounter some more Mat member functions that have been made available to aid the programmer with this task.

Continuity of the Mat data matrix

Before we start with the code for traversing Mat objects, we need to understand how (more precisely, in what order) the data matrix stores the pixel values in memory. To do that, we need to introduce the concept of continuity. A data matrix is said to be continuous if all its rows are stored at adjacent memory locations without any gap between the contents of two successive rows. If a matrix is not continuous, it is said to be non-continuous. Now, why do we care if our Mat object's underlying data matrix is continuous or not? Well, as it turns out that iterating a continuous data matrix is much faster than going over a non-continuous one because the former requires a smaller number of memory accesses. Having learnt about the benefits offered by the continuity property of a Mat object's data matrix, how do we take advantage of this feature in our applications? The answer to that can be found in the following code snippet:

```
int channels = image.channels();
int num_rows = image.rows;
int num_cols = (image.cols * channels);

if (image.isContinuous()) {
    num_cols = num_cols * num_rows;
    num_rows = 1;
}
```

This piece of code achieves what I like to call *flattening* of the data matrix, and this is typically performed as a precursor to the actual image traversal. If the rows of the data matrix are indeed saved in contiguous memory locations, this means that we can treat the entire matrix as a single one-dimensional array. This array will have one row and the number of columns will be equal to (numRows*numCols*numChannels), which is the total number of pixels in the image. The code snippet assumes that the image is an 8-bit Mat object. Also note that the *flattening* is performed only if the image is continuous.

In the case of non-continuous images, the value of `numRows` and `numCols` remain as they are read from the Mat object.

Matrices created by `imread()`, `clone()`, or a constructor will always be continuous. In fact, the only time a matrix will not be continuous is when it *borrows data* from an existing matrix. By borrowing data, I mean when a new matrix is created out of an ROI of a bigger matrix, for example:

```
Mat big (200, 300, CV_8UC1);
Mat roi (big, Rect(10, 10, 100, 100));
Mat col = big.col(0);
```

Both matrices, `roi` and `col`, will be non-continuous as they borrow data from `big`.

Image traversals

Now, we are ready for the actual traversal. As stated earlier, we will discuss a couple of different ways to go about this. The first technique uses the `ptr()` method of the `Mat` class. According to the documentation of the `Mat::ptr()` method, it returns a `pointer` to the specified matrix row. We specify the row by its `0` based index passed to the function as an argument. So, let's check out the `Mat::ptr()` method in action:

```
for (int i = 0; i < numRows; ++i) {
    uchar* row_ptr = image.ptr<uchar>(i);
    for (int j = 0; j < numCols; ++j) {
        // row_ptr[j] will give you access to the pixel value
        // any sort of computation/transformation is to be performed here
    }
}
```

What this technique essentially does is acquire the pointer to the start of each row with the statement `image.ptr<uchar>(i)` and save it in a `pointer` variable named `row_ptr` (the outer `for` loop); `loop` variable `i` is used to index the rows of the matrix. Once we have acquired the pointer to an image row, we iterate through the row to access the value of each and every pixel. This is precisely what the inner `for` loop, which has the `j` loop variable, accomplishes. What is elegant about this code is that it works in both cases, whether our data matrix is continuous (and flattened) or not. Just think about it; if our matrix were continuous and had been flattened using the code that we discussed a while back, then it would have had a single row (`numRows=1`) and the number of columns would have been the same as the number of pixels in the image, $(numRows * channels * numCols)$. This would mean that the outer loop runs only once and we call the `Mat::ptr()` method once to fetch all the pixels of the image in a single call. And if our matrix hasn't been flattened, then `image.ptr<uchar>(i)` will be called for each row that makes it a total of `numRows` times. This is also the reason that flattening a matrix is more efficient in terms of time taken.

Let's put together the code for the *flattening* and traversal of the image to get a complete picture of using the `pointer` method for Mat object traversal:

```
void scanImage(Mat& image) {
    int channels = image.channels();
    int num_rows = image.rows;
    int num_cols = (image.cols * channels);

    if (image.isContinuous()) {
        num_cols *= num_rows;
        num_rows = 1;
    }

    for (int i = 0; i < num_rows; ++i) {
        uchar* row_ptr = image.ptr<uchar>(i);
        for (int j = 0; j < num_cols; ++j) {
            // Perform operations on pixel value row_ptr[j]
        }
    }
}
```

So, in summary, the `Mat::ptr()` method essentially works by fetching the data one row at a time. In that sense, the access method here is sequential: when the data of one of the rows is fetched, we can go over the contents of only that particular row. Accessing a new row necessitates a new fetch call. *Flattening* the data matrix is just a way to speed up computation, which works by bringing in all the data in a single fetch. This might not be the most *aesthetic* way of doing things. Your code may sometimes be difficult to understand and/or debug, especially when it comes to handling multi-channel images (you need to know exactly how many columns to skip per pixel while traversing a row). Now, this is where our second approach comes in.

This method relies on the `Mat::at()` method. As per the OpenCV documentation, the `at()` method returns a reference to any specified array element. The pixel whose value we are interested in is specified via the row and column index. This approach provides us with a random access to the data matrix. Let's look at an example code in action that uses the `at()` method to access pixel values. In the following code snippet, assume that `I` is a single-channel, grayscale image:

```
for( int i = 0; i < I.rows; ++i) {
    for( int j = 0; j < I.cols; ++j) {
        // Matrix elements can be accessed via : I.at<uchar>(i,j)
```

```
        }
    }
```

The code looks much simpler, more compact, and easier to read than the earlier approach. We have a couple of `for` loops: the outer loop (with index variable i) which iterates over the rows and the inner loop (with index variable j) that goes over the columns. As we move over each pixel, we can access its value by calling `I.at<uchar>(i,j)`.

But what about the case when our image is multi-channeled? Let's say that we have a three-channel RGB image that we need to traverse. The code would have a very similar structure but with minor differences. Since our image is now three-channeled, the `uchar` data type will not be appropriate for the pixel values. The solution is presented in the following code snippet:

```
for( int i = 0; i < I.rows; ++i) {
    for( int j = 0; j < I.cols; ++j) {
        /**
        * The B, G and R components for the (i, j)-th pixel can be accessed
by:
        * I.at<Vec3b>(i, j)[0]
        * I.at<Vec3b>(i, j)[1]
        * I.at<Vec3b>(i, j)[2]
        **/
    }
}
```

The first thing you notice about the code is the use of what seems like a new OpenCV type named Vec_3b. All you need to know about Vec_3b at this point is that it stands for a vector of three byte values, that is, a vector of three numbers between 0 and 255 (inclusive). And that seems to be the perfect data type for representing what a pixel stands for in a three-channel RGB image (OpenCV always has the right tools made available to its users!). Now that we have established that the type of each value in the data matrix is Vec_3b, which means that the at() method returns a reference to Vec_3b, we can access the individual elements within Vec_3b using the [] operator, just like a C++ array or vector. Now, recall that when we discussed about image channels, we said that the OpenCV stores the *R*, *G*, and *B* components in the reverse order. This would mean that the zeroth, first and second elements of Vec_3b would each refer to the *blue*, *green*, and *red* components of the pixel, respectively. You should be extra careful about this fact as it can be a potential source of errors in your code.

Now, the library has gone a step further to provide another level of convenience for its users. Using the previously mentioned approach, we have to write the name of the data type `Vec_3b` every time we want to access the value for a particular channel of a particular pixel. In order to avoid that, OpenCV provides us with a template class named `Mat_`. As always, we demonstrate its use via an example code snippet:

```
Mat_<Vec3b> _I = I;
for( int i = 0; i < I.rows; ++i) {
    for( int j = 0; j < I.cols; ++j ) {
        /**
        * The B, G and R components for the (i, j)-th pixel can be accessed
by:
        * _I(i, j)[0]
        * _I(i, j)[1]
        * _I(i, j)[2]
        **/
    }
}
```

The first thing we do is declare an object of the `Mat_` class and initialize it with our original Mat object. `Mat_` is a thin template wrapper over the `Mat` class. It doesn't contain any extra data fields in addition to what is available with the Mat object. In fact, references to the two classes (`Mat` and `Mat_`) can be converted to each other. The only advantage `Mat_` offers is the notational convenience of having to skip writing the data type every time we have to access a pixel (this is because the data type has been specified during declaration of the `Mat_` object itself).

As stated earlier, the `Mat::at()` method is suited for random access (it requires both the row and column index), the code is much more readable and clean, but it is slower than the pointer-based approach because the `at()` method does some range checks each time it is called.

We combine both the code snippets for single as well as multi-channel traversal using `Mat::at()` and encapsulate that within a single C++ function:

```
void scanImage(Mat& image) {
    int channels = image.channels();
    if (channels == 1) {
        for( int i = 0; i < I.rows; ++i) {
            for( int j = 0; j < I.cols; ++j) {
                // Matrix elements can be accessed via : I.at<uchar>(i,j)
            }
        }
    }
    else if (channels == 3)  {
```

```
for( int i = 0; i < I.rows; ++i) {
  for( int j = 0; j < I.cols; ++j) {
    // The B, G and R components for the (i, j)-th pixel can be
    // accessed by:
    //    I.at<Vec3b>(i, j)[0]
    //    I.at<Vec3b>(i, j)[1]
    //    I.at<Vec3b>(i, j)[2]
  }
 }
 }
 }
```

This concludes our section on image traversals. But before we move on to the next topic, a few final words on Mat object traversals. We have gone over a lot of different methods to achieve what seems like a very basic task. We have seen the sequential-pointer approach and the random-access technique using the Mat::at() method. Personally, I tend to lean towards the latter due to its aesthetic appeal and a clear distinction between single and multichannel images that leaves no room for confusion. It's usually also safer, due to the range checks that we've mentioned before, and it's also easier to access the surrounding pixels if you need them for processing (something that we would be doing quite a lot from Chapter 2, *Image Filtering*.

Most of the example programs in the remainder of this book will stick to this too. However, you are encouraged to try out the former approach too, if and when you feel like, and compare the results with the ones shown in the text.

Now, we have been traversing Mat objects and images for quite some time now but haven't really been doing any sort of tangible *processing* with them. You will have noticed that when it came to the section of code where we had the chance to actually access and/or modify the pixel values, we stopped and hid behind those boring comment blocks that did nothing but tell us more theory about how to code. Very soon, in the next few sections, we are going to remove those comments and fill up that space with some actual code that performs some simple, yet cool transformations on our images!

Image enhancement

This section is all about performing some form of computation or *processing* on each pixel. Since this is the beginning of the book and we are dealing with the basics, we'll let the computations be fairly simplistic for now. The more complex algorithms will be saved for the next chapter. In addition to being simplistic in nature, the computations will also involve all the pixels undergoing the same nature of transformations. The transformation function to be applied to every pixel is dependent only on the value of the current pixel.

Putting it mathematically, such transformation functions can be represented as follows:

s=T(r)

Here, *s* is the output pixel value and *r* is the input. The transformation function, *T*, also known as the gray-level or intensity transformation function, can be thought of as a mapping between the input and output pixel values. Essentially, the pixel value at the (i, j) position in the output image is dependent only on the pixel value at the same (i, j) position in the input image. Hence, you do not see any dependency of coordinate positions (i, j) in the transformation function, just the pixel values s and r. However, these transformations are pretty naive to assume such a simple pixel-dependency model. Most of the image processing techniques work with a neighborhood of pixels around the (i, j) pixel. It is due to this reason that grayscale transformations are *simple*. However, they are a good starting point for our journey on image processing.

Assume that we are dealing with a grayscale image (even in the case of a color image, the *R*, *G*, and *B* channels can be treated separately and independently as three grayscale images). *T* is applied to each and every pixel in the input image to yield the output. By changing the nature of *T*, we can get different forms of transformations. The names of some of the transformations that we'll discuss and ultimately implement have been listed as follows:

- Linear transformations:
    - Identity
    - Negative
- Logarithmic transformations:
    - Log
    - Inverse log or exponential

At this point, you can probably see the path laid out in front of you. We implement these grayscale transformations by traversing the data matrix by taking help from the arsenal of techniques we have developed in the previous section, and we apply the transformation function independently at each pixel to get the resultant image. While this approach is perfectly correct, there is yet a scope for optimization.

Lookup tables

Consider an image 1000 pixels high and 800 pixels wide. If we are to follow the aforementioned approach of visiting each pixel and performing the transformation *T*, we will have to perform the computation $1000 \times 800 = 8 \times 10^5$ times. This number increases in direct proportion to the size of the image.

At the same time, we also know that the value of each pixel only lies between 0 and 255 (inclusive). What if we can pre-compute and store the transformed values *s=T(r)* for values s=T(r) for r∈{0,1,2,...,255}, that is, for all possible values of the input. If we do so, then irrespective of the dimensions (number of pixels) in our input image, we will never need more than 256 computations. So, using this strategy, we traverse our matrix and do a simple lookup of the pre-computed values. This is called a **lookup table** approach (often abbreviated as **LUT**). Using LUT affords us with yet another benefit with regards to implementing our transformations. The logic/code for image traversals is independent of the logic for the actual computation of the grayscale transformation. This decoupling makes our code more readable, easy to maintain, and scale (add more and more transformations to our suite). Let's have a look at an example to elucidate what I'm trying to convey:

```
vector<uchar> getLUT() {
  /**
   * This function holds the implementation details of a specific
   * grayscale transformation
   */
}

void processImage(Mat& I) {
  vector<uchar> LUT = getLUT();
  for (int i = 0; i < I.rows; ++i) {
    for (int j = 0; j < I.cols; ++j)
      I.at<uchar>(i, j) = LUT[I.at<uchar>(i, j)];
  }
}
```

As you can see, we have used a combination of `LUT` and the random-access using `Mat::ptr()` for matrix traversal to define a framework for implementing grayscale transformations. The `getLUT()` method basically returns the lookup table as a C++ vector. Usually, the vector is constructed in such a way that the input value `r` can be used as an index into the `LUT` and the value stored as the vector element is the target value `s`. This means that if I want to know what value the input intensity `185` is mapped to, we would simply call `LUT[185]` to get it. Naturally, `LUT` will have a size of `256` (so that the indices range from `0` to `255`, thereby covering all possible input values). Now, while we traverse the data matrix in the `processImage()` method, we take the intensity value of each input pixel, query the LUT vector to know the desired output pixel value, and assign the new value. If you remember the section where we talked about the internals of Mat, we mentioned that Mat objects are always passed by reference and then called, and the caller function, are working with the same underlying data matrix. So, in the implementation framework that we have presented here, the same matrix will be modified and overwritten. If you want to have the original image preserved, you should create a new matrix by cloning and passing the cloned copy to the processImage() function. I guess you might have begun to appreciate the importance of learning about the internal workings of Mat now!

Let's take a moment to pause and think about what we've accomplished so far and the path that lies ahead. We have learnt about traversal of data matrix of Mat objects using a couple of different approaches. Then, to demonstrate the utility of such traversals, we introduced the concept of grayscale transformations, and talked about the design of a framework that would allow us to implement such transformation techniques.

Going forward, in the next section, when we discuss these transformations in detail, you will realize that each one of them modifies the image in its own characteristic way. They are meant to act upon certain aspects of the image and bring out the details that they are designed to exploit. That is the reason that these transformations are also referred to as *image enhancement techniques*. Very soon, we are going to demonstrate the different kinds of enhancements that you can bring about in your images by just transforming pixel values in accordance to a predefined function. Everyone, I guess at some point in time, has used a web or mobile-based photo/video editing application. You might recall that there is a dedicated section in such applications whose purpose is to apply these *enhancements* to images. In common Internet terminology, these are often referred to as *filters* (for example, Instagram filters). As we take you through these grayscale transformations, you will realize that at the most basic level, this is what the fancy filters really are. Of course, to design a full-scale, production-level image filter would involve a lot of different steps other than the basic $s=T(r)$, but grayscale transformations do act as a good starting point. Without any further ado, let's learn about these transformations while building our own simple (yet cool) set of image filters by the side.

Linear transformations

As mentioned previously, we will be discussing two broad categories of grayscale transformations: linear and logarithmic. We will start with linear transformations first.

When it comes to grayscale transformations, there are broadly two types of transformations that are widely discussed:

- Identity
- Negative transformation

In theory, you can make up as many arbitrary linear transformations that you want, but for the purpose of this book, we will restrict ourselves to just the two.

Identity transformation

The identity transformation maps each input pixel to itself in the output. In other words:

$T(r)=r$

Obviously, this does nothing exciting. In fact, this transformation doesn't do anything at all! The output image is the same as the input image, because every pixel gets mapped to itself in the transformation. Nevertheless, we discuss it here for the sake of completeness.

Implementing a lookup table for identity transformations shouldn't be a hassle at all:

```
vector getIdentityLUT() {
  vector<uchar> LUT(256, 0);
  for (int i = 0; i < 256; ++i)
    LUT[i] = (uchar)i;
  return LUT;
}
```

The first line of the function declares and initializes the C++ vector that is going to serve as our lookup table. This same vector is then computed and returned by the function. We had discussed earlier (while talking about lookup tables) that the size of LUT will, in practically all cases, be 256 for the 256 different intensity values in a grayscale image. The for loop traverses over LUT and encodes the transformation. Notice that LUT[i]=i will map every input pixel to itself, thereby implementing the identity transformation.

As stated earlier, one of the secondary benefits of using a lookup table is that it modularizes your code and makes it cleaner. The preceding snippet that we showed for identity transformations only computes and returns the lookup table. You can use a matrix traversal method after this to actually apply the transformation to all the pixels of an image. In fact, we demonstrated this framework in our section on *Lookup Tables*.

```
void processImage(Mat& I) {
  vector<uchar> LUT = getLUT();
  for (int i = 0; i < I.rows; ++i) {
```

```
      for (int j = 0; j < I.cols; ++j)
        I.at<uchar>(i, j) = LUT[I.at<uchar>(i, j)];
    }
  }

void main() {
  Mat image = imread("lena.jpg", IMREAD_GRAYSCALE);
  Mat processed_image = image.clone();
  processImage(processed_image);

  imshow("Input image", image);
  imshow("Processed Image", processed_image);
  waitKey(0);
  return 0;
  }
```

Note that while invoking the `processImage()` method to do our bidding, we have passed it a clone of the matrix that we just read from the input. This is just so that we are able to compare the changes that the processing has made on our input (not that there is any, in this particular case!). From the next transformation onwards, we are not going to write down the full detailed code (along with the `processImage()` and `main()`). We'll focus on the computation of the lookup table because that is what varies from one transformation to the next.

Negative transformation

The negative transformation subtracts 255 from the input pixel intensity value and produces that as an output. Mathematically speaking, the negative transformation can be expressed as follows:

s=T(r)=(255-r)

This means that a value of 0 in the input (black) gets mapped to 255 (white) and vice versa. Similarly, lighter shades of gray will yield the corresponding darker shades from the other end of the grayscale spectrum. If the range of the input values lie between 0 and 255, then the output will also lie within the same range. If you aren't convinced, here is some mathematical proof for you:

$0 \leq r \leq 255$ (Assuming the input pixels are from an 8-bit grayscale color space)

$\Rightarrow 0 \geq -r \geq -255$ (Multiplying by-1)

$\Rightarrow 255 \geq (255 - r) \geq 0$ (Adding 255)

$\Rightarrow 0 \leq s \leq 255$

Some books prefer to express the negative transformation as follows:

s=T(r)=(N-1-r)

Here, N is the number of grayscale levels in the color space we are dealing with. We have decided to stick with the former definition because all the color spaces we'll be dealing with in this book will involve values between 0 and 255. Hence, we can avoid the unnecessary fastidiousness.

The implementation of a lookup table for the negative transform is also fairly straightforward. We just replace the i with (255-i):

```
vector<uchar> getNegativeLUT() {
  vector<uchar> LUT(256, 0);
  for (int i = 0; i < 256; ++i)
    LUT[i] = (uchar)(255 - i);
  return LUT;
}
```

Let's run the code for negative transformation on some images and check what kind of an effect it produces:

The preceding image serves as our input image and the output (negative transformed image) is as follows:.

You can notice the darker pixels that make up the woman's hair (and feathers on the cap) have been transformed to white, and so have the eyes. The shoulders, which were on the fairer side of the spectrum, have been turned darker by the transform. You can now start to appreciate the kind of visual changes that this conceptually simple transformation seems to bring about in images! We iterate, once again, that the image manipulation apps, at the most basic, operate on similar principles.

If you are wondering who the lady in the image is, she goes by the name, Lena. Rather surprisingly, Lena's photograph with her iconic pose has become the de facto standard in the image processing community. A lot of literature in the field of image processing and computer vision uses this photo as an example to demonstrate the workings of some algorithm or technique. So, this is not the first time you'll be seeing her in this book!

Before we finish the section on linear transformations, there is one more thought that I would like to leave you with. You might find some texts out there that like to visualize these transformations graphically as a plot between the input and output pixels. The reason that such visualization is made is because not all linear transformations are as simple as the ones discussed here. We will briefly discuss *piecewise linear transformations*, where a graphical plot provides a convenient medium to analyze the transformation. But, before that, you will find such a plot for both the identity and the negative transformation drawn on the same graph:

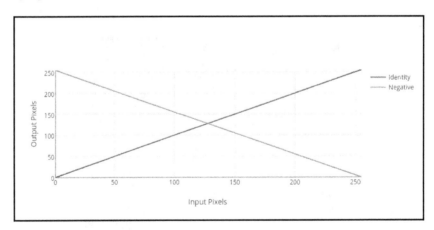

Both the linear transformations that we have discussed so far–identity and negative–are fairly trivial ones. You can have much more complicated forms for s=T(r). For example, instead of the transformation function being linear throughout the entire domain (0 to 255), we can make it piecewise linear. That would mean splitting the input domain into multiple, contiguous ranges and defining a linear transformation for each range, something along the lines of this:

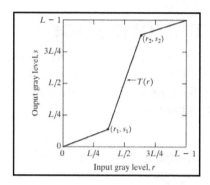

If you are wondering what purpose such a transformation achieves, the answer to that is *contrast enhancement*. When we say that an image has poor contrast, we mean that some (or all) parts of the image are not clearly distinguishable from their surroundings and neighbors. This happens when the pixels that make up the part of the image all belong to a very narrow band of intensity values. In the graph, consider the portion of the input intensity values that lie around L/2. You will notice that the narrow range of input pixels are mapped to a much wider range of output intensity values. This has been made possible by the steep line (greater slope), which defines the linear transformation around that region. As a result, all pixels that have intensity values within that range will get mapped to the wider output range, thereby improving the contrast of the image.

Now, astute readers might have realized that the shape of the piecewise linear transformation is dependent on the position of the points (r_1, s_1) and (r_2, s_2) So, how do we decide the location of the two points? Unfortunately, there is no single, specific answer to this question. As you will learn throughout the course of this book, in most cases, there can be no global correct answer for the selection of such parameters in image processing or computer vision. It depends on the kind of data (within the domain of computer vision, data often equates to images) that we are given to work with.

It would be a good exercise to try and implement the lookup table for a piecewise linear transformation. You can control the shape of the curve by varying the position of the two points and try to see what kind of an effect it has on the algorithm performance.

Logarithmic transformations

Having discussed linear transformations in the last section, we step into logarithmic transforms now. You will notice that they are mathematically more involved than their linear counterparts. Again, we'll be discussing two different types of enhancement techniques under logarithmic transforms:

- The log transform
- The exponential (or inverse log) transformation

Log transformation

Simply put, the log transform takes the (scaled) logarithm of every input pixel intensity value. Let's put it down in terms of a mathematical equation:

$$s = T(r) = c\log(r+1)$$

First, note that the input intensity values have all been incremented by *1 (r+1)*. This is because our input values vary from 0 to 255 $(0 \le r \le 255)$ and the logarithm of 0 is not defined. Secondly, there has been no mention regarding the base of the logarithm. Although conceptually the value of the base doesn't really matter (as long as it's kept same throughout the computation), for all practical purposes, we will assume it to be *10*. So, when we write *log*, we actually mean $\log_{10}$. Thirdly, you must be wondering about the constant *c* in the formula. What's it doing there? To answer that question, we need to know the range of output values for *log(r+1)* when $0 \le r \le 255$. To help us, I have plotted a graph of the function *log(r+1)*:

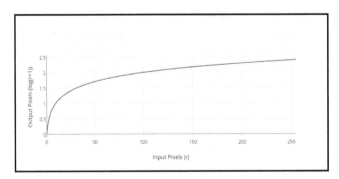

As *r* varies from 0 to 255, *log(r+1)* ranges from 0 to 2.4. It's in the nature of a logarithmic function to compress the range of input data, as is evident here: an input range spanning 256 values has been compressed to a mere range of 2.4. Does this mean that the output image will have a grayscale range of merely two or three values? It had better not, otherwise, the only thing you'll be able to see is complete darkness! This is where the multiplicative constant *c* comes into the picture. The role of the multiplier is to make the log-transformed pixel values span the entire range of 256 grayscale levels available for the output image. The way it's done is by choosing a value of *c* so that the maximum intensity available in the input image gets mapped to 255 in the output. This means that $255 = c log (r_{max} +1)$, further implies $c = 255/log (r_{max} +1)$. Often, for sufficiently large and contrast-rich images, it so happens that the maximum intensity in the input image is 255, that is, $r_{max} = 255$. In such cases, the value of the multiplier is *c=105.886*.

So far, we have been treating the log transformation in a highly mathematical context. Let's see what happens if we actually apply it to images. The image is made up of two horizontal bands. The first band depicts the grayscale color space from 0 (black) on the left and all the way up to 255 (white) on the right end of the spectrum:

The next band depicts the log transform of the corresponding grayscale values (again, from 0 to 255, as we move from left to right). A comparison between the two should give you an idea of what the log transform does to the grayscale spectrum. A glance will tell you that the log-transformed band is much more brighter than its counterpart. Why does this happen?

To give you a better perspective, intensity values of 0 and 15 in the input are mapped to 0 and 127 in the output. This means that if there are two adjacent pixels with intensities 0 and 15 in the input image, both of them would be almost indistinguishable. Human eyes will not be able to perceive such a subtle change in the grayscale intensity. However, in the log-transformed image, the pixel with the intensity value of 15 gets converted to 127 (which lies in the middle of the grayscale spectrum). This would render it clearly distinguishable from its neighbor, which is still completely black!

The exact opposite phenomenon takes place at the other end of the spectrum. For example, pixels with intensities of 205 and 255 are mapped to 245 and 255 by the log transform. This means that a significant difference of 50 in the grayscale spectrum has been reduced to a mere gap of 10. So, the log transform essentially magnifies the differences in intensity of pixels in the lower (darker) end of the grayscale spectrum at the cost of diminishing differences at the higher (brighter) end (notice the steepness of the log curve in the beginning and how it flattens as it reaches the end). In other words, the log transform will magnify details (by enhancing contrast) in the darker ends of the spectrum at the cost of decreasing the information content held by the higher end of the spectrum.

Now that you have an idea of the kind of changes brought forth in grayscale by a log transform, it's time we take a look at some real examples. If you have ever used a camera, you would know that pictures, when taken against a source of light (such as the sun or an artificial source such as a bulb or a tube-light) appear darker. The following image is an example of an image taken under such lighting conditions:

Now try to think of what would happen if we applied the log transform to such an image. We know that a log transform would enhance details from the darker region at the cost of information from the brighter regions of the image. The log-transformed image is shown next. We can see that the darker regions in our original image such as the face and the back of the chair in the background have been rendered more rich in contrast. On the other hand, there has been a significant loss in detail from the brighter segments, such as the table behind the person. This proves that the log transform can be effective in editing pictures that have been captured *against the light source* by digging out contrast information from the darker regions of an image at the cost of the brighter segments

Before we move on to the implementation, let's see one more application where a log transform may be considered useful. There are some scientific disciplines where we might come across patterns such as the one depicted in the following image:

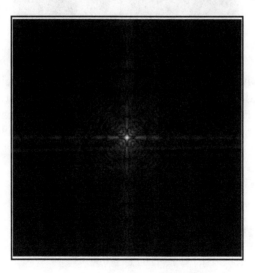

This image represents a pattern made by a light source on a dark background. More specifically, this is the representation of the Fourier transform of an image. As you can see, there definitely seems to be a pattern, but it's not clearly visible in its native form. We need a way to *magnify* and *enhance* these variations that are too subtle to be detected by the naked eye. Log transform to the rescue once more!

The log-transformed image is shown adjacent to the original one. We can observe the pattern quite clearly here:

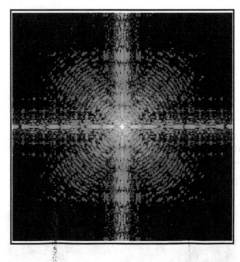

Now that we have familiarized ourselves with the mathematics behind the log transform and seen it operate on and transform images, we come to the most exciting part where we attempt to mimic their behavior via our OpenCV/C++ code. In accordance with the protocol we have adhered to so far, we first show the code that generates a lookup table for the log transform:

```cpp
#include <cmath>

vector<uchar> getLogLUT(uchar maxValue) {
    double C = 255 / log10(1 + maxValue);
    vector<uchar> LUT(256, 0);
    for (int i = 0; i < 256; ++i)
        LUT[i] = (int) round(C * log10(1+i));
    return LUT;
}
```

We notice that the lookup table function is a bit different and slightly more involved than the ones we have discussed thus far. This is mainly because it requires a parameter

to operate upon the maximum pixel intensity value in the input image. Recall the description of the log transform, where we discussed that the value of the multiplicative

constant c is calculated on the basis of the maximum intensity value, r_{max}, among the input pixels—$c = 255/log(r_{max} + 1)$. Knowing this fact, the remainder of the function is similar in structure to what we have seen so far.

Now, since the function that returns our lookup table (`getLogLUT()`) requires an additional parameter, we would have to make appropriate changes to the code that makes calls to it, that is, our `processImage()` method. The code for our `processImage()` method is as follows:

```
void processImage(Mat& I) {
    double maxVal;
    minMaxLoc(inputImage, NULL, &maxVal);
    vector<uchar> LUT = getLUT((uchar) maxVal);
    for (int i = 0; i < I.rows; ++i) {
        for (int j = 0; j < I.cols; ++j)
            I.at<uchar>(i, j) = LUT[I.at<uchar>(i, j)];
    }
}
```

The one thing that is noteworthy in the preceding snippet is the use of a method named `minMaxLoc()`. As per the documentation, the function is used to find the minimum and maximum element values and their positions within the array (and by array here, we are referring to a Mat object). The first argument is, of course, the name of the Mat object. The second and the third arguments are the pointers to the minimum and maximum elements, as computed by the function. We have passed the second argument as `null` because we aren't really interested in the minimum value for now. Apart from the call to `minMaxLoc()`, the structure of the remainder of `processImage()` should be familiar to you.

The implementation technique that we have employed for implementing the log transform has followed the framework that we established early on: lookup tables and image traversals. However, as we progress through this book, you will come to appreciate the fact that often, there are multiple ways to reach the same endpoint while implementing your programs in OpenCV. Although this is true for programming in general, we want to focus on how OpenCV provides us with options that allow us to perform and (more often than not) simplify tasks that otherwise would take a lot of tedious steps (iterations) to achieve. To that end, we will present another technique using OpenCV to compute the log transformation for images.

Like always, we first begin by including the relevant headers and namespaces:

```
#include <opencv2/core/core.hpp>
#include <opencv2/highgui/highgui.hpp>
#include <opencv2/imgproc/imgproc.hpp>

using namespace std;
using namespace cv;
```

Barring the declarations, our code that initially spanned a couple of user-defined functions and a `main()` class has now been essentially reduced to five lines of code that do all the work! Nowhere do we explicitly traverse any data matrix to modify pixel values based on some predefined transformation functions. The native methods that we use do that in the background for us. Have a look at the following code:

```
int main() {
    Mat input_image = imread("lena.jpg", IMREAD_GRAYSCALE);
    Mat processed_image;
    input_image.convertTo(processed_image, CV_32F);
    processed_image = processed_image + 1;
    log(processed_image, processed_image);
    normalize(processed_image, processed_image, 0, 255, NORM_MINIMAX);
    convertScaleAbs(processed_image, processed_image);

    imshow("Input image", image);
    imshow("Processed Image", processed_image);
    waitKey(0);
    return 0;
}
```

The five major functions used have been described in detail as follows:

1. The `convertTo()` function converts all the pixel values in the source array (Mat object) into the target data type. The destination array (which will store the corresponding converted pixel values) is the first and the target data type is the second argument that is passed to the function. Since we will be dealing with logarithmic calculations, it is best to shift to `float` as our data type.

2. The next statement after the `convertTo()` call increments all the pixel values by one. Recall that before applying the log operator, all pixel values have to be incremented by one as per the formula $s=T(r)=c\log(r+1)$. This is to avoid possible errors when a 0 is passed to a `log` function. The key thing to notice here is how operator overloading elegantly allows us to operate on entire data matrices with a single algebraic command.

3. The `log()` function calculates the natural logarithm of all the pixel values. After this step, what we have calculated so far would be `log(r+1)` for all pixels.

4. The `normalize()` method performs the same function as done by the multiplicative constant c in the formula $T(r)=clog(r+1)$. That is, it makes sure that the output lies in the range of 0 to 255 (as specified in the arguments passed to it). The way it does that is by applying the *MIN-MAX normalization* (again, another argument passed to it) technique, which is nothing but linearly scaling the data while making sure that the minimum and maximum of the transformed data take certain fixed values (0 and 255, respectively).

5. Finally, we apply `convertScaleAbs()`, which is the antithesis of `convertTo()`: it converts all the pixel values back to 8 bits (`uchar`).

One of the most prominent and striking differences that you will notice with this method is that it completely relies on the functions provided by the OpenCV API. What we have essentially done is avoid reinventing the wheel. Knowing how to traverse data matrices was, no doubt, an important skill to master. However, something as basic as iterating Mat objects becomes tedious, time consuming, and off-topic when we have big and complex computer vision systems to build. In such scenarios, it is good to utilize the features of the library if they have been made available to us. A classic example is the overloading of mathematical operators for the `Mat` class. Imagine if we had to implement a fully-fledged matrix traversal every single time we needed an operation as simple as *increment all pixels by 1*. To keep things concise and readable in our code and speed up the development cycle at the same time, the library has afforded us the luxury of writing *I=I+1*, even for the objects of the `Mat` class! Another advantage that we get if we rely on the OpenCV functions as much as possible is that we are guaranteed that the code that runs is heavily optimized and efficient in terms of memory and runtime.

The developers at OpenCV have built as many abstractions over such behind-the-scenes, *plumbing* operations as is required by programmers like us to seamlessly develop a varied set of applications that falls within the domain of computer vision and machine learning, without having to worry about the intricacies of implementation. This will be a recurrent theme in our book across most of the chapters.

Exponential or inverse-log transformation

Before we finish this section, we will visit our final transformation that goes by the name of exponential transform. What it does essentially is the complete opposite of the log transform (hence, it is also named inverse-log transform). While the log transform enhanced the pixels in the lower end of the spectrum, the exponential transform does the same for the pixels at the high intensity end of the spectrum. Mathematically, we have the following:

$$s = T(r) = c\left(b^r - 1\right)$$

Just like computing the log operator essentially involves taking the logarithm of the intensity values of every input pixel, the exponential transform raises a base value b to the power of the input pixel's intensity value. We subtract $^{1\left(b^r - 1\right)}$ so that when the input is 0, the output gets mapped to 0 as well. The constant c plays the same role as in the case of log transform, ensuring that the output lies in the range of 0 to 255. The value of the constant b decides the shape of the transform. Typically, b is chosen to lie close to 1. The following graph depicts a plot of both the log and the exponential transform (b=1.02):

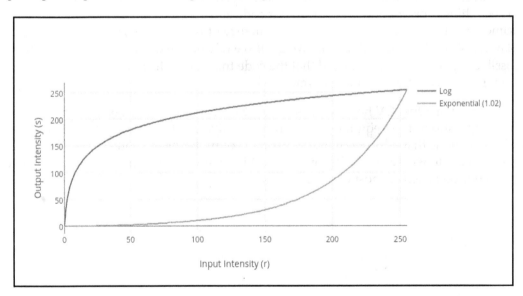

The shape of the plots brings out the complementary nature of both the transforms. On one hand, the log transform maps a narrow range of input intensity values at the lower end of the grayscale spectrum to a broader range at the output. On the other hand, the curve of the exponential transform becomes steep at the other end of the spectrum, thereby mapping a narrow range of input values to a much larger range at the output. To further illustrate the dichotomy between the two, the following figure demonstrates the changes that the exponential transform does to a grayscale spectrum. This is similar to the kind of grayscale comparisons that we did for the Log transformation. The following image depicts the original grayscale spectrum from 0 (on the left) all the way to 255 (on the right):

You'll find the corresponding spectrum for exponential transform in the following image. Note how the entire spectrum is *darker* (as opposed to *lighter*, in the case of log transforms) than the original grayscale band. Using the same line of reasoning that we presented in the section on log transforms, you can deduce why that happens:

As always, we share the code to compute the lookup table for the exponential transform:

```
const int BASE = 1.02;
vector<uchar> getExpLUT(uchar maxValue) {
   double C = 255.0 / (pow(BASE, maxValue) - 1);
vector<uchar> LUT(256, 0);
   for (int i = 0; i < 256; ++i)
     LUT[i] = (int) round(C * (pow(BASE, i) - 1));
   return LUT;
}
```

The code is exactly similar to the one for calculating log transforms except for the formula. We won't be going over the other functions, such as the traversal and the main() function once again. I would strongly suggest you to implement the exponential transform by using the OpenCV functions (and avoid reinventing the wheel by implementing matrix traversals) as we did in the case of log transforms. Take the help of online documentation (OpenCV has excellent online documentation) to find the function that would enable you to take the exponential of pixel values. This is an important skill to learn. There are so many different functions spread across different modules within OpenCV and the documentation is the only reliable and up-to-date source of information. As you go on to develop bigger and more powerful applications, the documentation will be your only ally to help you navigate your way through all the different functions.

Also, we show an example of how the exponential transformation works on images. The following is our original input image:

Applying an exponential transform leads us to the following:

The overall darkening of the input image is quite apparent!

We have discussed the advantages of using a lookup table-based approach for implementing grayscale transformations. In fact, we have also been implementing all our transformations using a framework based on a combination of computing the lookup table and traversing the data matrix. If this particular combination is so efficient as well as ubiquitous, haven't the OpenCV developers thought of implementing this for us already? If you've followed the trend of this chapter, you would've guessed the answer to the question by now! Yes, OpenCV does have a function that allows you to do exactly that: provide it with a lookup table and a Mat object, and it will transform each pixel of the Mat object on the basis of the rules laid down by the lookup table, and store the result in a new Mat object.

What's even better is that the function is named LUT()! Let's look at a sample code snippet that uses the LUT() method to implement the negative transform.

As we hinted just now, the LUT() method requires three parameters:

- The input matrix
- The lookup table
- The output matrix

We have been dealing with the first and the third throughout the chapter. How do we pass the lookup table to the LUT() method? Remember that a lookup table is essentially an array (or a vector). We have been treating it as such in all our implementations so far, and we also know that the Mat class in OpenCV is more than equipped to handle the processing of one-dimensional arrays. Hence, we would be passing our lookup table as another Mat object. Since our LUT is essentially a Mat object, we change our getLUT() function as follows:

```
Mat getNegativeLUT() {
vector<uchar> lut_array(256, 0);
for (int i = 0; i < 256; ++i)
  lut_array[i] = (uchar)(255 - i);

Mat LUT(1, 256, CV_8U);
for (int j = 0; j < 256; ++j)
  LUT.at<uchar>(0, j) = lut_array[j];
return LUT;
}
```

Notice that the first three lines are identical to what we have been doing so far–initializing and constructing our lookup table as a C++ vector. Now, we take that vector and transform it into a Mat object having one row and 256 columns and type CV_8U (which makes it the perfect container for the elements of a C++ vector of uchar). The remainder of the function makes that transition and returns the Mat object as our LUT.

Once the LUT has been created, applying it is as simple as calling OpenCV's LUT() method with all the necessary arguments:

```
LUT(input_image, lookup_table, output_image);
```

Summary

This concludes our first chapter. We have come a long way! We began our discourse on image processing and computer vision by talking about images and how they are represented inside a computing device. We also began our journey into the world of OpenCV by discussing how the library handles image data in its programs, thereby introducing the Mat class. A significant portion of the chapter was devoted to learning about how to use the Mat class, instantiating objects, learning about its internal structure, and getting intimate with some memory management that takes place under the hood. I hope that, by now, handling images in your code has been demystified for you and you are comfortable dealing with the different forms in which Mat objects appear in the code samples scattered throughout the remainder of the book.

This chapter also served a first taste of some processing that we can perform on images using OpenCV. You learnt a couple of different methods to iterate through the image data stored inside a Mat object, discussing the pros and cons of each. We went on to establish a framework for writing code to help us in the pixel-wise traversal and processing of images. This very framework came to life when we implemented some common grayscale transformations such as negative, log, and exponential transforms. We witnessed what sort of changes these transformations bring forth in our images.

A very important theme that we touched upon briefly in this chapter and would be repeated in the chapters to come is that there are multiple ways to accomplish the same image processing task. We saw that here when we talked about implementing log transformations. One of the alternatives is to implement everything from first principles (*reinvent the wheel*) and the other is to rely on the functions and APIs provided to us by the OpenCV developers. In the subsequent chapters, we will be relying less on the former and more heavily on the latter. Our approach henceforth will be to explain the theoretical concepts from scratch using the basic principles but demonstrating the implementations using OpenCV functions. We believe that it will give you the best of both worlds.

Finally, as we close off the first chapter, here is what you can expect going forward. We discussed transforms, which were quite simplistic in the way that they operate. Each pixel in the output image was dependent on only a single pixel in the input image. We will discuss some more sophisticated forms of transformations in the next chapter, where the output at a particular pixel location depends not only on the corresponding pixel intensity at the input, but rather on a neighborhood of values. Also, we will learn about a fundamental manner in which such transformations are visualized–using a filter or a kernel. Such a *filtering*-based approach is extremely common in the image processing and computer vision world and will make a reappearance in more than one chapter! We will also get an opportunity to extend our arsenal of cool image manipulation techniques that we started building in this chapter.

2
Image Filtering

In the previous chapter, we started off on our journey into the world of computer vision and image processing by familiarizing ourselves with some terms that occur frequently when we talk about images. We also had our first contact with OpenCV when we learnt about how the library provides us with efficient data structures to store and process image data. The chapter also helped us get acquainted with some basic algorithms within the realm of image processing by expounding the details of linear and logarithmic transformations. We familiarized ourselves with how these enhancement techniques essentially work to improve the image contrast (hence the name **image enhancement**), and saw them in action as they modified (stretched or compressed) the grayscale range of an image, thereby revealing details hidden in the darker and lighter regions of the image.

This chapter will take our journey forward. We will learn about more techniques that act on images, perform certain forms of computation, and produce better or improved versions of the input image. Such image processing algorithms form the prerequisites for more advanced computer vision techniques and frameworks. As we shall see, the algorithms discussed here form the preprocessing steps in the pipelines that we will design to solve sophisticated computer vision problems. Hence, it is an absolute necessity to have a firm grasp of the fundamentals that we will discuss in these initial chapters.

The pixel operations that we'll witness in the algorithms discussed in this chapter will no longer be as simple as the grayscale transformations presented in Chapter 1, *Laying the Foundation*. The intensity value at every pixel in the output image will not just be a function of the intensity of the corresponding pixel in the input, but rather it will depend on a neighborhood of pixels. This concept will allow us to define more sophisticated operations. It also affords us the power to visualize the operations using filters (that is, kernels)—a key concept in image processing. Representing image processing operations using filters will bring us to the mathematical concept of correlation that often comes up when we talk about image processing.

Due to the use of filters, the operations that form the topic of our discussions in this chapter are often referred to as **image filtering**. Filtering refers to a paradigm of operations rather than a single algorithm. It is essentially done to remove noise from digital images. *Noise* can be any arbitrary and random variation in the intensity values of a digital image and may be due to a myriad reasons. In this chapter, we discuss image filtering as a technique to combat the effect of random noise in digital images.

Before we start off, we present a list of topics that we propose to cover in this chapter:

- The basic neighborhood-of-a-pixel and image averaging concepts
- The box filter, its applications in the area of image averaging, and its implementation using OpenCV
- Introduction to the nature and form of the Gaussian function.
- Gaussian kernels and Gaussian filtering as an advanced form of image filtering
- The concept of image noise and how the process of averaging (or smoothing) helps to reduce it
- Implementing the Vignetting operation as a practical use case of a Gaussian filter

Neighborhood of a pixel

We have seen image processing operations where the value of a pixel at the output is dependent only on the value of the corresponding pixel at the input. By corresponding, we mean pixels at the same locations (row and column) in the input and output image. Such transformations were represented in mathematical form as follows:

$s = T(r)$

Here, s and r are the intensity values of a pixel in the output and input respectively. Since we are always dealing with pixels at the same locations, there is no mention of pixel coordinates in the preceding formula. That is to say, the grayscale value of the pixel at the 40th row and 30th column in the output depends on the grayscale value of the pixel at the same coordinates (the 40th row and 30th column) at the input.

This section will introduce you to a slightly more advanced form of image transformation. In the operations that we'll discuss now, the output value at a particular pixel (x, y) is not only dependent on the intensity at (x, y) in the input but also around a small neighborhood of (x, y). These transformations are represented mathematically as follows:

$g(x, y) = T [f(x, y)]$

Here, *f* is the input image, *g* is the processed image, and *T* is an operation defined over a neighborhood of *(x, y)*.

This allows for a greater variety in the kinds of transformation that we can allow. Also, you'll come to realize that a major chunk of sophisticated image processing algorithms work along these principles.

Before we delve into the details of the techniques, we need to discuss the notion of a *neighborhood* of a pixel. For that, imagine a set of coordinate axes laid across our image with the origin at the top-left corner, with the X-axis increasing downwards, indexing the rows from top to bottom, and the Y-axis increasing towards the right, indexing the columns from left to right. In such a system, the neighbors of a pixel are the ones that surround the target pixel, as shown in the following grid:

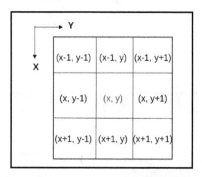

For the pixel *(x, y)*, its eight neighbors are: **(x – 1, y – 1), (x – 1, y), (x – 1, y + 1), (x, y + 1), (x + 1, y + 1), (x + 1, y), (x + 1, y – 1),** and **(x, y – 1)**. We have shown a 3 x 3 neighborhood around **(x, y)**. Note that, in some cases, you'll find the term *neighbors* to be a bit loosely defined. There are definitions and algorithms scattered across the image processing literature that might have a more liberal or restrictive definition of a neighborhood. For example, in some cases, the neighbors can include the eight *immediate neighbors* as shown here as well as their adjacent pixels (5 x 5, or even bigger neighborhoods). However, in some other places, you will find that only the four pixels that lie horizontally and vertically next to **(x, y)**, that is, **(x – 1, y), (x, y + 1), (x + 1, y),** and **(x, y-1)** are considered its neighbors. What I have shown here (the 3 x 3 neighborhood) is the one most commonly encountered. The 4-neighborhood won't be used unless specifically stated otherwise.

Image averaging

Now that we are familiar with the notion of a neighborhood, we are ready to delve into the details of an operation called image averaging. As the name suggests, image *averaging* involves taking the mean of pixel intensity values. More specifically, each pixel is replaced by the mean of all pixels in its neighborhood. The size of the neighborhood is one of the parameters that is usually passed to the function that implements this sort of an averaging procedure. For illustration purposes, we consider a neighborhood of 3 x 3 around the pixel (this would include the pixel and its eight immediate neighbors). For example, consider the next image (you can take it to be a small sub-section within the entire image). Let's say that we wish to compute the output intensity value corresponding to the pixel with an intensity of 6 in the input image. We take the 3 x 3 neighborhood of that pixel and calculate the mean of all those values (the values have been marked in bold-face). Hence, the corresponding value in the output is given by the following:

$$\frac{1}{9}\left(8+3+4+7+6+1+4+5+7\right) = 45/9 = 5$$

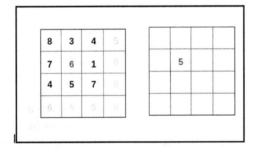

There is a subtle point that needs to be kept in mind while calculating the output pixel values. Let's say that we have computed the output corresponding to the pixel in red as **5**. Now, we move on to the pixel that lies on the immediate right (with an intensity value of 1). When we talk about the neighbors of that pixel, we consider **6** as its neighbor (from the input image) and not **5** (the output value we just computed). What we are trying to say is that the operations do not happen in place. That is to say, as we move across pixels and compute the averages in their respective neighborhoods, the input image remains unchanged and all the (new) output values that are generated are stored separately.

If we were to express this mathematically, it would be a little tedious but would look something like this:

$$J(x,y) = \frac{1}{9}\left(I(x-1,y-1) + I(x-1,y) + \cdots + I(x+1,y-1) + I(x,y-1)\right)$$

Here, the summation ranges over all the eight neighbors of (x, y), and I and J stand for the input and output images, respectively. As you can see, this is a rather inconvenient way to represent such classes of transformations. Imagine now that we used a 5 x 5 neighborhood instead of 3 x 3 as we have done here. Expressing such a transformation mathematically would involve dealing with 25 terms in summation. There should be a better way to express such averaging transformations, and of course there is! This brings us to the uber-important concept of filters in image processing.

Image filters

If you carefully observe the example that we discussed in the previous section, you will notice that during the process of computing the output intensity at (x, y), we basically multiplied the intensity values of all the 3 x 3 neighbors by **1/9** and added them all up. Let's create a small matrix of dimensions 3 x 3 (the size of the neighborhood under consideration) and fill all the cells with the value **1/9** as shown in the following image:

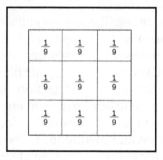

We'll call this a *filter* or a *kernel*. Now, we'll make use of this filter to calculate the output intensity value corresponding to any arbitrary input pixel (x, y), say the pixel having an intensity value of 6 (see the following image). How do we go about doing that? Well, we place the filter over the image in such a manner that the central grid in the filter lies right on top of the pixel at position *(x, y)*—*(2, 2)* in our case (I have assumed 1-based indexing for both rows and columns). Once we place the filter in this manner, it will completely cover the 3 x 3 neighborhood of our pixel at (2, 2) with every single grid of the filter lying exactly on top of one of the neighbors of our pixel with intensity 6. Now, all we have to do is multiply the corresponding values in the grid and the input image, and add them all up to get the output. We repeat this process for all pixels by simply sliding the filter across the input image and computing the average at all positions *(x, y)*!

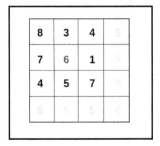

The process of multiplying the corresponding elements of a filter and the pixels in the image that it covers is called **correlation**. So, what we have essentially done is correlate our filter with the input image to perform the image averaging operation.

At this point, all of this must be seeming like an overkill: a fancy and visual technique to achieve something that is computationally straightforward. But the real power of image filters lies in the fact that we can represent different image processing techniques within the same framework of correlation by simply changing our filter. You'll witness later in this book that image derivatives and different edge detection algorithms essentially involve correlating different kinds of filters with our images. Even within averaging, using different types of filters leads to very different kinds of results! In fact, this process of correlation of an image using a filter is so common and ubiquitous in the realm of image processing that these techniques are given the name of image filtering algorithms. In the broadest sense of the term *filtering*, the value of the filtered image at a given location is a function of the values of the input image in a small neighborhood of the same location.

Before we move on to the exciting parts about implementation, I want you to ponder upon a couple of things. First, can all sorts of operations on images be represented using a filtering-based approach? Or does the process need to possess any inherent characteristics for it to have an analogous filter-based approach? Consider this operation: we need to replace each pixel by the mean of the squares of its neighbors. Can you think of any single filter that can perform this computation using the correlation technique that we just discussed? Clearly not. For an operation to have a corresponding filter, it needs to satisfy two properties:

- The same operation has to be performed at all pixel locations *(x, y)*
- The operation at any location must be linear

Second, do you think that knowing the nature of the filter and the input image is sufficient to calculate the output image? In the example that we have just discussed, what do you think should be the value for the pixel in the first row and third column, *I(1, 3)* with an intensity value of 4? Clearly, for such a pixel, there isn't a sufficient number of pixels available in the input image (neighborhood) to be covered by the filter. When positioned over the pixel, the top row of the filter would overshoot the boundaries of the image. In fact, this problem will persist for all pixels that lie along the boundary (first and last row, first and last column) of the image if we are using a 3 x 3 neighborhood. This problem will become more severe (with a greater number of outer rows and columns being affected) as we use a filter of higher dimensions. So, what do we do to overcome this?

We pad the input image with a sufficient number of extra pixels so that all the pixels of the original image will have a valid correlation. For example, if we are using a 3 x 3 filter, we pad our input image with two additional rows and columns at either ends as shown in the following image:

	8	3	4	5	
	7	6	1	0	
	4	5	7	8	
	6	5	5	6	

Now, what values are we to put into these extra pixels? There are quite a few options at our disposal. The most common technique that is used in the majority of cases is to replicate the value of the border pixels as shown in the next image. This is often a prudent thing to do because in a sufficiently large image, the pixel intensities do not change much with small changes in spatial coordinates. This means that if we are to predict the intensity values at the padded pixels, we can replicate the border pixels of the image as a reasonable guess.

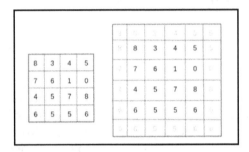

The other techniques (which we won't be discussing in detail) involve making the padded pixels all have the same intensity value (usually, 0 or 255), assuming that the image is cyclic (wrapped around) and replicating values from the opposite end or assuming that the boundary acts as a mirror and replicating values from the current edge of the image, reversing all the way to the opposite edge.

This brings us to the end of our discussions on the theoretical underpinnings of image averaging using image filtering techniques. Now, we will get down to the actual work–implementing these filters using our favorite combination of C++ and OpenCV!

Image averaging in OpenCV

While implementing the image transforms that we discussed in the previous chapter, we adopted an approach that was based on the fundamentals and involved quite a bit of *reinventing the wheel*. We could afford to do that because the traversals that we performed over the data matrix in our implementations were conceptually pretty straightforward. However, we will no longer do that for a couple of reasons:

- The kind of transformations that we are discussing at the moment (averaging using a filtering-based approach) no longer involves a simple pixel-by-pixel traversal of the data matrix. Rather, they involve a two-tiered approach where we have to traverse the neighborhood for each pixel that we encounter in our usual traversal of the data matrix. Implementing such a non-trivial traversal every single time can become time-consuming and error-prone.

- As we progress through the book, we want you to rely more and more on the functions and APIs provided by the OpenCV developers. After all, this is exactly what the book is supposed to teach you! We touched upon this briefly in the previous chapter as well when we demonstrated the code that utilizes OpenCV APIs to perform log transformations. While knowing how to traverse pixels is an important fundamental skill to master, we cannot afford to fall back on the basics every time we wish to implement an image-processing task. Using OpenCV functions will become the norm from now on.

Having said that, the `boxFilter()` method in OpenCV accomplishes the task of performing an image averaging operation by using a filter similar to the one we discussed in the last chapter. In fact, any such filter that computes the arithmetic mean of a neighborhood of pixel values is termed a **box filter**. So, let's jump straight in and see the method in action.

As always, we start with the relevant header files and namespaces:

```
#include <iostream>
#include <opencv2/core/core.hpp>
#include <opencv2/highgui/highgui.hpp>
#include <opencv2/imgproc/imgproc.hpp>

using namespace std;
using namespace cv;
```

You will have noticed the inclusion of a header named `imgproc.hpp`. This is the header file containing the declarations for OpenCV's image processing module. All of the image filtering functions that are going to be the subject of discussion in the current chapter, as well as a lot of functions aiding in other image processing tasks, fall under the dominion of `imgproc.hpp`. You are going to see a lot more of this header! Now, we write the body of code that actually performs the box filtering operation:

```
int main()
{
  Mat input_image = imread("lena.png", IMREAD_GRAYSCALE);
  Mat filtered_image;
  boxFilter(
    input_image,
    filtered_image,
    -1,
    Size(3, 3),
    Point(-1, -1),
    true,
    BORDER_REPLICATE
);
```

```
imshow("Original Image", input_image);
imshow("Filtered Image", filtered_image);
waitKey(0);
return 0;
}
```

As we can see, the boxFilter() function accepts a lot of arguments. Let's go over them one by one:

1. The first argument is, of course, the input image on which the averaging has to be performed.

2. The second argument is the output image. Most OpenCV functions follow the design rule of accepting a Mat object representing the output image as an argument in itself rather than returning one.

3. This function allows us to specify the depth (data type used to store the individual pixel values) of the output image as the third argument. Even if our input is a grayscale image having an 8-bit depth, averaging operations can give rise to floating point values. Hence, float CV_32F or a double CV_64F would be perfectly acceptable values to pass here. As you will notice, we have decided to pass on a value of -1, which signifies that we would be using the same depth as the source (input) image: unsigned char. All computed output pixel values will automatically be type-casted to the provided output type.

4. The next argument refers to the size of the kernel used for the averaging operation. You will notice the reappearance of the Size class here! If you remember the time when we introduced the Size object, we had used it to specify the dimensions for our Mat object initializations. Note that using an object of the Size class would mean allowing kernels of any arbitrary dimensions, not necessarily square, whereas, we have been using a square kernel for all our discussions. OpenCV does allow you to use rectangular kernels; however, we will rarely be using anything other than square kernels.

5. The fifth argument is what is known as the **anchor point**. The anchor point specifies the coordinate of the point within the filter that will lie on top of the input image pixel under consideration (the pixel at coordinate *(x, y)* in our examples). Note that we have passed it a value of *Point(-1, -1)*, which basically refers to the center of the kernel. If you are using a square filter with odd dimensions, using *Point(-1, -1)* is probably the best idea.

6. The sixth argument is a flag specifying whether the output of the filter has to be normalized. Now, in the context of image filtering, what does normalization mean? If you look at the OpenCV docs, the filter (or kernel) that is implemented by the library's boxFilter() method is given by the following equation:

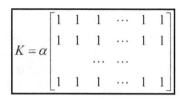

What has been done here is that the filter has been represented as a matrix. After all, both of them are a two-dimensional grid of values. By comparing the matrix form with the examples that we worked with in the last section, we can deduce that alpha is equal to 1/9, for our example. Where did the 9 in the denominator come from? It is quite easy to guess that the 9 here refers to the total number of elements in the kernel (we used a 3 x 3 kernel). So, generalizing this, we can state that the alpha in the preceding relation is nothing but the reciprocal of the size of the filter. When you come to think of it, it does make sense because the aim of the box filter is to compute the average of the pixel values that it encompasses, and that is only possible when you divide the sum of all the values by the number of terms (filter size). So, where does normalization fit into all of this? Well, as it turns out, alpha is not always what we have discussed. The expression for alpha is given by:

$$\alpha = \begin{cases} \dfrac{1}{width * height} & if\ normalize = true \\ 1 & if\ otherwise \end{cases}$$

So, essentially, the value of the normalization flag decides the value of alpha. When it is true, the behavior of the filter is as expected: it performs the averaging. When it is kept false, the function will only perform the summation of the neighborhood pixels (try to reason why!).

The last and final argument tells the function how to deal with borders. We touched upon the different possibilities that are available to us while discussing the basics of image filtering. Keeping those in mind, here is a table listing all the different values that you can pass to this argument (the | represents an image boundary in the descriptions):

Border Type	Description
BORDER_REPLICATE	aaaaa	abcdefgh	hhhhhhh
BORDER_REFLECT	fedcba	abcdefgh	hgfedcb
BORDER_WRAP	cdefgh	abcdefgh	abcdefg
BORDER_CONSTANT	iiiiii	abcdefgh	iiiiiii (for a specified value, i)

The descriptions have been provided via examples of 1D images; however, the concepts that they represent can very easily be extended to the 2D case. For example, we discussed a scenario where the padded pixels were filled in with the intensity values of the pixels at the boundaries of the image. This behavior is represented by the BORDER_REPLICATE flag. As you can see in the 1D example from the table, the values at the extreme ends of the 1D image (*a* and *h*) have been replicated for the bordering pixels (those lying outside the two / marks). You can deduce the behavior of the other flags using similar reasoning.

Judging by the variety and the number of arguments to the method, one can easily appreciate the wide spectrum of behavior that a single function encapsulates. We can return Mat objects of different types that can hold the result of averaging using a filter selected from a vast possibility of sizes, aligned over the image pixels in different ways and treating the pixels at the borders differently! On the other hand, it is not always mandatory to specify all the seven arguments with every single function call. The first four are mandatory (input and output image, output image depth, and kernel size) and the others are set to defaults. The following is another perfectly valid function call:

```
boxFilter(input_image, filtered_image, -1, Size(3, 3));
```

We discussed implementing an averaging filter in great detail in OpenCV. Now, we'll see what it actually does to an image by looking at some sample outputs generated by running the preceding code. As always, our input image will be a grayscale version of Lena. In the following set of four images, each one is an output generated by the boxFilter() method for different values of the kernel size. Starting from the first image (top-left) and moving along the top-right, bottom-left, and all the way to the last image on the bottom-right, our filter size progressively increases from 3 x 3, 7 x 7, 11 x 11, to 15 x 15, respectively (we have kept the kernel as a square of an odd size in order to have a well-defined and symmetric anchor point).

As you can clearly observe, with an increase in the filter size, the images become progressively blurry. If you think in terms of the nature of operations being performed at every pixel, it does make intuitive sense. As we replace each pixel with the average of its neighbors, the image starts losing its finer details. And this loss would be more pronounced as we increase the size of the neighborhood. When we talk about edge detection algorithms in the subsequent chapters, we'll discuss the fact that there is a sudden change in the variation (gradient, to be more scientific) of pixel intensity values across the edges of an image, as compared to the non-edge regions. Another way to put this would be to say that there is a sharp change in the pixel intensity values as we cross the edges of objects in an image (after all, edges are supposed to mark the boundaries between two different objects), and there is a comparatively more uniform distribution of pixel intensity values in the non-edge regions. This also means that the edges are the most sensitive when it comes to averaging operations and they seem to be the first regions in an image to get affected by the most subtle smoothing operations.

Before we move on, we want to give you a feel of the different border-pixel extrapolation techniques by showing results obtained from two different methods: BORDER_REPLICATE and BORDER_CONSTANT. As we have already discussed, the BORDER_REPLICATE method extrapolates the values by copying the pixel intensities from the pixels situated at the border and the BORDER_CONSTANT method will fill in all extrapolated pixels with the same value (black in our case). The following screenshot is an example of smoothing performed using BORDER_REPLICATE. In fact, all the four examples presented were also done using the same method for border extrapolation.

The next image has been averaged using the BORDER_CONSTANT method by filling in all extended pixels with black. You can clearly observe a thin strip of dark pixels surrounding the image from all four sides like a border. The image has been blurred using a kernel of size 25, which means a significant number of rows and columns has been padded with the edges of the image, leading to the dark strip that is visible:

To summarize the effect of image averaging, we can say that it performs a blurring operation on images. In fact, OpenCV has yet another function named `blur()`! Let us see what `blur()` accomplishes and whether it is any different from the `boxFilter()` method that we have discussed just now.

Blurring an image in OpenCV

Since we are already familiar with the basics, let's jump right into the code. I am skipping the header declarations because they remain the same as we saw in our previous code:

```
int main()
{
  Mat input_image = imread("lena.png", IMREAD_GRAYSCALE);
  Mat filtered_image;
  blur(input_image, filtered_image, Size(3, 3), Point(-1, -1),
BORDER_REPLICATE);
  imshow("Original Image", input_image);
  imshow("Filtered Image", filtered_image);
  waitKey(0);
  return 0;
}
```

The first thing that you notice about the blur() function is that the number of arguments is less than its counterpart. Upon a closer inspection, you'll find that the following two arguments are missing:

- **Depth of the output image**: According to OpenCV's documentation for blur(), the output image has the same size and type as the source image. Since the equality between the input and output image types is already enforced by the implementation of the function, there is no need to specify the type of the output separately as a parameter.
- **The normalize flag**: The absence of the normalize flag means that the blur() method doesn't afford us the versatility of choosing the value of alpha. Again, the structure of the kernel has been hardcoded within the implementation itself and is shown as follows:

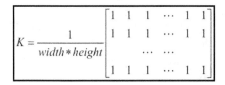

$$K = \frac{1}{width * height} \begin{bmatrix} 1 & 1 & 1 & \cdots & 1 & 1 \\ 1 & 1 & 1 & \cdots & 1 & 1 \\ & & \cdots & \cdots & & \\ 1 & 1 & 1 & \cdots & 1 & 1 \end{bmatrix}$$

The remaining arguments are exactly the same as we discussed while talking about the boxFilter() method. It should be pretty evident by now that the blur() function is much more restrictive than boxFilter(). While the latter allows us to perform both averaging and summation over the neighborhood of pixel values (by providing flexibility over the selection of alpha), the former can only be used for image smoothing and averaging (hence the name blur()). As an exercise, you should try out the preceding code on the same set of images that you used for running boxFilter() and compare the results.

Gaussian smoothing

In the image smoothing operation that we introduced in the last section, we used a 3 x 3 filter where every value was 1/9. When we discussed the working of a filter, we explained that every element in a filter multiplies itself with the intensity value of a pixel in the neighborhood and the result is added up (this was one way to visualize the averaging operation). Now, we will present one more technique to visualize the same!

I am guessing that you are aware of the concept of weighted averages. For those who are not, we reiterate the same here. Given a sequence of n values $x_1, x_2, \cdots, x_n$ and their corresponding weights $w_1, w_2, \cdots, w_n$, the weighted average of these n values is given by the following relation:

$$\bar{x} = \frac{w_1 x_1 + w_2 x_2 + \cdots + w_n x_n}{w_1 + w_2 + \cdots + w_n} = \frac{\sum_{i=1}^{n} w_i x_i}{\sum_{i=1}^{n} w_i}$$

In the special case where all of the weights sum up to 1, our equation reduces to the following:

$$\bar{x} = w_1 x_1 + w_2 x_2 + \cdots + w_n x_n = \sum_{i=1}^{n} w_i x_i$$

This form is starting to feel a little familiar now, isn't it? What if the weights $w_1, w_2, \cdots, w_n$ correspond to the values in our filter and the sequence $x_1, x_2, \cdots, x_n$ is our pixel intensity values? Well, in that case the preceding equation perfectly represents the filtering operation around a certain pixel in the input image! This is indeed the connection between weighted averages and image smoothing that we have been alluding to. The image smoothing that we have discussed (using a box filter) and implemented in this chapter is actually a special case of weighted averaging. All the weights are same and equal to the reciprocal of the filter size, that is, $w_1 = w_2 = \cdots = w_n = (1/n)$. Note that our weights are also adding up to unity.

Now, we come to the more important part. Expressing image smoothing as a weighted average (with the weights being specified by the filter) opens up a vast range of possibilities with respect to the types of filter we can employ. We have focused on a single type of filter till now, the box filter, where all weights are the same, causing the weighted average to reduce to a simple arithmetic mean.

The box filter is limited in its usability because of a rather trivial assumption that it inherently makes. Since all weights are equal, a box filter assumes an equal contribution from all its neighbors to a pixel's *smoothed* (output) value. This means that, for a pixel with an intensity of 6, as shown in the following figure, all its neighbors with intensities **8**, **3**, **4**, **1**, **7**, **5**, **4**, and **7** contribute equally (with a factor of *1/9*) to the calculation of the average value:

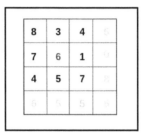

Obviously, this assumption of equal contribution is a rather naive one to make. The pixels lying nearby should have a greater impact on the output value than the ones lying farther away. This is precisely the notion that is captured by yet another type of filtering that is going to be the subject of our study in this section: **Gaussian filtering**.

Gaussian function and Gaussian filtering

Very shortly, we will be embarking on a long, but rather interesting discussion as we build our mathematical intuitions on Gaussian filtering. In order to motivate the same, we present to you some sample images that have been generated by applying the Gaussian filtering operation on Lena's image. A detailed description of each of the succeeding four output images will be presented at the end of this section. Right now, this is to motivate you and give you a glimpse of what to expect as we move ahead!

For the purpose of explaining the theoretical underpinnings and working of the Gaussian filtering method, we take a step back and consider 1D images. Just as regular 2D images are represented using a 2D grid of values, in the same manner (hypothetical) 1D images are nothing but a 1D array of pixel values.

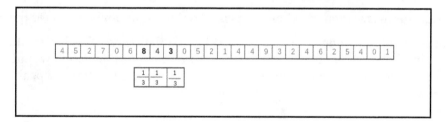

The preceding diagram attempts to visualize the workings of a simple 1×3 box filter that replaces each pixel with the average of itself and its immediate left and right neighbors. As you can see, the weights corresponding to all the elements are the same, that is, 1/3 (as is expected of a box filter). A Gaussian filter attempts to change that by giving each pixel a different weight in accordance with its distance from the center pixel (or anchor point). And how does it decide on the value of the weights? Well, it utilizes the Gaussian function.

The form of the Gaussian function is given here:

$$G(x) = \frac{1}{\sigma\sqrt{2x}}\,e^{-\frac{x^2}{2\sigma^2}}$$

Here, σ stands for the standard deviation. Those of you who have come across this function before might be having some questions in mind. What does the standard deviation represent in our case? Isn't the Gaussian function defined for a continuous domain? If yes, then aren't images discrete? How does the Gaussian function fit into our framework of filters and images? We will tackle each question, one by one!

First, let's take a look at what the Gaussian curve looks like. The following figure shows the shape of a Gaussian curve. You can see that the curve peaks in the middle and tapers off symmetrically as we move away from the peak in either direction. In other words, the values close to the peak (on both sides) have a higher output as per the Gaussian function. Similarly, for values that are distant, the output value rapidly diminishes:

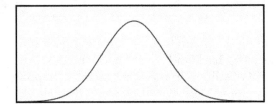

The Gaussian curve is symmetric about its peak. The standard deviation, σ (or the variance, σ^2) is a measure of how much the data is spread about the center. This information is represented by the width of the Gaussian curve. A low standard deviation would mean that the data is clustered in and around the central value giving rise to a narrow peak as shown in the following figure:

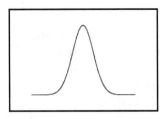

On the other hand, a large standard deviation means data that is spread far and wide leading to a Gaussian curve that is flattened and spread out, much like the one we showed when we introduced the Gaussian curve.

Now, you must have caught on to some similarity between the Gaussian curve and what we are trying to accomplish via the so-called Gaussian filtering. We want to compute the weighted average of pixels in a neighborhood where the weights gradually decrease as we move away from the center pixel (anchor point of the filter), and we have a mathematical function where the output values decrease symmetrically as we move away from the central peak! So, the only thing left is to provide a connection between the two. Now, imagine that we index our filters in the manner shown in the following diagram. The anchor point is given an index of **0**, and the locations to the right and left of the anchor point are indexed using positive and negative integers respectively (this is a somewhat non-conventional method of indexing 1D arrays). How does such an indexing help us? Essentially, what we have done is made the indexes reflect the relative positions of the filter coordinates with reference to the anchor point. That is, just by looking at the index positions, we can judge that a position with an index of **4** lies farther away (on the same side) from the anchor than another position having an index of **2**. Also, the positions having indices **-2** and **2** lie equidistant from the anchor point, but on opposite sides:

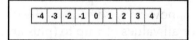

Now, these filter indices can serve as input values for the Gaussian and we can sample the Gaussian function at these discrete integral points. Note that sampling the Gaussian is another fancy way of saying *calculate the output of the Gaussian function at this discrete set of integral points*. So, the output that the Gaussian function gives for each of these indexes as input becomes the filter value at that index. For calculating the Gaussian, the standard deviation is a parameter that is passed on as an argument (much like the size of the kernel in the `boxFilter()` method). The following shows a sample computation for a filter of size 9, similar to the one that we previously presented. The standard deviation is set to 3.0:

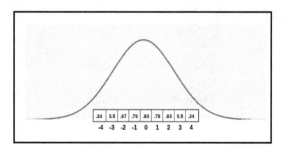

If you combine what you learnt about the nature and the shape of the Gaussian and the indexing of a filter, you can easily deduce that the filter that we obtained (the Gaussian filter) gives different weights to different pixels in accordance with their distance from the center pixel (or anchor point). If you have been following the discussion carefully, you will have noticed that we started off by saying that that the sum of the filter should be equal to 1 (this was true for the box filter, by design). However, the Gaussian filter does not ensure this. So, what we do is that after computing the values in the filter, in accordance with the Gaussian formula, we normalize the filter, that is, we divide each term by the sum of all the terms in the filter. So, for a filter of size $2N + 1$, the value at a particular index i, such that $-N <= i <= N$, is given by the following relation:

$$F(i) = \frac{G(i)}{\sum_{k=-N}^{N} G(k)} \; where \, G(x) = \frac{1}{\sigma\sqrt{2\pi}} e^{-\frac{x^2}{2\sigma^2}}$$

This raises one more very pertinent question—what size of filter do we go for? When we talked about box filtering in OpenCV, the size was one of the parameters for implementation. Also, the effects of changing the size of the filter are easy to visualize—it simply changed the amount of blurring. But here, for the same value of Sigma, we can have different sizes of filters; we are free to decide upon the choice of N in the preceding equations. So, for a given Sigma, how do we decide on the filter size? Theoretically, the Gaussian function is defined for all values of x up to (plus and minus) infinity. However, you might have noticed that the curve drops down to infinitesimally small values (practically zero) at either ends of the mean. This means that taking the filter size to be longer than necessary would lead to redundant computations: a lot of pixels with weights of zero (or very close to zero). On the other hand, taking a small filter size would mean missing out on the contributions of the neighborhood pixels (and only considering pixels which lie close to the anchor point). A good filter size should ideally involve a trade-off between the two.

In fact, OpenCV has a function named `getGaussianKernel()` which computes and returns the Gaussian filter values for a given size and standard deviation. Let's check out how it works. Following protocol, at the very outset, we include header files and namespaces:

```
#include <iostream>
#include <opencv2/core/core.hpp>
#include <opencv2/highgui/highgui.hpp>
#include <opencv2/imgproc/imgproc.hpp>

using namespace std;
using namespace cv;
```

The `main()` function given in the following code calls the `getGaussianKernel()` function and displays the result that is returned. The two arguments to the function are:

- Size of the kernel. As per the documentation, the kernel size must be odd and positive.
- The standard deviation of the Gaussian.

There is a third argument that specifies the datatype of the Gaussian kernel returned as a Mat object. You can pass two possible values: `CV_32F` (float) or `CV_64F` (double). The argument has a default value of `CV_64F`, so it has been skipped in the implementation given here:

```
int main() {

  Mat gaussian_kernel = getGaussianKernel(7, 1.0);
  int rows = gaussian_kernel.rows;
  int cols = gaussian_kernel.cols;
  if (gaussian_kernel.isContinuous()) {
    cols = (cols * rows);
    rows = 1;
  }

  cout << "Gaussian Kernel...\n";
  for (int row_idx = 0; row_idx < rows; ++row_idx) {
    double* row_ptr = gaussian_kernel.ptr<double>(row_idx);
    for (int col_idx = 0; col_idx < cols; ++col_idx)
      cout << row_ptr[col_idx] << " ";
    cout << "\n";
  }

  return 0;
}
```

You must have noticed that we resorted to the sequential approach of Mat object traversal in the preceding code snippet. However, it is known for a fact that the `getGaussianKernel()` function returns a column matrix. This means that the Mat object returned will always have one single column and the number of rows will be equal to the size of the filter. We can make use of this information to simplify our code. Take a look at the following snippet:

```
cout << "Gauusian kernel...\n";
for (int i = 0; i < gaussian_kernel.rows; ++i)
  cout << gaussian_kernel.at<double>(i, 0) << " ";
cout << "\n";
```

We have made use of the `at()` method of random access coupled with the fact that there is only a single column for each row. This looks to be a far more concise and aesthetic way of doing things. Also, note that the `getGaussianKernel()` method only computes the Gaussian kernel. It doesn't apply filtering using the same. We will be covering that very soon.

We have been dealing with hypothetical 1D images in our discussions so far. Let's now take a look at how all of this scales to 2D images. The two-dimensional Gaussian form is shown as follows:

$$G(x,y) = \frac{1}{2\pi\sigma_x\sigma_y} e^{-\frac{1}{2}\left(\frac{x^2}{\sigma_x^2} + \frac{y^2}{\sigma_y^2}\right)}$$

Note that there are two standard deviations–one for each of the dimensions. Here is a plot of the same. The 2D curve peaks at *(0, 0)* and gradually tapers off as we move away in either the **X** or the **Y** direction.

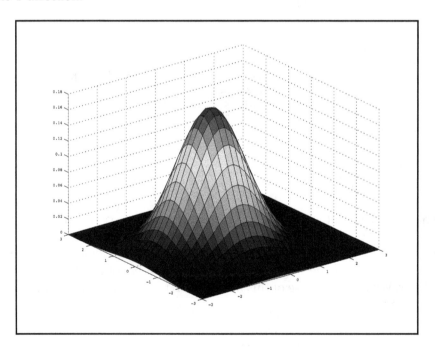

If you are intimidated by the form of the two-dimensional Gaussian, don't worry. It's just a product of two 1D Gaussian functions:

$$G(x, y) = \frac{1}{\sigma_x \sqrt{2\pi}} e^{-\frac{x^2}{2\sigma_x^2}} \cdot \frac{1}{\sigma_y \sqrt{2\pi}} e^{-\frac{y^2}{2\sigma_y^2}}$$

When we compute a two-dimensional Gaussian filter, we use a format of indexing as shown in the following figure:

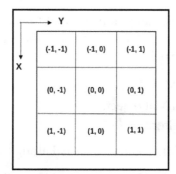

You can see that the filter coordinates for both the dimensions **X** and **Y** have been computed independently where each of the axes has been numbered identically to the format we used for the 1D filter. So, generating a 2D Gaussian filter is as simple as plugging the *(x, y)* coordinate values for each cell into the 2D Gaussian formula.

Gaussian filtering in OpenCV

We have spent a considerable amount of time understanding the theory behind Gaussian filtering. It is now time to jump into the implementation. The headers will remain the same as in the case of `boxFilter()`. The functions implementing Gaussian filtering also reside within the `imgproc` module:

```
#include <iostream>
#include <opencv2/core/core.hpp>
#include <opencv2/highgui/highgui.hpp>
#include <opencv2/imgproc/imgproc.hpp>

using namespace std;
using namespace cv;
```

Here is the code snippet that actually accomplishes the task of Gaussian filtering:

```
int main() {
    Mat input_image = imread("lena.jpg", IMREAD_GRAYSCALE);
    Mat filtered_image;

    GaussianBlur(input_image, filtered_image, Size(7, 7), 1.0, 1.0,
BORDER_REPLICATE);

    imshow("Filtered Image", filtered_image);
    waitKey(0);
    return 0;
}
```

One of the first things that you probably notice is that the arguments to `GaussianBlur()` are fewer than those to `boxFilter()`! In fact, most of the arguments (except a couple of them) serve exactly the same purpose. Let's discuss them one by one:

1. The input image as a Mat object.
2. The output image as a Mat object.
3. Size of the Gaussian filter.
4. Standard deviation of the Gaussian kernel along the X-direction: σ_x.
5. Standard deviation of the Gaussian kernel along the Y-direction: σ_y.
6. Border flag that tells the implementation how to deal with borders.

Apart from 4 and 5, all the other arguments are familiar to you and serve the same purpose as they did when we discussed them in the context of `boxFilter()`. The fourth and fifth arguments are double precision floating point values that specify the standard deviations along the X and Y directions, respectively (see the formula for the two-dimensional Gaussian curve in the *Gaussian function and Gaussian filtering* section).

Having written the code to implement Gaussian filtering, we will now demonstrate its effect on images. The following image shows the effect of changing the value of the standard deviation in a Gaussian filter (the size of the filter is constant). The image is a combined set of 4 images. In all four images, the standard deviation along X and Y has been kept equal. The top-left image starts of with a Sigma of 1.0. As we proceed from the top-right and move along the bottom-left and reach the bottom-right, the standard deviation changes from 2.0, 3.0, to 4.0, respectively.

As you can observe, increasing the standard deviation leads to more blurriness (try to reason why). In fact, when you use a Gaussian filter, you have two parameters through which you can control the extent to which you want the image to be smoothed: the size of the filter and standard deviation of the Gaussian kernel. Also, if you compare the preceding Gaussian smoothing results with the box-filter counterparts, you will notice that in the case of box filtering, the edges are more prone to blurring, whereas here the severity of the blur on edges and corners is less.

Using your own filters in OpenCV

So far, we have talked about a couple of different filtering techniques: box filtering and Gaussian filtering. Both of them had their own set of rules for defining a filter and also had a dedicated set of functions to help you apply the filters to images. When we introduced the concept of filtering, we said that different operations can be performed on our images by simply changing the value of the filter. So, if we design our own custom filter, how do we apply that to our image? There needs to exist a function that is more generic than `boxFilter()`, `blur()`, or `GaussianBlur()` and that will help us in applying the filter that we have designed to our input image. And OpenCV has the answer for you–the `filter2D()` function.

We have already hinted at what the `filter2D()` hopes to accomplish, so let's jump right into the code! I think at this point, I really don't need to say what the first few lines should look like:

```cpp
#include <iostream>
#include <opencv2/core/core.hpp>
#include <opencv2/highgui/highgui.hpp>
#include <opencv2/imgproc/imgproc.hpp>

using namespace std;
using namespace cv;
```

Although, in theory you can design and apply any possible filter using the `filter2D()` method, for convenience, we will demonstrate the application of a box filter using `filter2D()`. Note that we first create and then apply the box filter. Let us start by defining the size of the filter as a global integer variable:

```cpp
const int KSIZE = 7;

int main() {
    Mat input_image = imread("/home/samyak/Pictures/lena.jpg",
IMREAD_GRAYSCALE);
    Mat filtered_image;
    Mat kernel = Mat::ones(KSIZE, KSIZE, CV_32F) / (float)(KSIZE * KSIZE);

    filter2D(input_image, filtered_image, -1, kernel, Point(-1, 1), 0,
BORDER_REPLICATE);

    imshow("Filtered Image", filtered_image);
    waitKey(0);

    return 0;
}
```

As you can see, the arguments to `filter2D()` are very similar to the kind of arguments that we have been dealing with in all the functions discussed in this chapter. Nevertheless, here is a quick recap of what each of them accomplishes:

1. The input, or source image (as a Mat object).
2. The output, or filtered image (again as a Mat object).
3. The depth of the output Mat object. We have specified a value of *-1*, which makes the depth the same as that of the input image.
4. The fourth argument is unique to the `filter2D()` method and specifies the filter that has to be applied. Note that the filter has been specified as a Mat object. It is interesting to see how the filter has been constructed. While declaring the kernel,

we initialize it with a matrix of all 1's (having square dimensions of length KSIZE–already declared as a global integer variable). Then, we go on to divide each element of the matrix with the total number of elements in the filter (KSIZE * KSIZE). If you recall, this is exactly how the box filter is constructed. Also, it is important to note that a non-trivial, element-wise division operation for the entire Mat object has been performed using a simple division operator. In the previous chapter, when we were discussing the implementation of the log transform, we saw a case where a similar element-wise addition was performed using the addition operator. This is yet another way in which life has been made simple by the OpenCV developers!

5. The next argument is the anchor point. And by now, you know what *Point(-1, 1)* stands for.

6. The sixth argument is also something that we haven't encountered yet. It specifies an optional delta value that may be added to all the pixels, after filtering and before storing them in the output matrix. Since we have specified a value of 0, we don't really want any additions to be made to our output pixel values.

7. The final argument is, of course, the flag that tells OpenCV how the borders of the image are to be handled during the filtering operation.

Image noise

We have learnt in great detail about image filtering operations (box and Gaussian filtering). We have also seen that, in general, image averaging tends to blur our input image. Let us now stop and ponder why (and in what scenario) we would need to perform such averaging operations. What prompted the need to replace each pixel with an average (or a weighted average of its neighbors)? The answer to these questions lies in the concept of image noise.

Images are nothing but two-dimensional signals (mapping a pair of x and y coordinate values to corresponding pixel intensities) and just like any signal, they are susceptible to noise. When we say that an image is noisy, we mean that there is a small or large variation in the intensity values of the pixels from the ideal value that we would expect. Noise in an image creeps in due to defects in digital cameras or photographic film.

The following image demonstrates some examples of noisy photographs:

There are two different types of noise when we talk of images. We will not be going into detail, as that would involve going off on a tangent. A very brief and informal description follows:

- **Salt and Pepper noise**: In this category of noise, certain pixels are quite different in intensity from their surrounding pixels. Due to this large variation, salt and pepper noise appears as dark and white dots scattered across the image.
- **Gaussian noise**: In Gaussian noise, the changes in the intensity values are comparatively smaller than salt and pepper noise. In fact, this category of noise borrows its name from the fact that plotting the intensity changes introduced due to the noise and the frequency with which the changes have occurred in the image gives a Gaussian curve.

In most cases (across both types of noise), the change in intensity values at one pixel location is independent of the other pixels.

One of the methods that we have for removing (or reducing the effect of) noise is image averaging. Why does this happen? When we are replacing each pixel by a weighted average of its neighbors, we are, in a sense, distributing the effect of noise in the center pixel across all its neighbors (which are involved in the averaging). The abrupt changes in intensity values due to noise will *smooth* or *smear* across the neighborhood, thereby reducing the severity of the variations.

From the preceding discussion, it is quite evident that the mechanism at play when we attempt to remove noise introduces blurring. The blurring of images is, in fact, a by-product and not an end goal of the averaging operation. Apart from noise reduction, the image smoothing operation finds its utility in some other image processing applications (such as edge detection) as preprocessing steps. We will discuss the same in the chapter on edge detectors.

Vignetting

So far, we have introduced the concept of image filtering and discussed a couple of important filtering techniques, namely box filtering and Gaussian filtering. We also implemented the same using OpenCV and demonstrated the blurring effects that it produced on images. You can now experiment with the extent or degree of blurring by playing around with the size (and the standard deviation in the case of Gaussian filtering) of the image filters.

In this section, we are going to do something even more exciting! We are going to implement a basic version of a very cool image editing technique called Vignetting. For those of you who have come across this term in the context of popular image processing apps (such as Instagram), you will have seen it being referred to as the **Vignetting filter** or **Vignette filter**. However, since we are computer vision enthusiasts, we know that the term *filter* holds a very special meaning in our literature. Hence, we refrain from using the term *filter* for describing such image manipulation techniques. Rather, we would call it a **Vignette mask**. The exact meaning behind using the term *mask* will be evident when we discuss the implementation. For those who haven't heard of Vignetting before, fret not! By the end of this section, you will not only have seen a Vignetting filter in action, but also have implemented one by yourself.

So, what does a Vignetting filter do? Simply put, it *darkens* the image from the corners while keeping the central portions relatively brighter. Consider the following as our original image:

After we apply a Vignette mask to our original image, the result is shown in the next image. You can clearly see that the borders of the image have been considerably darkened, and as we move towards the center, the image starts getting brighter. In fact, right at the very center (some people call it the center of focus of the Vignetting mask), the image intensity is the brightest.

The example we have selected to demonstrate the working of a Vignette filter involves color images. However, as we will be discussing the implementation of Vignetting in OpenCV, we will be using grayscale images for the simple reason that we do not want to burden you with the unnecessary trouble of thinking about color channels. All the operations that we perform here, however, can be applied independently to the different color channels, thereby allowing us to operate upon color images.

Implementing Vignetting in OpenCV

Now that you know about the type of changes that a Vignette mask brings about in images, we can start to think about devising a strategy for the same and ultimately go about implementing the Vignetting operation. As we have discussed, the Vignette mask leaves the central portion of an image bright and darkens the borders in all directions as we move out of the center. Now, the input image (grayscale) that we will be dealing with will have a fixed intensity value for every pixel. What we essentially need to do is modify the value of every pixel in such a manner that the pixels in the center remain at their original intensity levels while the surrounding pixels get progressively darker as we approach the borders.

How can we bring about such a transformation? Well, one way to do that would be to multiply each pixel value with a scaling constant between 0 and 1. The pixels whose intensities need to be kept as is (the ones near the center of the image) should be scaled with a constant close to 1. On the other hand, the pixels that require a sufficient amount of *darkening* should be multiplied by constants close to 0. All intermediate pixels should undergo scaling by values that decrease gradually from 1 to 0 (center to edges). So, essentially, what we need is a grid (having the same size as the image) of scaling constant values: one constant for every pixel. Once we obtain such a grid, the only thing that is left is to multiply the corresponding pixel intensities and scaling constants to get the output image intensities. In our present context, we will call the grid by a special name: a mask.

The next logical question to ask is, How do we obtain such a mask? This is where our knowledge of Gaussian filters comes in! We need a set of values (scaling constants or weights) that are maximal at the center of the mask and gradually (and symmetrically) decrease as we move away towards the edges. The Gaussian function affords us with both qualities–of a gradual decline from a central peak and symmetry. But before we jump to hasty conclusions, this problem requires a little deeper introspection. Are we performing an image filtering operation here? Obviously not! The process that we just described in the previous paragraph involved multiplying the corresponding pixel intensities and scaling constants only once for the entire image (this is a one-time operation, unlike filtering where the same operation is performed at every pixel position). So, using `GaussianBlur()` is out of the question. Another function that we know of is `getGaussianKernel()`, which returns 1D Gaussian kernels. But, our Gaussian mask must be two-dimensional and of the same size as the original image. Let's see how we can build the required Gaussian mask using our output from the getGaussianKernel() function and a little bit of mathematics.

We will skip over the boring parts. I'm sure you know what these lines accomplish:

```cpp
#include <iostream>
#include <opencv2/core/core.hpp>
#include <opencv2/highgui/highgui.hpp>
#include <opencv2/imgproc/imgproc.hpp>

using namespace std;
using namespace cv;
```

Here is where the good things happen:

```cpp
int main() {
    Mat input_image = imread("lena.jpg", IMREAD_GRAYSCALE);
    Mat kernel_X = getGaussianKernel(input_image.cols, 50);
    Mat kernel_Y = getGaussianKernel(input_image.rows, 50);
    Mat kernel_X_transpose;
    transpose(kernel_X, kernel_X_transpose);
    Mat kernel = kernel_Y * kernel_X_transpose;
```

The five lines of the preceding code perform most of the magic of Vignetting. We are going to discuss the *what*, followed by the *why*, which basically means that we are going to describe the steps we have performed first and then tell you about how these steps ensure that our algorithm accomplishes what we expect it to do. The first problem that we address is that of obtaining a two-dimensional matrix of values (the mask) from the one-dimensional vectors that are returned by getGaussianKernel(). From the basic rules of matrix multiplication, you know that multiplying a column and a row vector of lengths *m* and *n* respectively yields a matrix of dimensions m×n. So, if we multiply two vectors: a column vector whose size is the same as the number of rows in our input image and a row vector whose size matches the number of columns, their product will be equal to a matrix whose dimensions exactly match that of our input image. Having said that, what would these vectors contain and where will they come from? The answer, as we have just hinted at, is the getGaussianKernel() function. Note the couple of lines where we define kernel_X and kernel_Y. This means a couple of things:

- kernel_X and kernel_Y are both column vectors (see the section where we discuss the getGaussianKernel() function) of different sizes (number of columns and rows respectively)

- The values stored in `kernel_X` and `kernel_Y` are sampled from a Gaussian distribution (the standard deviation has been kept the same in our example, 50) and normalized so that they sum up to 1

Now, since both `kernel_X` and `kernel_Y` are column vectors and we need a row vector to complete the matrix multiplication process, we use the `transpose()` method to convert `kernel_X` into a row vector. For those of you who aren't aware, a transpose operation converts the rows of a matrix into its columns (and vice-versa). Going by this definition, applying the `transpose()` function on a column vector would convert it to a row vector. And that is precisely what we have done: `kernel_X_transpose` is the transposed version of `kernel_X`. Finally, we use the binary multiplication operator to perform matrix multiplication and obtain a matrix whose dimensions match those of the input image (kernel).

Moving on:

```
Mat mask, processed_image;
normalize(kernel, mask, 0, 1, NORM_MINMAX);
input_image.convertTo(processed_image, CV_64F);
multiply(mask, processed_image, processed_image);
convertScaleAbs(processed_image, processed_image);
```

The next few lines of operation are quite straightforward. You might have witnessed something similar when we talked about implementing log transformations. We take the kernel that we had computed in the previous few steps and normalize all values to make them fall between 0 and 1 (the scaling constants). The `multiply()` function performs the per-pixel multiplication that we have already discussed. Also, you might recall that `convertTo()` and `convertScaleAbs()` are complementary functions that perform type-casting for the matrix data types:

```
imshow("Vignette", processed_image);
waitKey(0);

return 0;
}
```

At the end of the computation, we display the result in a window and quit.

In summary, what we have done is created a couple of 1D Gaussian filters of appropriate dimensions, multiplied them to obtain a mask of scaling constants (between 0 and 1), and then applied the mask onto our image by performing a per-pixel multiplication. From our previous sections, we know that the 1D kernels that we obtain from the getGaussianKernel() function (kernel_X and kernel_Y) will follow the nature of Gaussian kernels, peaking at the center and symmetrically decreasing values at either end. If you carefully follow the rules of matrix multiplication, you will realize that multiplying two such 1D Gaussian kernels will yield a matrix where the peak lies at the center and the values diminish as we move outwards towards the edges–exactly the kind of behavior we were aiming at. I strongly urge you to work out a few small examples and convince yourself of the same!

Now that we are done with the implementation, let us apply the code to some real images and check the output. If you have gone over the implementation carefully, you will have noticed that there is one parameter that is under our control–the standard deviations of the Gaussian kernel. For the sake of symmetry, we have kept the standard deviations the same for both the kernels —kernel_X and kernel_Y. The effect of varying the value of Sigma can be seen in the following image, which consists of four different images:

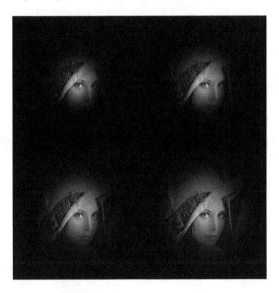

The images in the top row correspond to standard deviations of 50 and 60 (left and right, respectively). Similarly, the bottom row corresponds to Sigmas of 70 and 80 (again, left and right, respectively). It is evident that increasing the standard deviation means increasing the size of the brighter area (center of focus). This seems logical as well because a higher standard deviation would mean that a greater range (neighborhood) of pixels in and around the center get scaling constants that are close to 1 (recall that a Gaussian curve with a higher Sigma is broader near the peak). This would mean that a greater portion of the image at the center is brighter in comparison to the darker edges.

Before we close the section on Vignetting, I would like to leave you with a final comment. While devising a strategy on implementing Vignetting, we saw that what we essentially required was the darkening and brightening of image regions. If that is so, then why did we not go for a logarithmic or exponential transformation? After all, as per our discussions in the relevant sections of the previous chapter, isn't that what these transformations did? The reason behind not considering the grayscale transformations is that we need the gradual darkening of pixels in a spatially constrained manner. What I mean to say is that, irrespective of which image object the pixels form a part of, or what their original intensity values are, the pixels at the center will have to be kept as is (or darkened by a negligible amount); similarly, the pixels at the boundaries will undergo a much more rigorous darkening. This spatial pattern of darkening will remain the same for all images. Now, contrast this with what the logarithmic transformations achieve. They darken/brighten a pixel based on the grayscale value in the input image, and not on its position (coordinates) in the image.

I highlighted the difference between the two because when we deal with a real-world computer vision problem, the technique to apply is not inherently clear beforehand. A lot of tutorials online will tell you exactly *what* an algorithm does, but in order to be a *rockstar computer vision developer*, you need to understand *how* the algorithms work so that you get an insight into *when* to apply them. As we discuss and develop more sophisticated vision-based applications, we will be *weighing pros-and-cons* like this a lot more frequently.

Summary

In this chapter, we have continued our journey from the previous one. Filtering operations have been the primary focus of our study. The chapter started off by describing an image averaging operation and then went on to explain how such an operation may be conceptualized by visualizing the same in terms of *filters*. We then continued to generalize our concept of filters by demonstrating the basics of how any form of filtering is performed on images. By now, you must have realized that we are no longer dealing with simple pixel transformations similar to the ones that we discussed in the last chapter (grayscale transformations). When we talk of filtering operations, the computations at each pixel become much more sophisticated and involve a neighborhood around the pixel.

We learnt about a couple of different filtering techniques: box filtering and Gaussian filtering. Box filtering assumes an equal contribution from all the neighboring pixels in computing the weighted average. This assumption was relaxed during Gaussian filtering. Giving different weights to different pixels based on their relative distances from the central pixel (anchor point) is a much more natural way of doing things.

After learning about the theoretical underpinnings and implementations of both box and Gaussian filtering, we dipped our hands into a very practical application. We implemented the Vignetting operation from scratch. One of the key takeaways from this exercise is that more often than not, you won't be directly applying these filtering operations to images. Rather, you will be applying the concepts that power these operations. Both box and Gaussian filtering are straightforward in themselves (and their implementation is available). But, as we saw in the Vignetting example, quite often, you need to know and use concepts such as Gaussian filters, masks, and scaling constants to help you in the tasks that you seek to accomplish. Even if you do need to apply smoothing/filtering operations to images, it will be as a preprocessing step in the solution that spans a pipeline comprising several such processing steps. We will come back to this point later in the book.

In addition to teaching you about the applications of Gaussian kernels, the Vignetting operation also extended our set of cool image manipulation techniques that we have been building since the last chapter. Let's take a brief look at what we have covered so far:

- Image negatives, which give a *ghostly* appearance to your images
- Log and exponential transformations, which brighten or darken regions of an image
- Image smoothing (box and Gaussian filtering) imparting a blurring effect on your images
- Vignetting, which focuses on a central bright region and progressively darkens the edges

There you go! We have built our own arsenal of image manipulation operations while learning about the basics of computer vision and image processing! This will be a recurring theme in this book. We will keep on building cool stuff as and when we learn about new techniques or algorithms!

This concludes our chapter on image filtering. In the next chapter, we will learn about a new form of operation that is often applied on images–image thresholding. These thresholding operations produce what we call binary images. All pixels in binary images are either white (255) or black (0). There are no other grayscale levels. Although visually, they might not hold much information, as we'll see in the next chapter, they are immensely important when it comes to analyzing and processing images.

3
Image Thresholding

As part of our computer vision and image processing journey so far, we have essentially seen two different types of operation. The first and simpler ones were the grayscale transformations, where the output intensity value of a pixel depends only upon the intensity of the corresponding pixel in the input image. The second, slightly more complex form of processing that we saw is the image filtering operations, where the output intensity depends on a neighborhood rather than a single intensity value.

During our discourse on image filtering in Chapter 2, *Image Filtering*, we laid emphasis on how the aforementioned two approaches differ. However, there is some sense in which grayscale transformations and image filtering operations are alike. Algorithms belonging to both these classes produce grayscale images. Irrespective of the complexity of implementation, all the algorithms that we have discussed up to this point take a grayscale image as input and produce another grayscale image as output (all channels of a multi-channel colored image are treated independently as grayscale). We are now going to deal with the mechanisms that produce what we call *binary images*, rather than grayscale.

If you recall, our discussions on the basics of images in Chapter 1, *Laying the Foundation*, we made a clear distinction between grayscale and *black-and-white* images. Binary images are *black-and-white* images in the true sense of the word. That is, all pixels of a binary image possess either of the two possible color values-black or white! We will expound upon this distinction in the current chapter and talk about one of the processes that would lead us to binary images from grayscale ones–image thresholding.

We'll also look at yet another category of image processing algorithms called **morphological operations**. These algorithms are generally applied as a post-processing step after our thresholding operations have acted upon the input data. This sequential form of processing images where the output of one algorithm is fed as an input to the next algorithm in pipeline is quite common in the world of image processing and computer vision. We will witness a live example of such a pipeline in action towards the latter half of the book, when we talk about face detection and related processing.

Our main aim in this chapter is to familiarize you with binary images, image thresholding operations, and how the morphological operators act upon the binary images generated as a consequence of applying the thresholding operators. Keeping in mind these goals, here is a rough outline of the topics that we wish to cover in this chapter:

- Introduction to the concept of binary images and the basic framework of image thresholding algorithms. A key takeaway here is an understanding of how thresholding algorithms generate binary images
- Differences between the two major types of image thresholding algorithms: simple and adaptive
- Code examples and associated output images to demonstrate how both the types of thresholding algorithms can be implemented in OpenCV
- A discussion on two popular types of morphological operators: erosion and dilation

Binary images

The images that we have been dealing with so far are grayscale images. Programmatically, we have represented them using a Mat object having the equivalent of an unsigned `char` type. This means that each pixel value was permitted to be an integer between 0 and 255 (inclusive). This allowed us to represent not only black and white but also all the intermediate shades of gray as well. If you show these images to a layman (or anyone who isn't familiar with image processing parlance), they would no doubt label them as *black-and-white*. After all, grayscale images resemble the kind of pictures that you would expect to see on a black-and-white television.

However, this chapter will make a clear distinction between *grayscale* and *black-and-white* images. You will learn that in computer vision jargon, these two terms signify substantially different things. When we talk of *black-and-white* images in the context of image processing, we literally mean to say that the only allowable colors are black and white! The color space for these images is just two colors, instead of the 256 allowable shades in grayscale images. And for precisely this reason, these images have been given a special name: binary images.

So, from now on, we will be using the term binary images to refer to them instead of saying *black-and-white*. To give you an example, the following is a picture of Lena, displayed as a binary image:

If you recall the basics of the Mat class that we covered in chapter 1, *Laying the Foundation*, we talked about the fact that the type of the data matrix is dependent on the color space of the image. For example, we have been using CV_8U (unsigned char) as the type parameter while declaring Mat objects that are intended to store grayscale images because all values can be represented using eight bits. Following the same logic, it should be possible to represent a binary image using just a single bit! That is indeed true, theoretically. However, OpenCV doesn't provide a separate type parameter for binary images (that is to say, you do not have something along the lines of CV_2U at your disposal). So, in order to represent a binary image in our code, we use the same parameters for the Mat object as we would do for a grayscale image. We simply make sure that the pixel values are either 0 (black), or 255 (white).

You are aware that the three-channel RGB color images have the ability to store and process colors from a spectrum of *16 million+* possibilities. Similarly, a grayscale image can work with 256 different shades, whereas the color space reduces to merely two colors when we talk about binary images. There is a clear and sharp drop in the amount of color information as we move from color to grayscale to binary. Then, why are binary images used at all? The answer is that for a lot of computer vision algorithms, segregating the pixels into two binary classes (black and white) is an important step. An example of such an algorithm is image segmentation (into background and foreground). If you think of it, a binary image is the perfect way to visually represent the output of such segmentation algorithms. All pixels belonging to the foreground objects can be colored as white whereas all the pixels falling in the background can be black (or vice-versa, it's merely a matter of convention). Another application area of binary images is contour detection. As the name suggests, contour detection involves finding a series of points which demarcate the boundary of an object in an image. The contour detection algorithms accept a binary image as an input and return a set of points along the pixels that form the boundary of the black and white regions.

Now that we know what binary images are, how they differ from grayscale images, and the possible use-cases for binary images in computer vision, we are ready to dive into the remainder of the chapter. Over the course of this unit, we will talk about the different ways we can generate binary images from grayscale ones. All such techniques fall under the umbrella of what is known as **image thresholding operations**.

Image thresholding basics

Having learnt about binary images, let's now focus our attention on one of the processes that generate binary images: image thresholding. In the generic sense of the term, a threshold is some sort of a benchmark against which values are compared. Extending the same definition into our realm of computer vision, we use a threshold to compare pixel values. Let's try to understand how this happens.

The input to the thresholding functions are grayscale images, which means that every pixel has an intensity value in the range of 0 to 255 (inclusive). First, we predefine a threshold value for the operation. As expected, the threshold that we select is passed on to the function that implements the thresholding operation as a parameter. Now, what a thresholding operation essentially does is that it traverses the image pixel by pixel. At every pixel, it compares the intensity value with the threshold and decides on the corresponding output intensity value based on the result of the comparison. Since we are using a single threshold value, it means that any pixel intensity can either be greater than (or equal to) or less than the threshold value. That is, we have two possible outcomes of the comparison that we perform at every pixel location. This also means that we can map two possible output values (black or white), one for each of the decision outcomes; hence, such thresholding operations produce binary images.

The operation that I have just described is called **simple thresholding** because the threshold remains the same throughout the image. The input pixel intensities at all locations undergo a comparison using the same threshold value. This value is sometimes referred to as the **global threshold** to reinforce the fact that it remains constant throughout the entire image. We could also have a scenario where the threshold value is different for different pixels. Such thresholding operations are known as **adaptive thresholding** because the threshold value, in some sense, *adapts* its value according to each input pixel.

We will be learning about both types of thresholding operations in this chapter. Specifically, we'll be exploring the APIs provided by the OpenCV developers to help us generate binary images using image thresholding algorithms.

Image thresholding in OpenCV

We'll start with simple thresholding in this section and move on to adaptive thresholding in the next. OpenCV has a threshold() function in its imgproc module which implements different variants of simple thresholding. Where do these variants come from?

If you remember the working of thresholding operations, we map output intensity values to each of the two outcomes of the threshold comparison. The type of mapping that we perform gives rise to several different variants of simple thresholding. Before going into the details of these variants one by one, we will learn how to implement image thresholding in OpenCV. As in the case of image averaging, the implementation essentially boils down to a single line of code. However, a close inspection of the different parameters of the function call is imperative to enjoy a thorough understanding of image thresholding using OpenCV:

```cpp
#include <iostream>
#include <opencv2/core/core.hpp>
#include <opencv2/highgui/highgui.hpp>
#include <opencv2/imgproc/imgproc.hpp>

using namespace std;
using namespace cv;

int main() {
    Mat input_image = imread("lena.jpg", IMREAD_GRAYSCALE);
    Mat binary_image(input_image.size(), input_image.type());
    threshold(input_image, binary_image, 120, 255, THRESH_BINARY);
    imwrite("binary.png", binary_image);
    return 0;
}
```

As we have mentioned just now, all the work is done by the threshold() function. If you have been watching the design of OpenCV APIs closely, you can easily guess what the first two arguments in the function call stand for: the input and the output images, respectively. The remaining arguments are specific to the threshold() function and are worth discussing in detail:

1. **Threshold value**: The third argument is the threshold value. When we introduced the concept of image thresholding, we mentioned the fact that the threshold value is passed down to the implementation as a parameter. In the code sample shown in the preceding diagram, we have selected the threshold to be 120.

2. **Maximum value**: Simply put, this parameter specifies one of the values to be assigned to a pixel in line with the outcome of the comparison (the other possible value being zero). Hence, the output image that the function generates will be a binary image where each pixel will have an intensity value that is either 0 or maximum value. Now, you may argue by saying that since we are dealing with binary images, the only possible values in the output image can be 0 or 255. So, how can we afford this flexibility of choosing our own intensity value? This is not entirely correct. Recall that OpenCV represents binary images using an 8-bit, single channel Mat object, which means that we have the entire 256 grayscale color space at our disposal. This is what provides the freedom to select what one of the pixel intensities in the output can be (the other one being fixed at 0, and not under our control). Also, irrespective of our choice of the maximum intensity, the output image will continue to be binary because its color space would consist of only two color values: 0 and the maximum intensity).

3. **Thresholding type**: This flag specifies the type of simple thresholding operation that we can perform. We have passed a THRESH_BINARY flag in our implementation, which stands for binary thresholding. The other options available to us are: inverted binary, truncate, threshold-to-zero, and inverted threshold-to-zero. As we hinted earlier, these variations arise because of the different ways that we can assign the output intensity values based on the outcome of the comparison at the pixel locations. In the next section, we will take a look at all the different types of simple thresholding operations along with sample outputs for each.

Types of simple image thresholding

The following table describes the different types of simple image thresholding operations that have been made available by the OpenCV developers:

Threshold Type	Threshold Function
THRESH_BINARY	$dst(x,y) = \begin{cases} \text{maxval} & src(x,y) > thresh \\ 0 & otherwise \end{cases}$
THRESH_BINARY_INV	$dst(x,y) = \begin{cases} 0 & src(x,y) > thresh \\ \text{maxval} & otherwise \end{cases}$
THRESH_TRUNC	$dst(x,y) = \begin{cases} \text{threshold} & src(x,y) > thresh \\ src(x,y) & otherwise \end{cases}$
THRESH_TOZERO	$dst(x,y) = \begin{cases} src(x,y) & src(x,y) > thresh \\ 0 & otherwise \end{cases}$
THRESH_TOZERO_INV	$dst(x,y) = \begin{cases} 0 & src(x,y) > thresh \\ src(x,y) & otherwise \end{cases}$
THRESH_OTSU	Uses the Otsu's method to compute the optimal threshold value

The flag representing the last thresholding method–Otsu's method is a little different (slightly more complicated) than the others. It relies on Image Histograms, our topic of discussion for the next chapter. For those of you who know what histograms are, the Otsu's method essentially assumes that the histogram for the image consists of two peaks–one corresponding to the background (black) and the other for the foreground (white). The computational steps in the algorithm try to come up with a threshold value that best separates the two peaks in the image histogram. We won't be discussing Otsu's thresholding as part of this chapter. You are encouraged to try this out on their own.

As you can see, the threshold function in the second column specifies the values that are assigned to the output pixels as per the threshold decision. Different thresholding techniques have different functions. We are going to describe each of the thresholding types in detail.

Binary threshold

This is conceptually the simplest among all simple thresholding variants. If the intensity of a pixel is greater than the threshold value, the corresponding pixel in the output image is set to whatever we specify as the maximum intensity for the output image. Otherwise, it is set to zero (black). The transformation function, which looks like a step function is shown graphically in the following diagram:

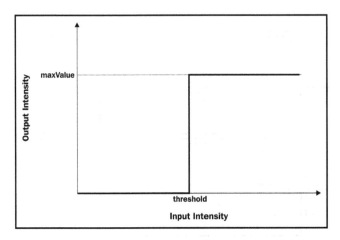

Also, the following image demonstrates the output when we run the THRESH_BINARY variant of the threshold() function with a threshold of 120 and a maximum intensity value of 255 (white):

Inverted binary threshold

The inverted binary threshold works in an opposite manner to simple binary thresholding. If you look at the thresholding functions for the two, you will realize that they perform exactly the same operations but under different conditions. That is, the inverted threshold will color a pixel black when the corresponding input pixel crosses the threshold and it will assign the maximum intensity when the input pixel lies below the threshold. The graph for the function is as follows:

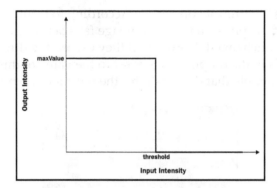

And here is the output for the THRESH_BINARY_INV variant of simple thresholding using the same set of parameters (threshold and maximum intensity value):

If you remember the negative intensity transformation from Chapter 1, *Laying the Foundation*, you'll realize that if our maximum intensity is 255 (as in our examples here), then the binary images generated by THRESH_BINARY and THRESH_BINARY_INV are negatives of each other!

Truncate

The type of simple thresholding that we'll discuss here and in the next two sections (threshold-to-zero and inverted threshold-to-zero) do not exactly behave like the conventional thresholding operations that we have been discussing so far. This is because the type of thresholding operations that will be the subject of our discourse from now on does not produce images whose color space is binary. That is, the output images will possess more than two possible colors (but still within the realm of 8-bit grayscale images).

The first among them is the truncate operation. According to its mathematical formulation, if the intensity values of the pixels in the input image falls below the threshold, then the intensity values remain unchanged. However, if they exceed the threshold, the intensity of the corresponding pixels in the output image is set to the value of threshold itself. The following image is an example that demonstrates the output of such a thresholding scheme:

Threshold-to-zero

This variant of simple thresholding is almost similar to binary thresholding in the sense that if the input pixel's intensity is less than the threshold, the corresponding output pixel will be black (0). However, in the other scenario, its behavior deviates from that of binary thresholding. When the input pixel intensity crosses the threshold, it is kept unchanged in the output image (as evident from the function's mathematical description). The following graph for threshold-to-zero will make things more clear:

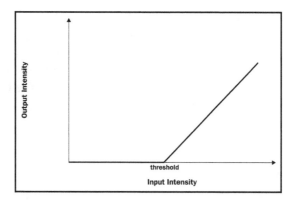

You can see that after the threshold point on the X-axis, the graph assumes the shape of $y = x$ (the identity transformation), and any input value is mapped to the same output value. As always, we present the output of the threshold-to-zero operation on our sample input image of Lena:

In line with our description of the algorithm, all the pixels that are colored black in the preceding image did not manage to cross the threshold. The remaining pixels that did have been left as they were in the input image. Also, similar to the line of reasoning that we adopted for truncate, the output images are not binary.

Inverted threshold-to-zero

As the name suggests, the inverted threshold-to-zero does the opposite of threshold-to-zero. These two operations are analogous to how the binary and inverted binary are inverses of each other. You can take a look at the function descriptions from the table. After learning about threshold-to-zero, the working of this transformation should be self-explanatory. The graph is plotted and shown in the following diagram:

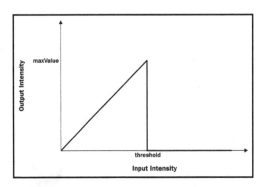

Also, the inverted threshold-to-zero is applied to a sample input and the result is shown in the following image:

During our discussions on binary and inverted binary thresholding, we claimed that if we select the maximum intensity value as 255, then the output images generated by the two thresholding operations are negatives of each other. But, is that the case here? Well, the answer is no. It will be a good mental exercise for you to convince yourself of the same!

At the outset of this chapter, we started off with a sufficiently strict definition of binary images where all pixels can either be black or white. When we saw the implementation of threshold() in OpenCV, we relaxed our earlier definition by allowing binary images to have any color from the grayscale spectrum to represent the *white* (the maximum intensity value parameter). Now, our earlier example of only allowing 0 and 255 became one specific instance (that we could achieve by setting the maximum value parameter to 255), from a much broader spectrum of possibilities. Finally, when we discussed the truncate and threshold-to-zero variants of simple thresholding operations, we realized another important fact. Simple thresholding won't always lead to a binary image! The output images generated by some of the variants that we have discussed retain the color space for certain sections of the image.

Although we have learnt that the scope and definition for binary images can be quite large when it comes to OpenCV, however, for most of the operations that require binary images, you'll be working with images that are binary in the strictest sense of the term. Even if we use binary images with a maximum value parameter other than 255, the algorithms that work with these images would treat all non-zero intensities in the binary image as 1 (or any suitable representation for white pixels that the algorithm deems fit).

Adaptive thresholding

In all of the thresholding operations that we have seen so far, the threshold value remained the same for all pixels in the image. However, most of the images that you would come across follow the principle of *spatial locality*. What this essentially means is that the intensity of a pixel is affected by a small neighborhood in space around that pixel's location and is relatively independent of pixels that are not in its immediate vicinity. When you come to think of it, it does make intuitive sense. Pixels make up objects in images, and these objects are well-separated in the spatial coordinate frame of the image. So, what we are trying to say is that the pixels which constitute the same object (or in more general terms, the same region in an image) will show a greater degree of similarity in their intensity values than those which are a part of totally different objects (or regions).

How does this concept of *spatial locality* fit into our discourse on adaptive thresholding? If we use the same threshold value in all spatial coordinates, we are essentially subjecting all the pixels to the same kind of treatment. This goes against the principles of spatial locality. To give you a more concrete example, let's say that we are dealing with a simple binary thresholding operation, and we have fixed the threshold value to be 128. Now, this seems like a decent threshold for a grayscale image. Consider a portion of the image which has pixels whose intensities are clustered around the higher end of the grayscale spectrum, that is, a relatively bright object or region in our image. Naturally, the thresholding operation will render all of those pixels white. This would mean a significant loss in detail (especially if the region of the image in discussion is sufficiently large) for our image. Why did this happen? This loss of information was a result of the fact that we chose to apply the same threshold of 128 in a region of the image where the distribution of pixel intensities was not suited to the choice of our threshold at all.

This is precisely what necessitates the need for selecting our threshold values as a function of the coordinate (more specifically, the neighborhood) of a pixel in the image, and adaptive thresholding accomplishes the same effect. It computes a separate threshold value for each pixel and then applies that threshold to the same pixel to generate the corresponding output intensity. Now, the next obvious question to ask is how does it compute the threshold for a particular pixel location? Well, the good news is that you are already aware of the method that adaptive thresholding uses to compute thresholds! It takes the mean of a neighborhood of a specified size centered on that pixel as the threshold corresponding to that pixel location. And as we saw in quite a bit of detail in the previous chapter, we have a couple of options available at our disposal when it comes to taking averages–the regular mean and the Gaussian mean. Not surprisingly, even in the case of adaptive thresholding, we have a couple of different possible ways in which we can compute the threshold at every location–(simple) mean and the Gaussian mean.

To sum up, adaptive thresholding computes the threshold at every pixel location *(x, y)* by taking the mean (or Gaussian mean) of a neighborhood of a specified size centered around *(x, y)*. The threshold is used to compute the output intensity corresponding to *(x, y)* and is then discarded. The same process is repeated at every other pixel location. It is obvious that adaptive thresholding does a lot more work internally than any variant of simple thresholding. However, as a trade-off, it also produces more detailed output images than its counterpart.

Now that we are through with our understanding of adaptive thresholding, we will take a look at the OpenCV API for the same operation. We won't be writing the entire code because barring a single line, it is exactly the same as the one for simple thresholding. And that one differing line is, of course, the call to the `adaptiveThreshold()` function as demonstrated in the following code segment:

```
adaptiveThreshold(
    input_image,
    binary_image,
    255,
    ADAPTIVE_THRESH_MEAN_C,
    THRESH_BINARY,
    25,
    0
);
```

As always, after presenting the code snippet, we indulge the readers in a description of the parameters and explain what each one of them accomplishes. The first couple of arguments, I believe, do not warrant any explanation. So, we'll start directly with the third:

- **maxValue**: This is one of the values (other than 0) that is assigned to the pixels in line with the outcome of the comparison. This serves exactly the same purpose as it did in the simple thresholding implementation that we discussed earlier. We have specified a value of 255 (white) in our code snippet. The couple of images shown in the following figure illustrate the effects of changing the value of the `maxValue` parameter (while keeping the other parameters constant). As expected, the output images get brighter as we increase the `maxValue` parameter from 128 to 255 (from left to right) because the same input pixels are now mapped to higher intensity values as dictated by `maxValue`:

- **Adaptive thresholding method**: This is the most important parameter when it comes to the adaptive threshold implementation. It dictates the manner in which the computation for the threshold at every pixel is carried out. As we had mentioned in our explanation of adaptive thresholding, there are two ways the threshold computation may be performed: the mean and the Gaussian mean. So, there are a couple of different flags that you can pass as acceptable values for this parameter–ADAPTIVE_THRESH_MEAN_C or ADAPTIVE_THRESH_GAUSSIAN_C. The following figure shows a sample output for each of the two different types of adaptive thresholding methods:

- **Thresholding type**: The thresholding type parameter serves the same purpose as it did in the implementation for simple thresholding–it defines a mapping between the outcomes of the comparison of the pixel intensity with the threshold and the output intensity. However, in the case of adaptive thresholding, only two thresholding types are permitted: THRESH_BINARY or THRESH_BINARY_INV. Once again, we demonstrate the output for each of the two different thresholding types in the following figure:

- **Block size**: This argument specifies the size of neighborhood that is used to calculate the threshold value for a pixel. We know that the adaptive threshold computes the mean (normal or Gaussian) centered around every pixel and uses that value as the threshold for that particular pixel location. The block size specifies the size of the neighborhood that must be used to compute this mean. Note that this size would be the same for the computations performed across all the different pixels in the image. What do you think will be the effect of increasing the block size on the output image? To answer this question, we need to take a step back and think about our discussions on the motivations behind migrating to adaptive thresholding from simple thresholding. We wanted the threshold at any pixel location to accurately reflect a sufficiently compact and local neighborhood of that particular location in order to avoid the loss in details that occurs as a result of treating all pixels in the same manner. This means that increasing the value of the block size is akin to taking a large neighborhood around each pixel for our threshold computations. And the larger the neighborhood that we select, the more loss in detail we have to put up with (we would be violating the spatial locality principle to a greater extent). This loss in detail can be observed in the following figure. Clockwise (from the top-left), the block-size is gradually increased and you can distinctly see the binary image losing its finer details:

- **C**: The constant subtracted from the mean or weighted mean, which can be positive, negative, or zero. This parameter is rarely useful; hence, it is best to set it as zero.

This concludes our discussion on adaptive thresholding. Note that, unlike a lot of other OpenCV APIs, the `adaptiveThreshold()` function doesn't offer us the luxury of default parameters. All the seven parameters have to be supplied along with each function call.

Morphological operations

So far in this chapter, we have looked at image thresholding operations. As we have stated a number of times, the end-result of these thresholding operations is binary images. These binary images are, of course, not very pleasant to look at! This means that we don't really create them for their aesthetic value. Rather, they serve as inputs to the subsequent processing stages of our image processing pipeline. The solutions to most of the common computer vision and image processing problems can be viewed as a pipeline, rather than a single algorithm. The outputs of the current operation serve as inputs to the next and so on until we reach the desired output stage. Image thresholding is one such stage that you might come across in any pipeline (and so is image smoothing/blurring).

What we are going to do in this section is learn in brief about one more operation that makes frequent appearances in the image processing pipelines that we just discussed–morphological operations. And on top of that, these morphological operations operate on binary images that have been produced as a result of thresholding operations. In other words, image thresholding and morphological operations occur as successive components of pipelines.

Now, as to what these operations actually accomplish, simply put, the morphological operations reduce the effect of noise in binary images. So, in some sense, these operations are to binary images what image averaging is to grayscale (or color) images. The next pertinent question that we might want to address is what does noise really mean in the context of binary images? To answer that, take a look at the following image:

Clearly, the original image was that of a man leaning slightly to his right. What is shown in the preceding image is the binary counterpart of the original grayscale image. Let us assume that the region-of-interest for us is the man himself, which means that we select the threshold value and other parameters of the thresholding operation (that we saw in the previous section) so that the region of the image depicting the man is highlighted. However, once we do that, we notice that in addition to the pixels making up the figure of the person, there are some other regions scattered throughout the image that have been turned white. This may be due to either a poor choice in our selection of parameters (which is under our control and correctable) or due to noise and other forms of aberrations present in the original input image itself. How do we get rid of such errors in binary images? That is exactly why we use morphological operations. As an example, acting as a prequel to what is to be discussed in this section, after we subject the preceding image to the remedies of morphological processing, we get an image that would look something like the one shown in the following image:

You can see that a majority of the undesirable chunks of white pixels have disappeared.

Similar to image thresholding, morphological operations refer to a spectrum of techniques rather than a single operation. In this chapter, we will be discussing a couple of simple, but very useful, morphological techniques: **erosion** and **dilation**.

Erosion and dilation

The good thing about erosion and dilation is that the fundamental principles that they operate upon are similar to image filtering. So, the basic concepts that you need to understand the nature of their operations are already known to you.

Now, when we talked about image filtering, we had mentioned that image averaging using a filter-based approach is a linear operation–the same type of operation is performed at all pixel locations and the output pixel intensity at any location is a linear combination of the intensities of its neighboring pixels. When we talk of erosion and dilation, we relax the constraints of linear combinations (the condition for the same operation to be performed at all locations still holds). In spite of the overwhelming similarity between filtering and morphological operations, there are some differences between the two. First, the *kernel* that is used in image thresholding is given the name of *structuring element*. And a change in the name always comes with certain changes in functioning as well. A structuring element, unlike a kernel, is always binary. It is composed of a matrix of *0s* and *1s*. The pattern of *0s* and *1s* in the structuring element defines its shape. For example, there are three types of structuring elements that are provided by the OpenCV API (along with an option of defining one on your own): rectangle, ellipse and cross. So, what type of non-linear computations do we exactly perform at each step along the way? What does a structuring element do and what functions do these specific shapes accomplish? All such questions will be answered as we describe the workings of these morphological operations.

Let's talk about dilation first. So, here is how dilation operates. As the structuring element is scanned over the image (much like a kernel), each input image pixel that lies beneath the anchor point is replaced by the maximum of the intensities of all neighboring pixels that the structuring element covers (the non-linear operation). So essentially, the weighted averaging operation in image smoothing is replaced by the maximum operator to give rise to the dilation operation. Also, there is an added condition that when the structuring element is placed on top of a pixel, only those neighbors which have a 1 in the corresponding location of the structuring element are considered for the maxima computation. Thus, the shape of the element determines which neighbors of pixels are to be considered at each location.

Although, conceptually, the dilation operation is quite straightforward, the consequences of its operation on binary images warrants a deeper look. Let's say that we are working with a thresholding operation which has produced a binary image that is to be operated upon subsequently by dilation. Assume the following figure to be the binary image:

Now, the input image to the dilation possesses only two possible pixel values: 0 and 255 (we assume `maxValue` to be 255, without any loss of generality). This also means that the maxima can be either of the two values. Let's try to approach this line of thought from the other side. In the dilation operation, if I tell you that the output intensity at any location is 255 (white), what can you say about the neighborhood of the input pixel at the location in question? Obviously, it means that at least one of the pixels in the neighborhood must have been white in the input image (thus taking the maxima to 255). Extending the same logic, if the output is 0 (black), we can be sure of the fact that all the pixels in the neighborhood that we have been considering are black (that is the only way of achieving a maximum of 0). In other words, even a single white pixel in the neighborhood of the anchor point is sufficient to turn it white in the output image, whereas for the same pixel to turn black, all its neighbors must be black themselves. Clearly, the condition for a pixel to turn white in the output is much more lenient than it is for it to be labelled black. As you might have expected, a dilation operation decreases the amount of black colored pixels in the image and consequently causes the brighter spots within the image to grow.

Having understood dilation, the erosion operation is the exact opposite. It replaces every pixel with the minimum among its neighbors. With this reversal in maxima-minima, the effect of erosion on binary images is also reversed. That is to say, erosion causes the darker patches in a binary image to grow. You can convince yourselves by following the same train of thought that we had adopted just now while reasoning about dilation.

As an example that would further demarcate the difference between the two different types of morphological operators covered so far, the following diagram shows the contrasting effects of erosion and dilation on the binary image that we introduced earlier:

The figure on the left is the dilated version of the original image, whereas the one on the right is the result of applying erosion to our input image. You can clearly compare and distinguish between the growth and shrinkage of the bright and dark regions.

Erosion and dilation in OpenCV

The morphological operations of erosion and dilation are implemented by the erode() and dilate() APIs of OpenCV. Since both of the APIs are quite similar in terms of the number and type of arguments that they accept, we would demonstrate them using a single snippet of code as shown here:

```
#include <iostream>
#include <opencv2/core/core.hpp>
#include <opencv2/highgui/highgui.hpp>
#include <opencv2/imgproc/imgproc.hpp>

using namespace std;
using namespace cv;

int main() {

    Mat input_image = imread("lena.jpg", CV_LOAD_IMAGE_GRAYSCALE);
    Mat dilated_image(input_image.size(), input_image.type());
    Mat eroded_image(input_image.size(), input_image.type());
    Mat element = getStructuringElement(MORPH_RECT, Size(5, 5), Point(-1,
```

```
-1));
    dilate(input_image, dilated_image, element, Point(-1, -1), 1);
    erode(input_image, eroded_image, element, Point(-1, -1), 1);

    imshow("Input_Image", input_image);
    imshow("Eroded_Image", eroded_image);
    imshow("Dilated_Image", dilated_image);
    waitKey(0);

    return 0;
}
```

The first thing that we turn our attention to in the code segment is a function that returns a structuring element: `getStructuringElement()`. The function accepts three arguments–the shape, size, and anchor point–and returns the structuring element as a Mat object. We have invoked the function to return a 5 x 5 sized square element having its anchor fixed at the center pixel. As we had briefly mentioned a little while back, OpenCV provides us with three different shapes for the structuring element, in addition to the option of defining our own custom shapes. They are listed as shown, along with the corresponding flags that need to be passed to the `getStructuringElement()` function:

- Rectangle: `MORPH_RECT`
- Ellipse: `MORPH_ELLIPSE`
- Cross: `MORPH_CROSS`

Now, jumping straight to the point, we will discuss the arguments to our functions of interest: `erode()` and `dilate()`:

- Source/Input image.
- Destination/Output image.
- **Structuring element**: The third argument is the structuring element that you want the operation to use. As demonstrated in the code snippet, a good idea would be to pass the Mat object that is returned by the `getStructuringElement()` method.
- **Anchor point**: The concept of the anchor point remains the same as we discussed with image filtering operations. This argument has a default value of *Point(-1, -1)*, which is represented using the central pixel as an anchor point. Although, there exists a default value, we have supplied the parameter for the function invocation nonetheless.

- **Iterations**: As opposed to image filtering, OpenCV APIs for both the morphological operations of `erode()` and `dilate()` provide an option for repeating the same process over multiple iterations. The fifth argument is an integer value that dictates the number of times the operation has to be performed. In our current implementation, we have restricted the iteration count to 1.
- **Border type**: We talked about the different types of border extrapolation methods available in `Chapter 2`, *Image Filtering*. This argument gives you the option of selecting an appropriate border extrapolation method. As you can see, we have opted for the replication of pixel values at the border (`BORDER_REPLICATE`).
- **Border value**: This parameter provides for a value in case a `BORDER_CONSTANT` flag was used in the previous argument.

This brings an end to our discussion on morphological operations and image thresholding as well. We have just given you a glimpse into a couple of basic operations that fall under the category of *morphological operations*: erosion and dilation. There are other, more complex operations that can be possible using a combination of erosion and dilation. You can read more about *opening* and *closing* operations on images.

Summary

This finishes our discussions on binary images and image thresholding algorithms. I hope that by now, the distinction between grayscale and binary images should be quite clear to you. We saw a lot of different variants of thresholding algorithms that are a part of OpenCV's arsenal. It is interesting to note that the most commonly used variant is the simplest one: binary thresholding!

We also showed you a couple of representative algorithms belonging to the category of morphological operators: erosion and dilation. We saw how the two operators improve the quality of binary images generated by the thresholding operations by reducing the adverse effect of aberrations and other forms of image noise.

All the algorithms that we have seen so far in this book–image enhancement (negative, log and exponential transformations), image filtering (Box and Gaussian filters), thresholding (simple and adaptive) and morphological operators (erosion and dilation)–have one thing in common. They operate and produce output on a per-pixel basis. What this means is that in each of these algorithms, we iterate over all the pixels in the image, perform some form of (algorithm-dependent) processing, and generate an output corresponding to each pixel. Thus, they produce a similar-sized image as an output. In the next chapter, we are going to look at some other possibilities when it comes to processing pixel values. More specifically, we will be looking at aggregating pixel values and constructing histograms.

4

Image Histograms

We started off with simple grayscale transformations and gradually moved to image filtering, thresholding, and morphological operations. At the most fundamental level, there is something in common among all the image-processing and computer vision algorithms that we have discussed in this book so far. In each of these processes, there was always some form of computation that was being performed at every pixel. The result of the computation at the input stage dictated the output value of a pixel in the output image (we usually termed it the *corresponding output pixel*). What this essentially meant was that the output of all of these operations was images of the same size (dimensions) as the input image, and there was one-to-one correspondence between the pixel locations in the input and the output images: this correspondence were governed by the nature of the computation that was performed. For example, when we talked about image averaging, we performed the average around a pixel neighborhood to obtain the corresponding output intensity value. Similarly, image thresholding involved comparing the input intensity with a threshold (static or dynamic) and fixing the output intensity on the basis of the result of the comparison.

In this chapter, we are going to focus our attention on a different style of processing pixel values. The output of the techniques, which will comprise our study in the current chapter, will not be images, but rather other forms of representation for images, namely image histograms. We have seen that a two-dimensional grid of intensity values is one default form of representing images in digital systems for processing as well as storage. However, such representations are not at all easy to scale. So, for an image with a reasonably low spatial resolution, say 512 x 512 pixels, working with a two-dimensional grid might not pose any serious issues. However, as the dimensions increase, the corresponding increase in the size of the grid may start to adversely affect the performance of the algorithms that work with the images. A primary advantage that an image histogram has to offer is that the size of a histogram is a constant that is independent of the dimensions of the image. As a consequence of this, we are guaranteed that irrespective of the spatial resolution of the images that we are dealing with, the algorithms that power our solutions will have to deal with a constant amount of data if they are working with image histograms.

Broadly speaking, histograms are a form of descriptors for images. We'll be discussing other forms of image descriptor in an upcoming chapter. For now, it is sufficient for you to understand that image descriptors are just another form of representation of images. Each descriptor captures some particular aspects or features of the image to construct its own form of representation. One of the common pitfalls of using histograms as a form of image representation as compared to its native form of using the entire two-dimensional grid of values is loss of information. A full-fledged image representation using pixel intensity values for all pixel locations naturally consists of all the information that you would need to reconstruct a digital image. However, the same cannot be said about histograms. When we study image histograms in detail, we'll get to see exactly what information do we stand to lose. And this loss in information is prevalent across all forms of image descriptors.

The following should give you a brief idea about what to expect in this chapter. We will be covering each of these topics in detail:

- The basic concept of a histogram
- Understanding image histograms and using OpenCV to construct the histogram of a given image
- Working with color histograms
- Image histograms and beyond, including understanding how the concept of histograms is used as an image descriptor and the manner in which it is adapted to other forms of image representation.

The basics of histograms

At the outset, we will briefly explain the concept of a histogram. Most of you might already know this from your lessons on basic statistics. However, we will reiterate this for the sake of completeness. Histogram is a form of data representation technique that relies on an aggregation of data points. The data is aggregated into a set of predefined bins that are represented along the x axis. The number of data points that fall within each of the bins makes up the corresponding counts on the y axis. For example, let's assume that our data looks something like the following:

$D=\{2,7,1,5,6,9,14,11,8,10,13\}$

If we define three bins, namely `Bin_1` `(1 - 5)`, `Bin_2` `(6 - 10)`, and `Bin_3` `(11 -`
`15)`, then the histogram corresponding to our data would look something like this:

Bins	Frequency
`Bin_1 (1 - 5)`	3
`Bin_2 (6 - 10)`	5
`Bin_3 (11 - 15)`	3

What this histogram data tells us is that we have three values between **1** and **5**, five between
6 and **10**, and three again between **11** and **15**. Note that it doesn't tell us what the values are,
just that some *n* values exist in a given bin. A more familiar visual representation of the
histogram in discussion is shown as follows:

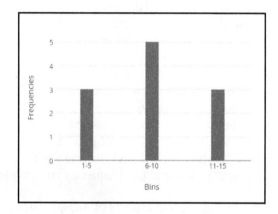

As you can see, the bins have been plotted along the *x* axis and their corresponding
frequencies along the *y* axis.

Now, in the context of images, how is a histogram computed? Well, it's not that difficult to
deduce. Since the data that we have comprise pixel intensity values, an image histogram is
computed by plotting a histogram using the intensity values of all its constituent pixels.
What this essentially means is that the sequence of pixel intensity values in our image
becomes the data. Well, this is in fact the simplest kind of histogram that you can compute
using the information available to you from the image. We will focus on such a histogram
throughout the entire chapter. However, towards the end, you will develop an intuition
regarding the other types of histograms that aggregate the other values associated with
pixels, apart from their pixel intensities. What exactly are those other values and how are
they computed? Such questions will form our topic of discussion in the chapter on image
descriptors.

Now, coming back to image histograms, there are some basic terminologies (pertaining to histograms in general) that you need to be aware of before you can dip your hands into code. We have explained them in detail here:

1. **Histogram size**: The histogram size refers to the number of bins in the histogram.
2. **Range**: The range of a histogram is the range of data that we are dealing with. The range of data as well as the histogram size are both important parameters that define a histogram.
3. **Dimensions**: Simply put, dimensions refer to the number of the type of items whose values we aggregate in the histogram bins. For example, consider a grayscale image. We might want to construct a histogram using the pixel intensity values for such an image. This would be an example of a single-dimensional histogram because we are just interested in aggregating the pixel intensity values and nothing else. The data, in this case, is spread over a range of 0 to 255. On account of being one-dimensional, such histograms can be represented graphically as 2D plots, the one-dimensional data (pixel intensity values) being plotted on the x axis (in the form of bins) along with the corresponding frequency counts along the y axis. We have already seen an example of this before. Now, imagine a color image with three channels: red, green, and blue. Let's say that we want to plot a histogram for the intensities in the red and green channels combined. This means that our data now becomes a pair of values (r, g). A histogram that is plotted for such data will have a dimensionality of 2. The plot for such a histogram will be a 3D plot with the data bins covering the x and y axes and the frequency counts plotted along the z axis.

Now that we have discussed the theoretical aspects of image histograms in detail, let's start thinking along the lines of code. We will start with the simplest (and in fact the most ubiquitous) design of image histograms. For starters, we'll consider grayscale images (we will be relaxing this condition in the later parts of this chapter). The range of our data will be from 0 to 255 (both inclusive), which means that all our data points will be integers that fall within the specified range. Also, the number of data points will equal the number of pixels that make up our input image. The simplicity in design comes from the fact that we fix the size of the histogram (the number of bins) as 256. Now, take a moment to think about what this means. There are 256 different possible values that our data points can take and we have a separate bin corresponding to each one of those values. So such an image histogram will essentially depict the 256 possible intensity values along with the counts of the number of pixels in the image that are colored with each of the different intensities.

Before taking a peek at what OpenCV has to offer, let's try to implement such a histogram on our own! We define a function named computeHistogram() that takes the grayscale image as an input argument and returns the image histogram. From our earlier discussions, it is evident that the histogram must contain 256 entries (for the 256 bins): one for each integer between 0 and 255. The value stored in the histogram corresponding to each of the 256 entries will be the count of the image pixels that have a particular intensity value. So, conceptually, we can use an array for our implementation such that the value stored in the histogram h[i](for 0≤i≤255) will be the count of the number of pixels in the image having the intensity of *i*. However, instead of using a C++ array, we will comply with the rules and standards followed by OpenCV and represent the histogram as a Mat object. We have already seen that a Mat object is nothing but a multidimensional array store. The implementation is outlined in the following code snippet:

```
Mat computeHistogram(Mat input_image) {
    Mat histogram = Mat::zeros(256, 1, CV_32S);

    for (int i = 0; i < input_image.rows; ++i) {
        for (int j = 0; j < input_image.cols; ++j) {
            int binIdx = (int) input_image.at<uchar>(i, j);
            histogram.at<int>(binIdx, 0) += 1;
        }
    }

    return histogram;
}
```

As you can see, we have chosen to represent the histogram as a 256-element-column-vector Mat object. We iterate over all the pixels in the input image and keep on incrementing the corresponding counts in the histogram (which had been initialized to 0). As per our description of the image histogram properties, it is easy to see that the intensity value of any pixel is the same as the bin index that is used to index into the appropriate histogram bin to increment the count.

Having such an implementation ready, let's test it out with the help of an actual image. The following code demonstrates a main() function that reads an input image, calls the computeHistogram() function that we have defined just now, and displays the contents of the histogram that is returned as a result:

```
int main()
{
    Mat input_image = imread("lena.jpg", IMREAD_GRAYSCALE);
    Mat histogram = computeHistogram(input_image);

    cout << "Histogram...\n";
    for (int i = 0; i < histogram.rows; ++i)
```

```
        cout << i << " : " << histogram.at<int>(i, 0) << "\n";

    return 0;
}
```

We have used the fact that the histogram that is returned from the function will be a single column `Mat` object. This makes the code that displays the contents of the histogram much cleaner.

Histograms in OpenCV

We have just seen the implementation of a very basic and minimalistic histogram using the first principles in OpenCV. The image histogram was basic in the sense that all the bins were uniform in size and comprised only a single pixel intensity. This made our lives simple when we designed our code for the implementation; there wasn't any need to explicitly check the membership of a data point (the intensity value of a pixel) with all the bins of our histograms. However, we know that a histogram can have bins whose sizes span more than one. Can you think of the changes that we might need to make in the code that we recently wrote to accommodate for bin sizes larger than 1? If this change seems doable to you, try to figure out how to incorporate the possibility of non-uniform bin sizes or multidimensional histograms. By now, things might have started to get a little overwhelming for you. No need to worry. As always, OpenCV has you covered!

The developers at OpenCV have provided you with a `calcHist()` function whose sole purpose is to calculate the histograms for a given set of arrays. By *arrays*, we refer to the images represented as `Mat` objects, and we use the term *set* because the function has the capability to compute multidimensional histograms from the given data:

```
Mat computeHistogram(Mat input_image) {
    Mat histogram;
    int channels[] = { 0 };
    int histSize[] = { 256 };
    float range[] = { 0, 256 };
    const float* ranges[] = { range };
    calcHist(&input_image, 1, channels, Mat(), histogram, 1, histSize,
ranges, true, false);

    return histogram;

}
```

Before we move on to an explanation of the different parameters involved in the `calcHist()` function call, I want to bring your attention to the abundant use of arrays in the preceding code snippet. Even arguments as simple as histogram sizes are passed to the function in the form of arrays rather than integer values, which at first glance seems quite unnecessary and counter-intuitive. The usage of arrays is due to the fact that the implementation of `calcHist()` is equipped to handle multidimensional histograms as well, and when we are dealing with such multidimensional histogram data, we require multiple parameters to be passed, one for each dimension. This will become clearer once we demonstrate an example of calculating multidimensional histograms using the `calcHist()` function. For the time being, we just wanted to clear up any confusion that might have popped up in your minds upon seeing the `array` parameters. Here is a detailed list of the arguments in the `calcHist()` function call:

- Source images
- Number of source images
- Channel indices
- Mask
- Dimensions (dims)
- Histogram size
- Ranges
- Uniform flag
- Accumulate flag

The last couple of arguments (the uniform and accumulate flags) have default values of true and false, respectively. Hence, the function call that you have seen just now can very well be written as follows:

```
calcHist(&input_image, 1, channels, Mat(), histogram, 1, histSize, ranges);
```

Plotting histograms in OpenCV

Now that we are familiar with the process of computing histograms using the APIs provided by OpenCV, we turn our attention to the problem of representing the information inside a histogram. In the previous section, we saw that we could easily traverse the Mat object representing our histogram to get a glimpse of the values (frequency counts). Also, in the section on the basics of histogram processing, we saw that a visual representation of a histogram in the form of a bar chart has the advantage of possessing a greater visual appeal. This section essentially attempts to the answer this question: Given a histogram that has been computed by the `calcHist()` function (or any other method for that matter), how do we represent the same graphically using OpenCV/C++? The key thing to note here is that we are trying to plot the histogram graphically using the same framework of OpenCV and C++ that we have been working with throughout this book. If we relax this restriction, we have a lot of online tools and programming language library packages (for example, matplotlib in Python) at our disposal that will perform such tasks for us. But, wouldn't it be nice if we are able to implement the same using OpenCV itself?

Let's see how we can go ahead with plotting a histogram. Our very first task is to decide upon the parameters of our canvas. As the name suggests, *canvas* is nothing but a blank image that serves as the chart on which histogram values are actually plotted. The parameters of a canvas include the width and height of the blank image, which in turn depend upon the number of bins (size) of our histogram. We know that we need to plot 256 bins. So, in order to have a well-spaced plot of a histogram, let's give each bin a space of 4 pixels along the *x* axis. This would mean setting the width of the canvas to 256×4=1024. Similarly, we select the canvas height at 400. The first few lines of our code provide the necessary declarations for our canvas:

```
void plotHistogram(Mat histogram) {

    int plotWidth = 1024, plotHeight = 400;
    int binWidth = (plotWidth / histogram.rows);
    Mat histogramPlot(plotHeight, plotWidth, CV_8UC3, Scalar(0, 0, 0));
```

Since the height of the canvas has been fixed at 400 pixels, we also have to normalize the values in the histogram so that they are spread uniformly over the entire height of the canvas (recall that the frequency counts are plotted along the *y* axis). We use OpenCV's `normalize()` function call to do our bidding. Recall that we have already used the `normalize()` function in a couple of places before: while implementing log transformations and the Vignette effect:

```
    normalize(histogram, histogram, 0, plotHeight, NORM_MINMAX);
```

Having initialized our canvas and properly calibrated our data, we are ready to do the actual *painting*: plotting the points that represent our histogram. The following lines of code achieve this:

```
    for (int i = 1; i < histogram.rows; ++i) {
        line (
            histogramPlot,
            Point((binWidth*(i-1)), (plotHeight -
cvRound(histogram.at<float>(i-1, 0)))),
            Point(binWidth*i, (plotHeight - cvRound(histogram.at<float>(i,
0)))),
            Scalar(255, 0, 0), 2
        );
```

```
    }
```

We use the line() function provided by OpenCV to actually draw the lines that make up our histogram plot. Since this is the first time that you are seeing the line() method being used, we will spend some time explaining the details of its usage. The line() function is part of an arsenal of drawing functions that have been provided by the OpenCV developers to aid programmers to draw some basic geometric entities, such as lines, rectangles, ellipses, and circles on images. The parameters that the line() method accepts are as follows:

1. The first is the source image on which the line is drawn.
2. The next two arguments provide the two endpoints of the line segment as Point() objects. The coordinates of the points are mentioned within the framework of the coordinates of the source image. The top-left corner of the image is taken as the origin with the x and y axes extending along the columns and rows of the image, respectively.
3. The next argument is the color of the line segment to be drawn. It is usually provided in the form of a Scalar object or can also be specified using the macro CV_RGB (r, g, b).
4. The fifth argument is an integer that specifies the thickness of the line segment.
5. Apart from the five arguments, there are a couple of extra arguments that also possess defaults and hence have been omitted from the code snippet we just saw. These arguments specify the line type (with options for either the 8-connected, 4-connected, or anti-aliased line with the default being an 8-connected line) and the number of fractional bits in point coordinates (default being 0, integral point coordinates).

Now that you can understand what the line() function does with the parameters that are passed to it, we provide you with an explanation of how we use the function to plot our histogram. What we essentially do is loop through the histogram values that we have and represent each frequency value as a point that has to be plotted on our canvas. Now, drawing a line between each pair of the adjacent points will give rise to the kind of output that we want to plot.

Finally, after everything is done, we display the results in an OpenCV window:

```
    imshow("Histogram", histogramPlot);
    waitKey(0);
}
```

Here is the output when the preceding function is executed by passing the histogram that we computed in the previous code examples:

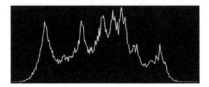

Instead of using line segments to join the points that represent the frequency counts for the various bins, we can adopt another approach that is more prevalent when it comes to plotting histograms. In our alternate approach, we draw rectangles for each of the bins, where the height of the rectangle is equal to the frequency count and the width of all the rectangles is constant at 4 pixels. Similar to `line()`, the drawing functions within OpenCV provide us with the `rectangle()` function whose usage has been shown as follows:

```
rectangle (
          histogramPlot,
          Point( (binWidth * (i-1)), (plotHeight -
cvRound(histogram.at<float>(i-1, 0))) ),
          Point(binWidth*i, plotHeight),
          CV_RGB(200, 200, 200),
          CV_FILLED
        );
```

The arguments to `rectangle()` are very similar to that of `line()`, expect for certain subtle differences. The two point objects (the second and the third arguments) represent two opposite vertices of the rectangle. Also, the `CV_FILLED` flag, which forms the last argument in the preceding code, draws a filled rectangle. Now that you know about the `rectangle()` API provided by OpenCV, it would be a good mental exercise for you to reason out how we plot the various rectangles that form the histogram (the logic is quite similar to what we discussed using points). The following is the output when we plot our histogram using rectangles:

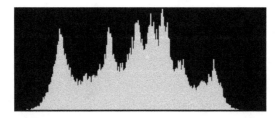

This brings us to the end of the current section, based on plotting histograms using OpenCV. We started off with computing histograms from images using the `calcHist()` function call and then saw how to visually represent the histogram data in the form of line/bar charts. Before we close this section, we consolidate all of the histogram-related code in a single place (one single C++ source file) for the benefit of the readers:

```cpp
#include <iostream>
#include <opencv2/core/core.hpp>
#include <opencv2/highgui/highgui.hpp>
#include <opencv2/imgproc/imgproc.hpp>

using namespace std;
using namespace cv;

Mat computeHistogram(Mat input_image) {
    Mat histogram;
    int channels[] = { 0 };
    int histSize[] = { 256 };
    float range[] = { 0, 256 };
    const float* ranges[] = { range };
    calcHist(&input_image, 1, channels, Mat(), histogram, 1, histSize,
ranges);

    return histogram;

}

void plotHistogram(Mat histogram) {
    int plotWidth = 1024, plotHeight = 400;
    int binWidth = (plotWidth / histogram.rows);
    Mat histogramPlot(plotHeight, plotWidth, CV_8UC3, Scalar(0, 0, 0));

    normalize(histogram, histogram, 0, plotHeight, NORM_MINMAX);

    for (int i = 1; i < histogram.rows; ++i) {

        rectangle (
            histogramPlot,
            Point( (binWidth * (i-1)), (plotHeight -
cvRound(histogram.at<float>(i-1, 0))) ),
            Point (binWidth*i, plotHeight),
            CV_RGB(200, 200, 200),
            CV_FILLED
        );
    }
    imshow("Histogram", histogramPlot);
    waitKey(0);
```

```
    }

int main() {

    Mat input_image = imread("/home/samyak/Pictures/lena.jpg",
IMREAD_GRAYSCALE);
    Mat histogram = computeHistogram(input_image);
    plotHistogram(histogram);
    return 0;
}
```

Color histograms in OpenCV

In this chapter so far, we have been working with grayscale images. Let's take a moment to understand the concept of histograms when applied to multichannel color images. For all demonstration purposes in this section, we will be working with the color version of Lena's picture as our input image:

While talking about the transition from grayscale to color images, we have always visualized color images as being composed of three channels of red, green, and blue. We have maintained that all three channels can be treated independently as grayscale images themselves. And this is exactly what we will do in the case of color histograms as well.

In the last few sections, we have seen how to compute as well as plot histograms for single-channel grayscale images. Now imagine performing the same operation across all the three channels of a color image to obtain three separate histograms. Since each individual channel is exactly the same as a grayscale image (all pixel intensities lying in the range of 0 to 255), there is no change in the histogram computation logic when we deal with it separately. This is exactly what we have done in the following code. As we take you through the different modules, we will emphasize the portions that are either different or new from what we have already seen.

At the very outset, we have the header files and namespace declarations out of the way:

```
#include <iostream>
#include <opencv2/core/core.hpp>
#include <opencv2/highgui/highgui.hpp>
#include <opencv2/imgproc/imgproc.hpp>

using namespace std;
using namespace cv'
```

The logic and design of the computeHistogram() method remain the same. Recall that the function accepts a single-channel image and computes the 256-bin histogram for the same. We have said that in the case of a three-channel color image, the histogram computation logic will essentially remain the same as for a single-channel grayscale image and is just replicated across all the three channels. Therefore, it does make sense to keep the computeHistogram() function unchanged and simply mirror the function calls across all the channels of the input image (we will see that happening soon):

```
Mat computeHistogram(Mat input_image) {
    Mat histogram;
    int channels[] = { 0 };
    int histSize[] = { 256 };
    float range[] = { 0, 256 };
    const float* ranges[] = { range };
    calcHist(&input_image, 1, channels, Mat(), histogram, 1, histSize,
ranges);

    return histogram;

}
```

We now come to the plotHistogram() function. You can notice some significant changes to the function from its previous versions. Let's take a moment to understand what the changes are and why they need to be made. While we were working with grayscale images in the previous sections, there was just a single histogram that needed a plot. So our function took the Mat object representing the histogram as an argument, created the plot using the drawing functions available through the OpenCV API, and displayed it in an OpenCV window. However, since we are dealing with multichannel images and hence multiple histograms here, we need to share our plot across three different calls of the plotHistogram() function. The different histograms for the red, green, and blue channels will be provided to the function as the first argument in each of the function calls, whereas the second argument is the plot that needs to be shared across all the three invocations of plotHistogram(). Imagine it this way: when the first call to plotHistogram() is made, the histogram for the blue channel is passed along with an empty canvas. When the function returns, the blue-channel histogram is plotted on the empty canvas. Now, in the subsequent call, we pass the green-channel histogram as an argument along with the canvas that now has the blue-channel histogram already plotted on it. And when the second function call returns, the canvas will have both the blue and the green histogram plots. You can extend the same line of reasoning for the third and the final function call.

From our discussions so far, it is also obvious that the design of our code necessitates that the histogram plot (the second argument) be an object that has a global scope, rather than being local to the function definition (the Mat object histogramPlot was kept as a local object in the previous code snippet).

Now there is a third argument to the function call as well, named chIdx. This is nothing but an index that identifies which color channel is being processed right now. Why would the function need to know which channel it is processing as long as the relevant histogram is a Mat object (the first argument). After all, didn't we just state that all the three channels are to be treated independently? As it turns out, the channel information becomes crucial when we want to plot the histogram on a canvas. If you recall the description of the line() function, there was an argument that specified the color of the line to be plotted. Since we were dealing with the plot of a single histogram, we simply selected white. However, we now have three separate histograms to plot on the same canvas, and we cannot simply afford to have them of the same color. Therefore, each of the three histograms are plotted using their respective channel colors: blue, green, and red.

The way we handle this in the code is by declaring another helper function called getPlotColor(). The sole purpose of this function is to return the appropriate Scalar in accordance with the channel index passed to it as an argument. As you can see in the following code, the function body consists of a simple switch case statement:

```
Scalar getPlotColor(int chIdx) {
    switch (chIdx) {
        case 0:
            return Scalar(255, 0, 0);
            break;

        case 1:
            return Scalar(0, 255, 0);
            break;

        case 2:
            return Scalar(0, 0, 255);
```

```
        break;
    }
    return Scalar(255, 255, 255);
}
```

Now that we have discussed all the aspects of the plotHistogram() function in detail, here is its implementation:

```
void plotHistogram(Mat histogram, Mat histogramPlot, int chIdx) {
    int plotWidth = histogramPlot.cols;
    int plotHeight = histogramPlot.rows;
    int binWidth = (plotWidth / histogram.rows);
    normalize(histogram, histogram, 0, plotHeight, NORM_MINMAX);

    for (int i = 1; i < histogram.rows; ++i) {
        Scalar plotColor = getPlotColor(chIdx);
        line (
                histogramPlot,
                Point((binWidth*(i-1)), (plotHeight -
cvRound(histogram.at<float>(i-1, 0)))),
                Point(binWidth*i, (plotHeight -
cvRound(histogram.at<float>(i, 0)))),
                plotColor, 2, CV_AA, 0
        );

    }
}
```

Finally, we have the main() function where everything comes together:

```
int main() {
```

We first read the input image to a Mat object and subsequently use the split() function to split it into its constituent channels. The channels are saved in a C++ vector of Mat objects:

```
    Mat input_image = imread("/home/samyak/Pictures/lena.jpg");
    vector<Mat> channels;
    split(input_image, channels);
```

As discussed, the Mat object representing our histogram plots (the canvas) should have a global scope. We declare the same here. The parameters (dimensions) remain the same as we had used previously:

```
    int plotWidth = 1024, plotHeight = 400;
    Mat histogramPlot(plotHeight, plotWidth, CV_8UC3, Scalar(0, 0, 0));
```

We now loop through all the channels in the vector. For each channel, we first calculate its corresponding histogram by calling the computeHistogram() function and then plotting the same on the canvas by invoking plotHistogram() and passing all the relevant parameters:

```
for (int chIdx = 0; chIdx < channels.size(); ++chIdx) {
    Mat channel = channels[chIdx];
    Mat histogram = computeHistogram(channel);
    plotHistogram(histogram, histogramPlot, chIdx);
}
```

After all the channels have been processed, we display our plot in an OpenCV window and quit:

```
imshow("Histogram", histogramPlot);
waitKey(0);

return 0;
}
```

Before we end this section, I would like to leave you with a glimpse of the output from running the code that we have just described in great detail. In the next image, you can clearly see the three separate plots, each drawn using the color of the corresponding channels that they represent:

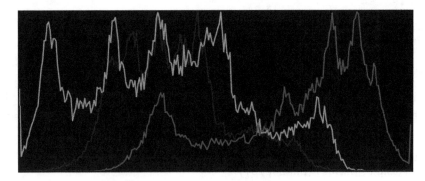

Multidimensional histograms in OpenCV

All the histograms that we have seen being computed and/or plotted in this chapter so far have been one-dimensional histograms. This is because the pixel intensities were the only entities that were being aggregated into bins. Also, if you recall the parameters that we discussed for OpenCV's `calcHist()` function, you would remember that one of them explicitly specified the number of dimensions that the function is supposed to work with (we have passed the integer 1 as the parameter for all the invocations in the chapter so far). In this section, we will take a brief look at the concept of multidimensional image histograms and also see how we can modify the code that we have been working with to enable the `calcHist()` function to return a multidimensional histogram.

Before we dive into the code, let's understand what multidimensional histograms are and what they represent. If you think of the one-dimensional histograms that we have been dealing with so far, they essentially answer questions of this type: How many pixels in the image have the intensity value x? We saw that x could vary from 0 to 255. If we specifically talk of color images, we may re-phrase the question as this: How many pixels in the image have the intensity value of x in their red channel? We can get the answer to this question by taking a peek at the histogram corresponding to the *red* channel that we have plotted. Now, what if I want answers to questions of this form: How many pixels in the image have the intensity values of r in their red channel and b in their blue channel? Note that the keyword here is *and*. We must count only those pixels in our answer that satisfy both the conditions. It is pretty evident that the histograms that we have been dealing with so far are not equipped to handle such queries. And this is precisely the task of multidimensional histograms.

To answer queries of the type that we have just discussed, we essentially need to simultaneously keep track of the intensity values of both the red and blue channels. Earlier, each bin of our histogram corresponded to a single intensity (or a range of intensities, if there was an increase in the bin width) from a single channel. Each bin of our two-dimensional histogram will now correspond to two intensity values (or two ranges): one for each channel (red and blue in our example).

As always, we dive into the code for computing and plotting a multidimensional histogram (2D, in our case). We have left out the header and namespace declarations as they would remain exactly the same as before. While running the code in your machines, you can simply copy and paste the required lines:

```
int main()
{
```

Like before, we read an image from the disk and load its contents to a `Mat` object.

```
Mat input_image = imread("lena.jpg");
```

The basic format (structure and order of arguments) remains the same. However, there is a difference when it comes to the values that we pass to the `calcHist()` function. You must have noted the use of single-element arrays when we dealt with one-dimensional histograms. At the time, we briefly mentioned that the usage of arrays is for the case of multidimensional histograms. The code snippet shown next demonstrates exactly how:

```
int rBins = 32, bBins = 32;
int histSize[] = { rBins, bBins };

float rRange[] = { 0, 255 };
float bRange[] = { 0, 255 };
const float* ranges[] = { rRange, bRange };

int channels[] = { 2, 0 };
```

Note that the array elements are the parameters for the separate channels that compose our multidimensional histogram. Since we are working with a two-dimensional histogram with our data being taken from the *R* and *B* channels, all `array` parameters will have a size of 2: one of each of the two channels. So, for example, if we want 32 bins each for the *R* and *B* channels, then we pass the array that comprises those two values as the `histSize` parameter:

```
Mat histogram;
calcHist(&input_image, 1, channels, Mat(), histogram, 2, histSize,
ranges, true, false);
```

Having understood the logic behind computing a two-dimensional histogram, let's now turn our attention to the ways in which we can create a plot of the same. In the case of a simple one-dimensional histogram, it was quite easy to visualize its graphical version. We plot the bins along one of the axes (usually, the *x* axis) and the frequency counts go along the other axis (the *y* axis). But, we have seen that for a 2D histogram, we need two dimensions to represent the bins, which means that the bins themselves take up the entire *x*-*y* plane! So, how do we go about the frequency counts that accompany each bin? There are a couple of options that emerge. One is to represent the plot using a 3D diagram with the frequency plots along the *z* axis. An example of such a plot is as follows:

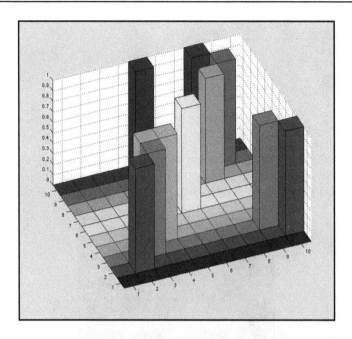

Unfortunately, as of now, OpenCV doesn't provide us with the tools to create such plots. So we move to our second alternative. We visualize the 2D histogram plot as an image where we have the bins correspond to our two channels (red and blue) instead of the rows and columns. So essentially, in the image representation of a 2D histogram, each pixel is indexed by the two-dimensional bins (instead of row and column values) and they store the frequency counts (in place of intensity values). Expressing the histogram in such a manner allows you to have easy visualization because the frequency counts can be normalized to a 0-255 scale, and we can display the 2D histogram as a regular grayscale image. The following code snippet achieves what we have just described:

```
double maxVal=0;
minMaxLoc(histogram, 0, &maxVal, 0, 0);

int scale = 10;
Mat histImg = Mat::zeros((bBins * scale), (rBins * scale), CV_8UC3);
for (int r = 0; r < rBins; r++) {
    for (int b = 0; b < bBins; s++) {
        float binVal = histogram.at<float>(r, b);
        int intensity = cvRound(binVal * 255 / maxVal);
        rectangle(
            histImg,
            Point(r * scale, b * scale),
            Point((r+1)*scale - 1, (b+1)*scale - 1),
            Scalar::all(intensity),
            CV_FILLED
```

```
        );
    }
}

imshow( "H-S Histogram", histImg );
waitKey(0);
return 0;
}
```

Expressing the histogram in such a manner allows you to have easy visualization because the frequency counts can be normalized to a 0-255 scale, and we can display the 2D histogram as a regular grayscale image. The following is an example of this:

If you have followed the explanation closely, it is not at all difficult to interpret the preceding image. The brighter spots represent those combinations of red and blue for which the frequency of pixel counts is high, whereas the corresponding counts are lower for the combinations that belong to the comparatively darker regions of the image.

You can also appreciate the difficulty in the representation that comes along with an increase in the dimensionality of the histograms. Although more complex than a one-dimensional histogram, plotting 2D histograms was still manageable. However there is no straightforward technique for plotting three- or four-dimensional histograms or higher.

Summary

In this chapter, we covered a new genre of image processing algorithms. Moving from performing per-pixel computations, we introduced the notion of aggregating pixel values into structures called histograms.

Delving into the details, you learnt about the nomenclature associated with histograms and also went through the implementations of histogram-related routines available in OpenCV. We also briefly touched upon the idea that a histogram acts as a form of representation or descriptor for images. In fact, histograms are one of the simplest forms of image descriptors that are used quite extensively in computer vision literature. We will look at descriptors in much greater detail in the subsequent chapters of the book.

If you recall, at the beginning of the book, we made a distinction between image processing and computer vision algorithms. Note that in all the programs we have developed in this chapter, none of the outputs were images. We might have used an image to represent the plot of a histogram, but the essential output that we were interested in has always been a histogram–an array/sequence of numeric values. This marks our foray into the realm of computer vision from the earlier image processing algorithms that we have been discussing in this book so far.

In the next chapter, we would be looking at yet another computer vision algorithm: detection of edges in images.

5

Image Derivatives and Edge Detection

In the very first chapter, we made a distinction between the terms *image processing* and *computer vision*. We made it clear that the outputs of the operations that fall under the umbrella of image processing are images themselves. So, an image-processing operation will take an image as input and produce yet another image as its output. Essentially, all the techniques that we have covered so far are image-processing operations: grayscale transformations, image filtering, and image thresholding. Computer vision tasks are slightly more interesting. The inputs for computer vision algorithms are again, images. But, the outputs are what we call *symbols*. These symbols represent some form of semantic information that the algorithm has derived from the image. The kind of semantic inference that is done by vision algorithms is quite close to what human beings would do. An example of a computer vision task in an image would be to separate the foreground from the background. Needless to say, most of the computer vision tasks certainly pose a much greater challenge than the traditional image-processing operations.

In this chapter, we take a plunge into the world of vision algorithms by studying one of the most fundamental topics in the computer vision literature: **edge detection**. Before we talk about the techniques that help us detect edges, we must know what edges are. And in order to define edges, we have to introduce the concept of a derivative as it is applied to images. At the most basic level, the definition of a derivative remains the same as you will have studied in your high-school calculus class: it is a quantitative measure of the rate of change. The center of attention for us in this chapter would be to transfer the knowledge of derivatives that we have and apply it to the domain of images. From then on, the course of study is quite clear. We see how the notion of image derivatives is used to provide a quantitative definition of edges. Then, we take a look at the various frameworks for edge detection that exist in the computer vision literature. We will touch upon the Sobel and Canny edge detectors, two very popular and commercially used edge detection algorithms.

Towards the end of this chapter, we will extrapolate the concept of derivatives to introduce second-order derivatives of images. Just like we implemented the Vignette mask to reinforce our concepts of Gaussian filters, we will see a practical application of image derivatives (particularly, a second-order derivative) to perform blur detection on images. Hopefully, that section will once again demonstrate how the simple theoretical concepts have wide-ranging applications in practical life.

So, in a nutshell, the following list gives us a pointwise timeline of the topics to be covered in this chapter:

- An introduction to the concept of an image derivative as it is applied to images
- Implementing a derivative calculation method in OpenCV and drawing inferences from the output
- Using derivatives to define edges
- A little bit of theory and implementation of some of the most popular edge detection algorithms, namely Sobel and Canny
- An introduction to the concept of a second-order derivative of images (Laplacian) and see how it helps us solve an interesting practical problem

Like always, our focus will be on implementing whatever we learn in OpenCV. As we move along the chapter and cover the various concepts we have outlined in the introduction, we will simultaneously share the code snippets that implement the same. Following such a policy will make it much easier for you to visualize the things that happen as a result of the operations that we apply. Such visualization is sometimes difficult to achieve when talking about computer vision tasks.

Image derivatives

Those of you who may have taken up a basic calculus course in your high school will know the definition of a derivative as it applies to functions. For the sake of others, we repeat the same here, albeit very briefly. Mathematically, a derivative is represented as follows:

$$\frac{d}{dx}f(x)|_{x'} = \lim_{h \to 0} \frac{f(x+h) - f(x)}{h}$$

Note that we are not trying to be mathematically fastidious, our only intention here is to give you an intuition into the concept of a derivative and how it applies to images. So, this chapter won't go into the intricacies behind the mathematics that is involved. Rather, our focus will be on how the principles of derivatives of functions are transferred to the domain of images.

What the preceding formula essentially tells you is that the derivative of a function $f(x)$ at any point is the ratio of the change in the output to the input, as the input is varied by an infinitesimal amount in and around that point. Imagine that you have a 2D plot of the graph of the function $f(x)$. You sample the function at any point, say x, and obtain the value $f(x')$. Now, we move a little further along the x axis and sample the function again at another nearby point, namely $(x' + h)$, to get $f(x' + h)$. Now, in the limiting case when the two points x' and $(x' + h)$ are closely spaced (another way to put this is if h tends to zero), then this ratio of the change in the value of the function output to the change in the input is a good approximation of the derivative of the function at the point x'. This is what derivatives are all about, how the function changes around a point.

When we introduced the concept of Gaussian filtering, we started off by applying it to one-dimensional images and then eventually scaled up to two dimensions, remember? In the same manner, we will first describe how we can transfer this definition of image derivatives to a one-dimensional image (hypothetical 1D numerical arrays) before we move on to proper 2D images. When we think about applying the preceding equation to a 1D array, the first problem that comes to the fore is the fact that the equation has been defined for continuous functions, but arrays (or images) are discrete. So, the notion of limits (*infinitesimally small* or the notion of being *as close as possible*) doesn't really apply here. The closest that we can go from a particular location is to the next immediate neighbor (left or right). Keeping this in mind and drawing parallels from our explanations of the derivative for a continuous function, what a discrete derivative does is that it samples the discrete function at a particular location, say x', and moves it forward by some distance. Since this distance is to be kept as small as possible, we choose $h = 1$ (the shortest distance possible in the discrete domain), which essentially means we move to the neighboring cell in the 1D array. The difference between the values of the function at these two adjacent locations gives you the magnitude of the derivative for a discrete function.

So how does all of this look for a 1D image? To calculate the derivative of an image that is represented in the form of a 1D array, we simply make a traversal and compute the derivative at each pixel location by making a note of the difference between the current intensity value and the intensity at the immediate next location.

This operation has been shown graphically in the following image:

In the preceding figure, the 1D array on the top represents our input whereas the corresponding array given at the bottom is the derivative output that has been calculated using the rules that we have just described.

In terms of mathematical equations, the formula for the derivative of a 1D image looks something like this:

$$f'[x]\big|_{x=x'} = f[x'] - f[x'+1]$$

Note that we have shifted to square brackets instead of the usual round ones. This is because it is a common practice to use square brackets to represent discrete functions in order to differentiate them from their continuous counterparts.

If you have been following the explanations closely, you might have noticed the scope for some variations in the manner in which we compute differences (derivatives). To calculate the derivative at a pixel location, we take its difference with its immediate neighbor on the right-hand side. Can we do the same using its left neighbor? Yes, of course! In such a scenario, we are essentially computing our derivatives using the following formula:

$$f'[x]\big|_{x=x'} = f[x'] - f[x'-1]$$

In fact, both these methods are well-recognized forms of computing derivatives for one-dimensional image sequences. There are in total three such variations that have been described in the following list:

1. **Forward difference**: The derivative is computed by taking the difference between the current pixel and the immediate next pixel on the right-hand side.
2. **Backward difference**: The derivative is computed by taking the difference between the current pixel and the previous pixel on the left-hand side.
3. **Central difference**: For the current pixel location, the derivative is computed by taking the difference between the intensities of the immediate next and previous pixels.

For the sake of completeness, we also present the formula for computing the derivative using the central difference rule. Note the factor of *1/2* in the formula. Can you figure out why this appears? This is because when we are taking the difference of pixel intensities at the locations *(x'+1)* and *(x'-1)*, we are essentially skipping a distance of 2 pixels; this is why the value of *h* here is 2:

$$f'[x]|_{x=x'} = \frac{1}{2}\left(f[x'+1] - f[x'-1]\right)$$

What we have seen so far is that computing derivatives for hypothetical one-dimensional images essentially boils down to taking the difference of pixel values. A fairly complex and important mathematical idea has been reduced to something simple in the domain of images. Before we move on and extend this to real-world (two-dimensional) images, let's visualize these pixel differences as filtering operations.

Back in Chapter 2, *Image Filtering* when we introduced the notion of filters, we had demonstrated their operation in the context of image averaging. We stated that the true strength of visualizing tasks, such as image averaging, as filtering operations lies in the fact that a lot of computer vision tasks can be molded into the same framework. You have just learned yet another operation: image derivatives. Do you think that we can model the same using filters and the concept of correlation (let's stick to 1D images for the time being)? Before reading on, I would strongly urge you to take some time to think about the answer yourselves.

The answer to the question is indeed, yes! Image derivatives can be very easily computed using filters. In fact, the filters that we use for taking derivatives are much simpler than their image averaging counterparts. The following image demonstrates a simple filter that computes the derivative of a 1D image using forward difference:

Note that since the filter size here is 2, there isn't a well-defined central point for the filter. In fact, the anchor point is the first pixel itself. Given the anchor point, it is quite easy to visualize its operation. As you slide the filter over the 1D array, for each pixel location, it will multiply the intensity of the current pixel (that overlaps the anchor point) by **1** and its immediate right-hand side neighbor by **-1**. Also, it will add the results to compute the derivative value for that pixel location. This is nothing but using forward difference, as discussed earlier.

Now that we know how the forward-difference derivative calculation works using a filter, it is quite easy to design filters that perform the backward-difference derivative computation:

While using the preceding filter, the second element will act as the anchor point rather than the first, as we saw in the case of the forward-difference filter. Finally, we have the filter for central difference:

This again is a symmetric filter with a well-defined anchor point at its center. You may have noticed that the anchor point kept shifting as we went from forward- to backward- to central-difference filters. This makes it a rather inconvenient representation to work with. In order to overcome this, we represent the preceding three filters in a slightly modified fashion, as shown in the following image:

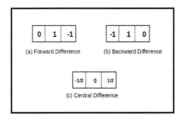

As you can see, we have padded the forward- and backward-derivative filters with zeros to make their size even (padding a filter with zeros does not change its behavior). All the three filters now have well-defined anchor points at the center.

Since there are three different variants, a natural question that arises is, which one is the best? For most applications where an image derivative may be required, we generally prefer to go with central difference. This is mainly due to the fact that it is symmetric and is able to capture the variations (differences or gradients) across the pixel in a better manner (since it takes into account the intensities to the left and right, both). In fact, when we extend the derivative computation logic to two dimensions, we will stick with central difference.

Image derivatives in two dimensions

Now that we are comfortable with the theory behind image derivatives in one dimension, we will see how the concept can be scaled to two dimensions. After all, when we start our OpenCV implementation from the next section onward, we will deal with images: two-dimensional data.

From what we have gathered in this chapter until now, derivatives essentially measure how our function changes. When we are dealing with one-dimensional data, there is only one possible *direction* along which this change can take place. When we talk about two-dimensional functions, we have two variables that we can vary independently, typically x and y. So, changing one of them (while keeping the other constant) allows us to measure the change in our function value (the thing we call derivative) along two directions as opposed to one. Therefore, it is prudent to assume that for two-dimensional functions (such as images), two different derivatives are computed. One derivative measures the change in pixel values across rows and the other across columns.

Let's understand what we've just written using some concrete examples. For this, we present the two kernels that allow us to compute the two derivatives that we have been talking about. Let's start with the derivative along the horizontal direction:

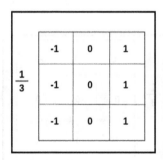

Take a moment to study this filter and try to understand what it accomplishes. At the outset, let's get the obvious things out of the way. This is a 3 x 3 filter, which means that it works with 8 neighbors of the central pixel (which coincides with the filter's anchor point). You might have already noticed some forms of similarity between the central-difference filter and the filter that we have shown here. In fact, all the rows of the preceding filter are the same as and (ignoring the multiplicative factor of *1/3*)equal to the one-dimensional central-difference filter that we saw in the previous section. Having said that, let's try to visualize what this accomplishes. When we place the preceding filter on top of a pixel in the image, it will compute the sum of the central differences of three pixels: the pixel overlapping the anchor point and the one lying above and below it. This is because all the rows independently function as central-difference filters. I strongly advise you to take a moment so that this visualization is registered in your mind, as this will remain a key idea when we work with such derivative filters in the upcoming sections on edge detection. Once this filter has computed the sum of the central differences for the three pixels, the factor of *1/3* averages out the horizontal differences to produce a single value as the output of the filter. If you look at it, essentially what the filter does is that it computes the derivative at the three pixels (anchor point and one pixel above and below) and then takes the average of the three values to produce the derivative at the central pixel. By looking at the direction in which the difference is being computed, you can check for yourself why we named this filter as the horizontal derivative filter (or kernel). Now, we focus our attention on the following image:

$$\frac{1}{3}
\begin{array}{|c|c|c|}
\hline
-1 & -1 & -1 \\
\hline
0 & 0 & 0 \\
\hline
1 & 1 & 1 \\
\hline
\end{array}$$

The preceding diagram shows the filter used to compute the vertical derivative for an image. Since we have already grasped how the horizontal difference filter operates, we will not spend much time in the explanation of the working of its vertical counterpart. Rather, we will only highlight some of the differences that exist between the two. As opposed to rows, all the columns of this filter are similar to the one-dimensional central-difference filter. This means that this filter computes the difference in the vertical direction for three pixels (the central pixel and one to the left and the right) and averages these derivatives in order to generate the derivative at the central pixel. Again, since the difference computations are oriented along the columns, this filter is named as the vertical derivative filter (or kernel).

Why are we insisting on repeating the difference computations (horizontal and vertical) across three different pixels and averaging the results? This is done so that the derivative value that is computed is a good approximation of the actual derivative. Factoring the differences (horizontal or vertical) that exist in the neighboring (left-right or top-bottom corners) pixels in the form of an average will give us a better estimate of the variations in the center pixel that we are trying to capture.

This brings us to the end of our discourse on image derivatives. Before we move on to edge detection, let's implement all that we have learned until now (and a little more) using OpenCV.

Visualizing image derivatives with OpenCV

In this section, our focus will be on the implementation of the concepts for image derivatives that we have covered in the last couple of sections. In terms of code, this section doesn't really present anything radically different from what we have worked on so far. In the last section, we presented two-dimensional image derivatives within the framework of image filters. All that remains to be done for calculating the derivative is that we implement the filters. And we already know from Chapter 2, *Image Filtering* that OpenCV's filter2D() function allows us to do exactly that. So without any further ado, let's delve into our code:

```cpp
#include <iostream>
#include <opencv2/core/core.hpp>
#include <opencv2/highgui/highgui.hpp>
#include <opencv2/imgproc/imgproc.hpp>

using namespace std;
using namespace cv;
```

If you recall our discourse on the `filter2D()` function, one of the foremost things that we need to do while using `filter2D()` is to define (and populate) a Mat object that would serve as the custom filter we want to apply to our image. We have already discussed the contents of the filters, so let's initialize the corresponding Mat objects in our code.

To do this, we define a couple of C++ functions, namely `getHorizontalDerKernel()` and `getVerticalDerKernel()`, that return Mat objects corresponding to the 3 x 3 horizontal and vertical derivative kernels. The implementation of both the functions are conceptually identical and simple enough to not warrant any explanation:

```cpp
Mat getHorizontalDerKernel() {
    Mat horizontalDerKernel = Mat::zeros(3, 3, CV_32F);
    horizontalDerKernel.at<float>(0, 0) = -1.0;
    horizontalDerKernel.at<float>(1, 0) = -1.0;
    horizontalDerKernel.at<float>(2, 0) = -1.0;

    horizontalDerKernel.at<float>(0, 2) = 1.0;
    horizontalDerKernel.at<float>(1, 2) = 1.0;
    horizontalDerKernel.at<float>(2, 2) = 1.0;

    return (horizontalDerKernel / 3);
}

Mat getVerticalDerKernel() {
    Mat verticalDerKernel = Mat::zeros(3, 3, CV_32F);
    verticalDerKernel.at<float>(0, 0) = -1.0;
    verticalDerKernel.at<float>(0, 1) = -1.0;
    verticalDerKernel.at<float>(0, 2) = -1.0;

    verticalDerKernel.at<float>(2, 0) = 1.0;
    verticalDerKernel.at<float>(2, 1) = 1.0;
    verticalDerKernel.at<float>(2, 2) = 1.0;

    return (verticalDerKernel / 3);
}
```

Having implemented both the kernels, we make a simple call to the `filter2D()` function and pass the required parameters. The filtered output images are saved in a couple of different Mat objects: `derivative_horizontal` and `derivative_vertical` for the horizontal and vertical derivatives, respectively.

Note that in the `filter2D()` function, we fixed the depth of the output as `CV_16S`, which basically stands for `short int` (or simply, `short`). This has been done because keeping it as an 8-bit `unsigned char` (`CV_8U`) might lead to an overflow. We are performing the derivative operation, which involves taking differences. This might lead to the possibility of some of the entries turning out to be negative, and a `CV_8U` Mat is incapable of handling this.

Since derivative images are of the type `CV_16S`, we use the `convertScaleAbs()` function to bring them to `CV_8U` and subsequently display the images using `imshow()`:

```cpp
int main()
{
    Mat input_image = imread("/home/samyak/Pictures/lena.jpg",
IMREAD_GRAYSCALE);
    Mat derivative_horizontal, derivative_vertical;
    Mat scaled_derivative_horizontal, scaled_derivative_vertical;

    Mat horizontalDerKernel = getHorizontalDerKernel();
    Mat verticalDereKernel = getVerticalDerKernel();

    filter2D(input_image, derivative_horizontal, CV_16S,
horizontalDerKernel);
    filter2D(input_image, derivative_vertical, CV_16S, verticalDerKernel);

    convertScaleAbs(derivative_horizontal, scaled_derivative_X);
    convertScaleAbs(derivative_vertical, scaled_derivative_Y);
    imshow("Horizontal_Derivative", scaled_derivative_horizontal);
    imshow("Vertical_Derivative", scaled_derivative_vertical);
    waitKey(0);
    return 0;
}
```

Now that we have the code for computing two-dimensional image derivatives up-and-running, it would be interesting to visualize the kinds of image that it will produce as output and check whether these images reconcile with our understanding of image derivatives.

As always, the input for the preceding code is the grayscale version of Lena, as follows:

The output for both the horizontal and vertical derivatives are presented side by side in the following image (the image on the left-hand side is of the horizontal derivative and the one on the right is for the vertical derivative). In both the images, the white patches represent the pixels across which the change in the intensity values (derivative or gradient) is high. Similarly, the darker regions in the image correspond to areas that are more or less homogenous with respect to intensity variations.

From a single glance, you can say that the areas that are at the boundaries of objects, such as the outline of the hat or the curvature of the eyes, are the ones where the concentration of white pixels is maximal (in either of the two directions). You should hold on to this observation because this forms the basis of our discussions in one of our subsequent sections on the relationship between image derivatives and edge detection.

The Sobel derivative filter

We have just implemented and applied our own derivative filter to an image. Since computing the derivative is quite a fundamental operation in computer vision and image processing, we typically do not want to burden the programmer with the task of having to populate the filter all by himself (as we just did). It is no surprise that OpenCV provides you with a function that can return the final output of the image derivative operation. Also, by varying the parameters of the function call, you can compute both the x and y derivatives. The function's name is `Sobel()`, named after Irwin Sobel, who came up with the design of this filter along with Gary Feldman in 1968.

What is so special about this filter? Well, the design is slightly different from what we implemented just now. For example, the x-derivative filter is shown as follows:

$$\begin{bmatrix} -1 & 0 & 1 \\ -2 & 0 & 2 \\ -1 & 0 & 1 \end{bmatrix}$$

If you look carefully, you will notice a subtle difference in the Sobel filter. The middle row has been multiplied by two. What this essentially means is that while computing the differences and averaging them up, the difference that is calculated across the pixel at the anchor point is given more weightage (multiplied by a factor of two) than the remaining pixels. A similar difference exists in the y-derivative filter as well:

$$\begin{bmatrix} -1 & -2 & -1 \\ 0 & 0 & 0 \\ 1 & 2 & 1 \end{bmatrix}$$

When we presented the motivation for using a Gaussian filter instead of a box filter for averaging, we said that the pixels near the center should have greater weight (in the weighted average) than the ones that are further away. If you think about it, the same principle is at play here as well. The pixel that is at the center is given more weight during the averaging process than its neighbors (although there is no evident gradual decline in weights in the case of the Sobel derivative). It is for this reason that the Sobel filter is said to compute the gradient with smoothing.

This is also due to the reason that it is a separable kernel that can be expressed as a product of a smoothing and differentiation kernel, as follows:

$$\begin{bmatrix} -1 & 0 & 1 \\ -2 & 0 & 2 \\ -1 & 0 & 1 \end{bmatrix} = \begin{bmatrix} 1 \\ 2 \\ 1 \end{bmatrix} \begin{bmatrix} -1 & 0 & 1 \end{bmatrix}$$

Let's quickly implement the Sobel operator in C++, and in the process, take a look at all the different parameters that it requires:

```cpp
#include <iostream>
#include <opencv2/core/core.hpp>
#include <opencv2/highgui/highgui.hpp>
#include <opencv2/imgproc/imgproc.hpp>

using namespace std;
using namespace cv;

int main()
{
    Mat input_image = imread("/home/samyak/Pictures/lena.jpg",
IMREAD_GRAYSCALE);
    Mat sobel_filtered_horizontal, sobel_filtered_vertical;
    Mat horizontal_der_scaled, vertical_der_scaled;

    Sobel(input_image, sobel_filtered_horizontal, CV_16S, 1, 0);
    Sobel(input_image, sobel_filtered_vertical, CV_16S, 0, 1);

    convertScaleAbs(sobel_filtered_horizontal, horizontal_der_scaled);
    convertScaleAbs(sobel_filtered_vertical, vertical_der_scaled);

    imshow("Horizontal_Derivative", horizontal_der_scaled);
    imshow("Vertical_Derivative", vertical_der_scaled);
    waitKey(0);

    return 0;
}
```

The parameters for the Sobel operator have been listed as follows:

- The source image.
- The destination image.
- Destination depth; again, we take CV_16S to avoid overflow.

- The x-order derivative, which is the order of the derivative to be computed along the x direction. The derivatives that we have been talking about are first-order derivatives. If we move on to take the derivative of our derivative image, it becomes a second-order derivative, and so on.
- The y-order derivative, which is the order of the derivative to be computed along the y direction. Usually, while computing the Sobel derivative for images, the x order and y order parameters are kept at either 1 and 0 (for the x derivative) or 0 and 1 (for the y derivative). This is precisely what we have done in our code.
- The size of the Sobel kernel.
- The last three arguments, namely `scale`, `delta`, and `border_type` have default values of 1, 0, and `BORDER_DEFAULT`, respectively. Hence, they have been omitted from the preceding function call.

The following is the output of the Sobel derivative kernel (*left* = x derivative and *right* = y derivative). If you compare the same with the output that we generated with our own kernels, you can see that the edges are more distinctly visible.

Before we close this section and move on, I want to present another variation of the derivative kernel, called the Scharr kernel. The design of the kernel (for the x derivative) is as follows:

$$\begin{bmatrix} -3 & 0 & 3 \\ -10 & 0 & 10 \\ -3 & 0 & 3 \end{bmatrix}$$

You can see that the scaling weights are different from Sobel, but the basic concept remains the same. If you wish to implement the Scharr kernel, the function call is almost identical (in terms of parameters) to Sobel:

```
Scharr(input_image, sobel_filtered_horizontal, -1, 1, 0);
Scharr(input_image, sobel_filtered_vertical, -1, 0, 1);
```

Here is the output of the preceding code:

From derivatives to edges

This chapter covers both image derivatives and edge detection. So far, we are done with the first half of the chapter, that is, image derivatives. The remainder of the chapter will be based on edge detection algorithms. Before we embark on an explanation of the various edge detection algorithms out there and the nuances of implementing them using OpenCV/C++, let's take a moment to get a feeling for how these two topics are related. This would not only help you appreciate why these two topics have been put together in the same chapter, but will also make the transition from derivatives to edge detection seamless.

For a moment, let's forget about computer vision or OpenCV and think as a layman. Now if I ask you, what do you understand by edges in images, what would your answer be? Well, to put it simply, we refer to the boundaries of objects as *edges*. Most of the natural images that one might expect to come across would consist of a finite number of objects (some of the objects might be more dominant than the others), and each object will have a boundary or an edge that demarcates it from its surroundings. If you observe the following image, the left-hand panel is a picture of an assortment of tools kept on a surface, whereas on the right, you can see that the edges of the objects have been highlighted:

In fact, this was one of the motivating factors behind pioneering research in the field of edge detection–segregating objects so that they can be isolated within the image for subsequent processing. As a consequence of the research, we have some efficient as well as accurate algorithms that detect edges in images.

Let's go back to our realm of OpenCV and try to define edges in a manner that befits a student of computer vision. We say that an edge occurs in an image whenever there is a sharp change in pixel intensity values. To get a clearer idea, once again consider the image of the group of tools placed on top of a surface. On the bottom-right hand corner of the image, you will see a circular disk (that looks like a CD-ROM). Within this disk, consider a patch where the pixels lie within the circular periphery. Clearly, there is very little change or variation in the intensity values across any such patch that you might assume. However, as soon as you try to move out of the circular boundary (and on to the surface of the table), you will experience a drastic change in the grayscale value (white to gray). This sudden change in intensity values is the clue that the algorithms for edge detection aim to exploit.

Now you know the basic principle on which the edge detection algorithms operate, so the next question is how do they find such *discontinuities* in the image intensities? Well, the answer has been staring us in the face for quite some time now: derivatives! We have spent the last few sections learning about the fact that derivatives essentially provide a quantitative measurement of the change in pixel intensity values along a particular direction. And this is precisely what makes derivatives the preferred choice when it comes to detecting edges. Let's try to get an intuition of how the image derivatives that we have studied so far feature in the framework of common edge detection algorithms.

The Sobel detector – a basic framework for edge detection

In the last section, we touched upon the foundation on which the frameworks for edge detection are built on. Let's partake in a deeper analysis of the same here.

The very first step in a common edge detection framework that you might come across is the computation of derivatives. The derivatives along both the x and the y direction are computed separately and stored in, say, two different matrices. So, for every pixel (x, y) in the input image, we essentially have the gradient in the x and the y direction: G_x and G_y (these gradient values will be stored in the locations that correspond to pixel (x, y) in both the matrices). From these two values of gradients, we compute what is known as the gradient magnitude at (x, y). The gradient magnitude is given by the following formula:

$$G = \sqrt{G_x^2 + G_y^2}$$

If you recall, this is the same as the magnitude of a two-dimensional vector that has components G_x and G_y. In fact, derivatives (or gradients) in multiple dimensions are often visualized conceptually as 2D vectors. Furthermore, in addition to having a magnitude, the gradient also has a direction given by this formula:

$$\theta = \tan^{-1}\left(\frac{G_y}{G_x}\right)$$

However, we will keep things simple and not use the gradient direction in our computations as of now. Coming back to our edge detection framework, for each pixel location, we now have the magnitude of the gradient at that point: G. Since G takes into account the gradients from both the directions, it is a good quantitative estimate of the amount of variations in the pixel intensity values around each location (x, y). So what needs to be done next?

Well, in our definition of edges, we have already stated that edges are those regions where the change in pixel intensities is high, and we have a quantitative measure of the amount of this *change* for every pixel in the image. All that remains to be done is to figure out which pixels have a value of G that we deem to be high enough to be classified as edges. And the way we decide on this is by doing a simple thresholding operation as the last step of our edge detection framework.

All the steps that we have explained so far have been beautifully summarized in the following flowchart:

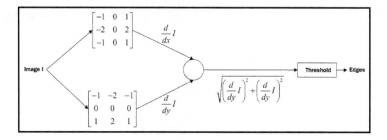

This flowchart actually depicts what we call the Sobel edge detector. This is because if you notice carefully, the kernels that have been used to compute the derivatives are Sobel kernels. The explanation behind the different modules in the chart should be evident to you.

Now that we know how edge detection works and we have seen the detailed steps behind the Sobel edge detection frameworks in theory, it is time to bring the algorithms to life using OpenCV/C++. In the previous sections, we have already seen how to compute the two Sobel derivatives G_x and G_y. Moving ahead, we have introduced a couple of steps:

1. Calculating the overall gradient magnitude at every pixel location.
2. Using a threshold to find pixels where the gradient (calculated just now) is high and marking them as belonging to edges in the image.

During the explanation of the code, our focus will be to highlight the implementation of the preceding two steps. So here goes:

```
#include <iostream>
#include <cstdlib>
#include <opencv2/core/core.hpp>
#include <opencv2/imgproc/imgproc.hpp>
#include <opencv2/highgui/highgui.hpp>

using namespace std;
using namespace cv;
```

The getGradientMagnitude() function takes two Mat objects that represent the *x* and the *y* gradient of our input image as parameters, and it returns another Mat that holds the gradient magnitude for every pixel location. It must be obvious to you that the sizes of all the three Mat objects (the two arguments and the one that is returned) are same and equal to those of our original input image:

```
Mat getGradientMagnitude(Mat xGrad, Mat yGrad) {
    CV_Assert((xGrad.rows == yGrad.rows) && (xGrad.cols == yGrad.cols));
    Mat gradient_magnitude(xGrad.rows, xGrad.cols, CV_16S);
    for (int i = 0; i < xGrad.rows; ++i) {
        for (int j = 0; j < xGrad.cols; ++j)
            gradient_magnitude.at<short>(i, j) =
                abs(xGrad.at<short>(i, j)) + abs(yGrad.at<short>(i,
j));
    }
    return gradient_magnitude;
}
```

The first thing that you would have noticed with regard to the implementation is the very first line itself. The CV_Assert() statement hasn't been introduced in the book until this point. This function takes an expression as an argument and throws an exception if it is evaluated to be false at runtime. As you might have guessed, using CV_Assert(), we have tried to enforce the fact that the two input arguments are of the same size (which in the next line also becomes the size of the Mat that is to be returned). CV_Assert() is quite useful when you want to enforce such conditions in your code. In fact, this function is extensively used in most of the internal implementations of the OpenCV library.

The remainder of the function is self-explanatory. We create a new Mat object to hold the gradient magnitude and iterate over the pixels of the two input arguments. At each location, indexed by (*i* and *j*), we compute and store the gradient magnitude in the Mat object that is ultimately returned. However, there is one difference between what we have explained in theory and our implementation. In our implementation of getGradientMagnitude() as shown in the preceding code, we calculated the gradient as the sum of the absolute values of G_x and G_y, instead of using the usual formula for calculating the magnitude. So, we implemented the following as the magnitude of our gradient:

$$G = |G_x| + |G_y|$$

This is because calculating square roots is computationally more expensive than taking absolute values. You might argue that we can always leave out the square root part and work with the sum of squares because after all, we are only bothered about the relative values of the gradients at the pixel locations. A sound argument, but if we take the sum of squares, then we would be dealing with quite large numeric values. Note that the maximum possible value for either G_x or G_y can be 255. Working with the sum of squares would mean having to deal with integers as large as 1,30,050. Taking the sum of the absolute values poses no such problems and gives us good results. Most of the implementations of edge detectors rely on this for calculating the gradient magnitude.

Having computed the gradient magnitude, we now show you the implementation of a function that implements a thresholding operation on the gradient magnitudes. It takes a couple of parameters: the Mat object storing the gradient magnitudes for all the pixels in the image and the threshold. The Mat object that it returns corresponds to a binary image where the pixels that cross the threshold (have a sufficiently high magnitude of gradient, which in turn means that they are part of a region that has an edge) have been displayed in white (255) and all the other pixels in black:

```
Mat thresholdGradientMagnitude(Mat gradient_magnitude, int threshold) {
    Mat edges = Mat::zeros(gradient_magnitude.rows,
gradient_magnitude.cols, CV_8U);
    for(int i = 0; i < gradient_magnitude.rows; ++i) {
        for (int j = 0; j < gradient_magnitude.cols; ++j) {
            if (gradient_magnitude.at<short>(i, j) >= threshold)
                edges.at<uchar>(i, j) = 255;
        }
    }

    return edges;
}
```

You can go through the implementation details of the preceding function. There is nothing different that we have done here. Just make sure that you are careful with the data types; the `gradient_magnitude` Mat object is of the type `CV_16S`, which translates to a `short int` (or simply, a `short`) in C++. If you look at `main()`, notice that we called this function by passing it a value of `200` for the threshold parameter.

Finally, this is the main function where we put everything in place. If you go line by line, you will be able to trace out the flowchart that we shared earlier. We calculate the gradients along *x* and *y*, use them to compute the magnitude of the net gradient, and finally do a threshold operation to mark the pixels that belong to edges:

```
int main()
{
```

```
    Mat input_image = imread("/home/samyak/Pictures/lena.jpg",
IMREAD_GRAYSCALE);
    Mat x_gradient, y_gradient;

    Sobel(input_image, x_gradient, CV_16S, 1, 0);
    Sobel(input_image, y_gradient, CV_16S, 0, 1);


    Mat gradient_magnitude = getGradientMagnitude(x_gradient, y_gradient);
    Mat edges_output = thresholdGradientMagnitude(gradient_magnitude, 200);

    imshow("Edges", edges_output);
    waitKey(0);
    return 0;
}
```

This brings us to the end of our implementation of the Sobel operator. There is still one aspect that you can experiment with in the code that we have shared in this section, that is, the threshold value. You should run this code with different values of thresholds and try to reconcile the kinds of output that you obtain with your understanding of the process. Check out the following image:

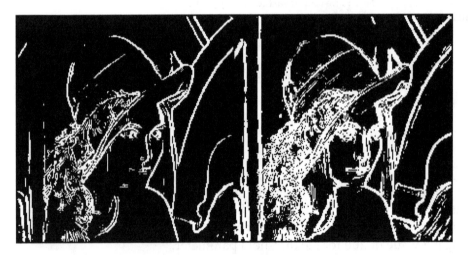

This image shows the output for the Sobel detector for two different values of the threshold. The image on the left-hand side has been generated using a threshold value of 200, whereas the one on the right with a threshold of 100. Can you reason out the differences with your understanding of how Sobel works?

The Canny edge detector

Having learned about and also implemented the Sobel edge detector in the previous section, we now turn our attention to yet another edge detection algorithm, namely the Canny edge detector. It's named after its inventor John F. Canny who came up with the algorithm in 1986. The algorithm is much more involved than the Sobel edge detector and is considered to be superior to the latter.

The basic guiding principles powering the Canny detector remain the same. This means that we will still use the gradient values as indicators of whether the pixel belongs to a potential edge region or not. However, there are certain additional steps that are performed by the detector to improve the quality of detected edges. We provide a brief explanation of the same. Note that we won't be getting into the intricate mathematical details behind Canny. Rather, we would only be sharing the intuitions that motivate the additional steps that the algorithm performs. In addition to improving our knowledge of how the detector works, it would also help us to get a feel of the role that each of the parameters plays in the working of the algorithm as a whole. Here are the steps we spoke about:

1. **Non-maximum suppression**: This step is performed after we have calculated the gradient magnitude and direction (G and θ). Non-maximum suppression is basically used to *thin* the edges. For each pixel in the gradient image, we compare its gradient magnitude with a small neighborhood of pixels that lie along the same direction as that of the gradient. If the gradient magnitude of the pixel is indeed the highest among all such neighbors, the value is preserved; otherwise, it is suppressed. This step is essential because the edges that have been deduced from the gradient values alone are quite blurred (thick) around the edge regions (you can verify the same by checking the output of the Sobel detectors). So, non-maximum suppression improves the quality of the edges by making them as thin and as close to real life as possible.

2. **Double threshold**: After performing non-maximum suppression, we use the double thresholding technique to reduce the effect of false positives. False positives are those regions that have been detected as edges but are actually not. These mainly occur due to the presence of noise in images, a topic that we would briefly touch upon in the next section. We define two threshold values (instead of a single threshold as in the case of Sobel): a low and a high threshold. After defining the values, we will subject each pixel to the following classification criteria:

   - If the gradient magnitude is above the high threshold, it is classified as an edge pixel and is called a strong edge pixel.

- If the gradient magnitude is lower than the low threshold, it is discarded.
- If the magnitude lies between the low and the high threshold, then the pixel is classified as a weak edge pixel. Weak edge pixels are subject to a process called hysteresis, where they are kept only if one of their eight neighbors are a strong-edge pixel; otherwise, they are discarded.

Now that we are done with the explanation of the Canny detector, it is time to see it in action. The following code snippet applies the Canny algorithm on a single-channel grayscale image:

```cpp
#include <iostream>
#include "opencv2/core/core.hpp"
#include "opencv2/highgui/highgui.hpp"
#include "opencv2/imgproc/imgproc.hpp"

using namespace std;
using namespace cv;

int main()
{
    Mat input_image = imread("/home/samyak/Pictures/cannyInput.jpg");
    cvtColor(input_image, input_image, CV_BGR2GRAY);

    Mat edges;
    Canny(input_image, edges, 100, 300, 3, false);

    imshow("Edge-Detection", edges);
    waitKey(0);
    return 0;
}
```

The structure of the code is quite self-explanatory, and I don't think that it demands an explanation. The parameters for the `Canny()` function are listed as follows:

- **Image**: A single-channel 8-bit input image.
- **Edges**: The output image that will store the edge map.
- **Threshold1**: The low threshold as described in the *double threshold* step of the Canny edge detection framework.
- **Threshold2**: The high threshold. The two thresholds (`threshold1` and `threshold2`) are used to work out the hysteresis procedure. We recommended that you keep the ratio between the two, `threshold2` and `threshold1`, as 3. Going along the same lines, we empirically set the values to 100 and 300 in the code.

- **Size of the kernel**: This is the size of the edge detection kernel.
- **L2 flag**: This flag indicates whether the `L2` norm must be used to compute the gradient magnitude, instead of the sum of absolute values. We discussed the tradeoffs for the same in our section on Sobel edge detection.

In the course of the entire book so far, we have come across several instances where we wanted to play around with some parameters of the functions involved. For example, we tried out several different values for the kernel size during filtering, or more recently, different thresholds for our edge detection algorithms. The way we went ahead was that we made the desired change in the source code, recompiled it, and ran the code again to check the results. Now there are several problems with this style of working. It is inconvenient; it requires us to compile our source files after each minute change in the code, and there is no obvious way to compare our results as we gradually alter the values.

What we present to you now is a cool and convenient way to visualize the effect of such parameter changes in real time! Before we delve into the code, we would like to explain what we are trying to build here. Our aim here is to put up an interactive user interface where we are able to conveniently modify the value of the parameter that we wish to experiment with. This modification will be done through a sliding trackbar that goes from a minimum to a maximum value (see the following image). As we move the slider over the trackbar, thereby changing the value of our parameter, our code should compute the new output in a synchronous fashion and refresh the display window with the same. What makes all of this even more exciting is that everything happens during a single execution of your code, making it real-time in its true sense.

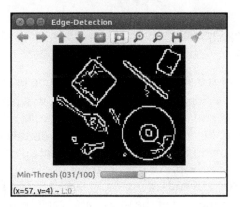

The code for achieving what we have just described is as follows:

```
#include <iostream>
#include "opencv2/core/core.hpp"
#include "opencv2/highgui/highgui.hpp"
```

```
#include "opencv2/imgproc/imgproc.hpp"

using namespace std;
using namespace cv;

Mat input_image, edges;
char* window_name = "Edge-Detection";
int lowThreshold;

void CannyThreshold(int, void*) {
    Canny(input_image, edges, lowThreshold, (lowThreshold * 3), 3);
    imshow(window_name, edges);
}

int main()
{
    input_image = imread("/home/samyak/Pictures/cannyInput.jpg");
    cvtColor(input_image, input_image, CV_BGR2GRAY);

    edges.create(input_image.size(), input_image.type());

    namedWindow(window_name, CV_WINDOW_AUTOSIZE);
    createTrackbar("Min-Threshold:", window_name, &lowThreshold, 100,
CannyThreshold);
    CannyThreshold(0, 0);

    waitKey(0);
    return 0;
}
```

Most of the work is done by OpenCV's `createTrackbar()` function. The following are the arguments of this function:

1. The first argument is a string that acts as the name of the trackbar.
2. Each trackbar is associated with a parent window where it appears which is specified by the second argument of `createTrackbar()`. The `namedWindow()` function in OpenCV is used to create a window. It takes two arguments: the name of the window to be created and a flag that specifies the type of the window. There are a couple of flags that are used quite often, namely `CV_WINDOW_AUTOSIZE` and `CV_WINDOW_NORMAL`. The former adjusts the size of the window as per the size of the image and can't be modified by the user, whereas the latter allows the user to change the window dimensions by dragging the corners.

3. A trackbar is essentially used to keep track of the changes made to an integer parameter as the slider is moved over it. The third argument is a pointer to such integers.

4. The next argument specifies the maximum limit to which the slider may be extended (the minimum is always zero).

5. Finally, the last (and the most important) argument is the callback function. This is a function that is called every time there is a change in the value of the integer by virtue of a change in the slider position. No prizes for guessing that all of the actual processing (Canny edge detection, in this case) is encapsulated inside the body of the callback function so that it can be run every single time there is a change in the slider position.

Having explained the various parameters of the `createTrackbar()` call, the preceding code should be self-explanatory now. As we have mentioned, the flow of logic works something like this. Every time the slider is moved across the trackbar, a call to the callback function named `CannyThreshold()` is triggered. This function does the Canny edge detection using the latest value of the threshold, as received from the slider, and displays (refreshes) the result in the output window (note that the `imshow()` function call inside the callback function is important if we want our latest results to get refreshed and updated in real time).

Image noise and edge detection

We are almost at the end of our chapter on edge detection. Before we close off the topic, I want to stress a practical aspect concerning edge detection algorithms. While talking about image filtering in Chapter 2, *Image Filtering* we discussed image noise. We said that noise in an image is not that uncommon and can occur due to a variety of factors. In this section, we're going to look at image noise with reference to edge detection.

So far, we have learned that edge detection algorithms rely on detecting abrupt changes in pixel intensity values. Now try to think of the effect that noise has on the pixel values in an image. It can do two things:

1. It can change the intensity of the group of pixels in an otherwise uniform area of the original image in such a manner that it becomes considerably different from its surroundings, thereby getting classified as an edge.

2. It can alter the intensity values of the pixels that actually belong to edges or regions near the edges in such a manner that they are no longer captured by our detection algorithms.

In either case, it is not difficult to see that the accuracy of the edge detection framework decreases. The following image shows the effect of adding random Gaussian noise to an input image and the corresponding accuracies of the Canny edge detector. The top-left and right-hand side images have been generated by adding zero-mean Gaussian noise with variance 10 and 30, respectively. For each of these two successive images, you can see the corresponding output of Canny edge detection. As stated, with an increase in image noise, the edge detection becomes less and less accurate.

The addition of Gaussian noise has been done using the following lines of code:

```
Mat gaussian_noise = input_image.clone();
randn(gaussian_noise, 0, 50);
input_image += gaussian_noise;
```

In order to combat the effect of noise, it is always advisable to do a blurring (or smoothing) operation on our input images to reduce noise, just before putting them through the edge detection pipeline.

Laplacian – yet another edge detection technique

In this section, we are going to look at yet another technique that is available for edge detection: Laplacian. Simply put, Laplacian is nothing but the second derivative of the image, where the second derivative refers to the derivative of the derivative. Mathematically, this is represented as follows:

$$dst = \frac{d^2 src}{dx^2} + \frac{d^2 src}{dy^2}$$

When we were looking for edges using the first derivative, we saw that regions that are potentially edge regions have a sufficiently high magnitude of the derivative (gradient). As it turns out, in the same edge regions, the second derivative is zero. This phenomenon is used as a criterion to detect edges using the Laplacian operator.

The `Laplacian()` function in OpenCV implements the Laplacian operator that we just discussed. In fact, a single call to `Laplacian()` will handle both the dimensions, x and y. Internally, it calls the `Sobel()` function to calculate gradients. A code snippet showing the implementation of `Laplacian()` is as follows:

```
#include <iostream>
#include <cstdlib>
#include <opencv2/core/core.hpp>
#include <opencv2/imgproc/imgproc.hpp>
#include <opencv2/highgui/highgui.hpp>

using namespace std;
using namespace cv;

int main()
{
    Mat input_image = imread("/home/samyak/Pictures/lena.jpg",
IMREAD_GRAYSCALE);
    Mat output, scaled_output;

    Laplacian(input_image, output, CV_16S, 3);
```

```
convertScaleAbs(output, scaled_output);

imshow("Laplacian", scaled_output);
waitKey(0);
return 0;
}
```

As you can see, the call to Laplacian takes some parameters, which have been described in the following list:

1. The first parameter is the source image.
2. The destination image, which must be of the same size and number of channels as the source.
3. The desired depth of the destination image; we have defined it to be `CV_16S` (`short` in C++) to avoid overflow.
4. The size of the kernel that is used for computing the derivatives.
5. The last three arguments, namely `scale`, `delta`, and `border_type` have default values of `1`, `0`, and `BORDER_DEFAULT`, respectively. Hence, they have been omitted from the preceding function call.

All of the arguments should seem familiar to you by now. Their meanings are the same as what your intuition may suggest. Also, we ran the grayscale version of Lena's image through the Laplacian operator. The result is presented as follows:

You can see that the pixels that make up the edges have been highlighted in the output.

Blur detection using OpenCV

Let's take a look at one of the applications of the Laplacian operator: detecting the amount of blur in images. Often, the pictures that we take in our day-to-day lives using digital cameras, DSLRs, and so on. turn out to be not that clear, sharp, and well-focused. This can arise due to a variety of factors ranging from the motion of the subject that is being captured to the sudden movement of the capturing device just before the picture was taken. The problem that we are going to solve is that given an image, can you detect whether it is blurry or not?

The approach that we are going to take here is to use the Laplacian operator to quantify the amount of blur that is present in the image. As we'll soon see, the higher the value of our metric, the less blurry our image would be.

Now, how do we arrive at such a metric? As it turns out, it has been proven (through peer-reviewed research that we are not going to get into) that the variance of Laplacian gives a sufficiently good numeric indicator of the blurriness of an image. When we explored the Laplacian() function in the previous section, we saw a particular parameter for the kernel size to be used. This parameter has a default value of 1, and when the value of the parameter is indeed 1, the following kernel is used to calculate Laplacian:

$$\begin{bmatrix} 0 & 1 & 0 \\ 1 & -4 & 1 \\ 0 & 1 & 0 \end{bmatrix}$$

It is easy to see that the kernel basically computes the difference between the sum of the intensities of the four neighbors and the central pixel value scaled four times. Why do you think that such a metric might work? Well, one way to think through this is that a relatively blurry image will have patches that are uniform with respect to the distribution of intensity values, that is, there will be no well-defined edge-like boundaries where the intensities change abruptly. This would make the difference that is being computed by the kernel small throughout all the patches of the image, thereby leading to a smaller variance (recall that variance is a measure of how our data samples are spread out). On the other hand, the complete opposite effect is observed when we are dealing with sharp non-blurry pictures.

Now that we have a basic framework for our solution, let's delve into the code:

```
#include <iostream>
#include <opencv2/core/core.hpp>
#include <opencv2/highgui/highgui.hpp>
#include <opencv2/imgproc/imgproc.hpp>
```

```
using namespace std;
using namespace cv;
```

First, we have a couple of helper functions to calculate the mean and variance of the elements of a Mat object. The functions implement the straightforward formulas that compute the mean and variance:

```
float getMean(Mat input) {
    int num_elements = (input.rows * input.cols);
    float sum = 0.0;
    for (int i = 0; i < input.rows; ++i) {
        for (int j = 0; j < input.cols; ++j)
            sum += input.at<float>(i, j);
    }

    return (sum / num_elements);
}

float getVariance(Mat input) {
    float mean = getMean(input);
    float sum_of_biases = 0.0;
    int num_of_elements = (input.rows * input.cols);

    for (int i = 0; i < input.rows; ++i) {
        for (int j = 0; j < input.cols; ++j) {
            float element_value = input.at<float>(i, j);
            sum_of_biases += ((element_value - mean) * (element_value -
mean));
        }
    }
    return (sum_of_biases / num_of_elements);
}
```

Now, in the `main()` function, we evaluate the Laplacian value of the input image and pass the Mat object (that stores the Laplacian image) to the function that calculates the variance. The value returned by the `getVariance()` function is then displayed as an output:

```
int main() {
    Mat input_image = imread("/home/samyak/Pictures/lena.jpg",
IMREAD_GRAYSCALE);
    Mat laplacian_output;

    Laplacian(input_image, laplacian_output, CV_32F);
    float std_dev = getVariance(laplacian_output);
    cout << std_dev << "\n";

    return 0;
}
```

Now that we have the implementation ready, it is time to test it on some real images. I have shown the variance values for a couple of different images that have been taken from the Internet (Google images). The first one is a rather blurry image that has a variance of approximately 208:

Variance of Laplacian = 208.01

The second image is a comparatively well-focused and sharper image that has a significantly higher variance of **9105.69**:

Variance of Laplacian = 9105.69

Now that we have a metric that quantifies the blurriness in an image, it is easy to modify the solution to have a yes/no answer to the question, "Is the given image blurry?" All you have to do is set a threshold and all the images that come up with a value that is less than the threshold are blurry. The obvious question to ask at this point is, "Where do we set the threshold at?" Unfortunately, there is no well-defined answer to this question. The choice of a threshold would be highly application-dependent and can be set heuristically after manually looking at the variance values of a set of images.

Summary

This brings us to the end of our discourse on image derivatives and edge detection. We started off by discussing the concept of the derivatives of functions. Similar to some other mathematical concepts that we have covered (Gaussian functions), we saw that discrete approximation of the continuous derivatives can be applied to images. Image derivatives were a precursor to edge detection frameworks. We introduced a couple of different frameworks, namely Sobel and Canny. Toward the end of the chapter, we saw yet another technique that helps detect edge-like regions in images: the Laplacian (or the second derivative) operator. Apart from edge detection, Laplacian lends its utility to other related, practical use cases, such as quantifying the amount of blur in images.

As we progress through the book, you would notice a clear shift in our focus towards discussing processes that identify themselves as being core *computer vision* algorithms. You will realize, and perhaps you have started to do that already, that these vision techniques are able to provide us with a much more nuanced understanding of the underlying images. Moreover, the kind of information that they extract not only helps us build a semantic understanding of the contents of the image, but are also useful for running machine learning algorithms on top of them. In fact, you have already seen examples of the former when we saw how histograms allowed us to judge the color/intensity distribution of an image or how edge detection allowed us to detect the boundaries of images by finding regions with a sharp intensity difference. Very soon, in the upcoming chapters, you will learn about feature descriptors. Running an image through a feature descriptor algorithm and then expressing it as a feature vector is one of the prerequisites before we can apply machine learning algorithms to images (our focus in the last chapter).

6
Face Detection Using OpenCV

We started our OpenCV journey by learning about techniques that could be best described as image processing algorithms. During the previous chapters, the focus was on taking an image and applying certain pixel-wise transformations or processing operations that ultimately produced images as an output. Grayscale transformations, image filtering, and thresholding are some examples that were illustrated as falling within the aforementioned framework of operations. Then, we moved on to slightly more mature forms of processing images and introduced techniques such as image histograms and edge detection that fall under the umbrella of computer vision algorithms.

In this chapter, we plunge deeper into the world of vision. In fact, we will take a look at one of the most exciting problems in vision–detecting faces in images. This was an active area of research for quite a few years. Even today, there are research papers that are published in the area of face detection as new algorithms are continuously being developed and implemented. Face detection algorithms find a myriad uses in our everyday lives. Most of the modern digital cameras have face detection algorithms embedded inside them. More recently, face detection has found its uses in biometric security systems. In particular, we are going to focus on the Viola and Jones face detection framework, which is arguably the most popular face detection algorithm out there. It is of no surprise that OpenCV has a ready-to-use implementation of the same. Once again, you will get to witness the power of OpenCV as it packs tons of behind-the-scene computations into a single line of API code (which is exposed to the end user!).

The idea of jumping into face detection might seem a little ambitious to you at this point in time. After all, just a few pages ago, we were taking differences of pixel values in the hope of detecting edges! And here we are, talking about the seemingly impossible task of detecting entire faces in images! You are right about the fact that this is no trivial task. In fact, even after devoting one complete chapter, we are not going to go into all the mathematical underpinnings of the algorithms. Our focus here is to show how a face detector can be set up in OpenCV/C++ by minimal coding on our behalf. Also, detecting faces is okay, but ideally we would want to do something even more fancy and useful with the faces that we detect. To that end, we are going to be developing an application that not only detects faces, but can also classify the gender of the face that has been detected! Now, this is not one of those projects like the Vignette filter or the blur detection that can fit into one single section in a chapter. The solution to this problem, much like the optical character recognition problem that we introduced earlier, borrows concepts from a lot of different aspects of computer vision—all of which we are going to cover in the remainder of the book. We will be developing the solution to our facial gender classification task part-by-part, inching towards the final system as we progress through the remaining chapters (including this one).

Before we embark onto our chapter on face detection, here is a quick peek at what you can expect:

- A brief mathematical overview of the Viola-Jones face detection framework
- A demonstration of the face detector in OpenCV
- A detailed explanation of the parameters involved and the effect of tweaking certain parameters on the quality of detection
- An introduction and motivation to the gender classification problem
- A brief outline of the steps involved in its solution with special emphasis on how face detection is an important preliminary process

Image classification systems

As we had mentioned, this chapter marks our foray into the very real life and challenging task of detecting faces in images. Like all major problems that computer vision strives to address, face detection also has a defining property. It is a fairly easy (some would say, trivial) task for humans to accomplish, but not that straight-forward at all for a computer to do so!

Before we dive into the details of face detection frameworks in this chapter, we will take a moment to talk in brief about how classification systems typically operate in the realm of computer vision. Note that our discussions right now would be very brief—we'll be sharing only the gist of how classification algorithms work for images. An in-depth explanation of the same will be undertaken in our final chapter, that is, Chapter 9, *Machine Learning with OpenCV*. We are introducing a few key notions at this point in time because they would help us understand object detection frameworks (the subject of interest in the current chapter) better.

Now, the topic of this chapter clearly states *detection*, then why are we taking this sudden interest in talking about *classification* algorithms? After all, *detection* problems talk about detecting certain objects (for example, faces) in images whereas *classification* algorithms are mainly involved in classifying the input into one of the pre-defined and fixed set of classes. You'll find that these two paradigms of *detection* and *classification* are often related in a subtle manner. For example, I can re-phrase the face detection problem in the following manner: "Given an image (or a local region within an image), classify it as being either a face or a non-face region". It's pretty evident what we did here–we took a detection problem and re-phrased it so that it becomes a classification problem (or, the solution to the detection problem now involves the solutions to several classification problems–more on this very soon).

Now, back to how classification algorithms operate. The following flowchart is more or less, the general sequence of steps that are adopted for the solution to any classification problem. We'll discuss in the Chapter 9, *Machine Learning with OpenCV* that classification algorithms fall under the subcategory of what we call **supervised learning algorithms**. In fact, the schematics that we discuss are valid for any supervised learning algorithm.

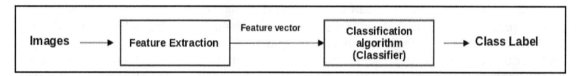

The very first step/module that we see here is feature extraction. The feature extraction module takes the image (a two-dimensional grid of values) as input and produces a feature vector (a list of numbers) as its output. In other words, it transforms our image from the two-dimensional grid of spatially-arranged pixel intensity values into a representation (the feature vector) that it deems to be more useful. The notion of what constitutes a useful representation is dependent on the application domain, that is, what problem we are trying to solve. When we talk about feature descriptors in Chapter 8, *Feature Descriptors in OpenCV* we will look at some of the techniques that fall under the umbrella of this module. In fact, we have already covered a very simple and basic feature extraction technique–image histograms. If you recall, histograms are the frequency counts of the intensity values arranged into a certain number of pre-defined bins. In the examples that we covered, the input image was converted into a 256-sized vector of frequency counts. This vector (the histogram) can serve as our image descriptor and hence, calculating image histograms is a valid feature extraction technique. In fact, you'll be surprised to know that it is not necessary to design an elaborate module that computes features for our image. There are instances in literature where the raw pixel values are used as features themselves. What I mean by this is that all the pixels that appear in the input image are *stretched out* in the form of a vector (by writing them one after the other) so that the feature vector representation contains all the information that was present in the original image (this is, contrast to histograms and feature descriptors in general, where there is a loss in information). Note that this is a very naive way of doing things and has a lot of disadvantages (more on that in `Chapter 9`, *Machine Learning with OpenCV*).

So, now we have a smaller and more compact representation of our image in the form of a feature vector. This vector goes into the classification module (or classifier). Here is where most of the magic happens. The classifier takes the feature vector and makes its own prediction as to which of the pre-defined classes is it most likely to belong to. For example, if we are working with a classifier that is supposed to decide whether an image is that of a face or not, then it'll be dealing with two classes:

- Face (positive class)
- No face (negative class)

Such classifiers are termed as binary classifiers. How does it know, given a feature vector, which class to segregate it into? Well, that is quite a non-trivial question to ask! In fact, there is an entire branch within computer science that started off in an attempt to address this question. Loosely speaking, a classifier applies certain *rules* on the input that it gets–the feature vector. And where do these *rules* come from? The classifier *learns* these rules during what we call its training phase. So, in the example of a binary classifier that detects a face region, during the training phase, we might show the algorithm examples of both kinds of images–ones that contain faces and ones that do not. Seeing these, the classifier constructs its set of rules as to which feature vectors should belong to which of the two classes. Once it is armed with such kind of knowledge, it can (up to a certain degree of accuracy) predict the classes of unseen images (those that it had never seen during training). Again, we will demystify the apparent magic that goes on behind the scenes in `Chapter 9`, *Machine Learning with OpenCV*.

Face detection

So, now that you have an idea of how a classification system operates on images, it is time to focus on face detection. In this section, we will give you an idea on the major steps that go into the popular Viola-Jones face detection framework. As we take you through the steps, we will simultaneously also draw parallels with the steps that we have just covered under *Image Classification Frameworks*. This would give you a good idea as to how these classification systems are implemented in practice (by Viola Jones, in particular).

For ease of explanation, I have divided the framework for Viola and Jones into four major parts, as described as the following:

1. **Haar features**
2. **Integral image**: an efficient way to compute Haar features
3. **AdaBoost learning**: an ensemble of classifiers
4. **Cascaded classifiers**: the secret to making the detection framework fast

We will be going through each of these sections one by one, in an attempt to build an understanding of face detection. Before we proceed, a disclaimer is in order. Each of the four sections are quite mathematically involved and one can go into any depth if they wish to. Instead, we are going to explain all of this in very simple terms–simple enough to enable us to use the OpenCV implementation with relative ease.

Haar features

This section will describe the kind of features that are extracted from the input images when we are trying to develop a face detection system. Since we have already stated that detecting faces in images is no trivial task for machines, you would expect the feature extraction step to be fairly complicated. Surprisingly, it is not so! As it turns out, extracting features is as simple as taking the sum of pixel values values over arbitrary rectangular sub-regions within images! One of the reasons for the popularity of the Viola-Jones detector is its simplicity. Let us learn a bit more about these features.

The feature-set that we are going to talk about in brief here are known as Haar-like features, or simply Haar features. They are nothing but the difference of the sum of intensity values within rectangular regions. If you look at the figure shown in a while, you will notice that each of the four given arrangements of rectangular regions (A, B, C, and D) have some clear and shaded rectangles. The computation of Haar features is not very different from the functioning of image filters that we are aware of. When these rectangular arrangements are placed over a section of the image, the feature value (at that particular location, for the given size of the rectangular region) is computed as the sum of the pixels within clear rectangles subtracted from the sum of the pixels within shaded rectangles. Specifically, three different types of Haar features are computed:

1. **2-rectangle features**: We consider two rectangular regions that are either horizontally (figure **A**) or vertically (figure **B**) adjacent to each other.
2. **3-rectangle features**: A central rectangular region is flanked by two other rectangular regions on either of its sides (figure **C**).

3. **4-rectangle features**: Four rectangular regions are arranged in a grid-like fashion, as shown in figure **D**.

Irrespective of the type of Haar feature that we are computing, the basic concept remains the same–subtract the sum of pixel values covered by the clear rectangles from the sum of pixel values encompassed by the shaded ones.

We have already hinted at the fact that the computation of Haar features is quite similar to the functioning of image filters. But unlike filters, we haven't specified the sizes of the rectangular regions that help us in the computation of our Haar features. That is because, inside any given region of the input image, the Haar features are computed for different possible sizes of the rectangles. So, in effect, given any sub-image, we take one of the configurations (A, B, C, or D), slide it across the different spatial locations within the sub-image (much like the correlation operation using filters) and compute the Haar features at each spatial location. Then, we change the dimensions of the Haar filter and repeat the same operation across the sub-image. When we are done with that, we repeat the process for each of the three other configurations.

At this point of time, if you feel that this seems like too much work, then you are absolutely right! In fact, in their paper that introduced the face detection framework, Viola and Jones stated that even for a modest 24 x 24 sized sub-image, the number of Haar features possible were a staggering 18,000! This raises a couple of pertinent questions:

- How is it possible to compute so many features in a reasonable amount of time? Bear in mind that calculating each of the 18,000 features involves taking the sum of pixels in a rectangular region and subtracting them.
- How do we make sure that the classifier doesn't blow up?

Both these questions will be answered in the subsequent sections on Integral Image and AdaBoost learning.

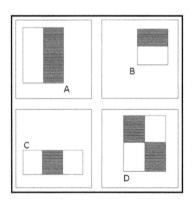

Before we finish this section on Haar features–one natural question to ponder upon is regarding the choice of this specific set of features. After all, if we are simply taking the sum/difference of intensity values in neighboring regions, there is only a very small amount of basic visual information that we can encode within these features. Although these features are indeed quite simple, they do a pretty decent job in capturing the variations that are idiosyncratic to faces. For example, consider the image shown as follows:

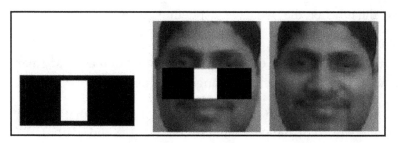

In the case of faces, it is quite natural to expect the nose region offers a slightly different intensity distribution than the regions that are adjacent to it horizontally: on either cheeks.

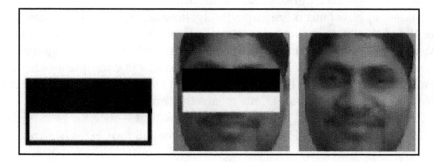

Similarly, as shown in the preceding figure, the eye-region is darker than the adjoining regions, just above and below the eyes.

Integral image

We saw in the previous section that computing Haar features involves calculating the sum of pixel intensity values over arbitrary rectangular regions placed over various parts of the image. Now, the naive way to accomplish this would be to traverse the rectangular region of interest (using nested for loops) and compute the sum. Here is what you would typically write in C++ to implement such behavior:

```
int sumOfRectRegionNaive(Mat image, int x, int y, int height, int width) {
```

```
        int sum = 0;
  for (int i = x; i < (x + height); ++i) {
        for (int j = y; j < (y + width); ++j)
            sum += image.at<uchar>(i, j);
  }
  return sum;
}
```

As you can see, the function that we have just defined takes the following inputs:

- The image
- The x and y coordinates of the upper-left corner of the rectangular region
- The width and height of the rectangular region of interest

The function returns the sum of intensity values of all the pixels that lie within our rectangular region defined by the parameters (x, y, height, and width). An alternative design is also possible where we provide functions with the x and y coordinates of two opposite corners of the rectangular region (upper-left and lower-right).

Now, while this seems to be a perfectly sound algorithm for achieving what we set out to do, try to think about how (and more importantly, how often) will such a computation be needed. We stated that these rectangular intensity sums help us in calculating Haar features. Also, as we saw in the section, *Haar features*, these rectangular regions can lie anywhere within the entire image. Basically, we would like to compute a particular Haar feature for all possible regions of the input image (and remember that there are multiple such Haar features that we compute). This means that our function sumOfRectRegionNaive(), will get called quite a few times—once for each possible location in the input image for a Haar feature, and across all four Haar features!

Having said that, what is the problem if our function is indeed called multiple times? Consider the following figure:

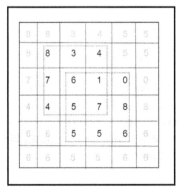

The dotted lines demarcate rectangular regions that we wish to sum over. Let us say that we have already computed the intensity sum for the upper rectangular region (the one starting with a pixel having an intensity of 8). And we now wish to compute the sum for the other (lower) rectangular region. Note that there are a few (four, to be precise) pixels that are shared between the two regions. This means that when we had computed the sum of the previous block, we had summed over these four values as well. And now that these four pixels are part of our next block, we have to sum over them again! While summing over just four pixel values might not seem like an issue to you now, consider the degree of overlap when the size of the rectangular regions are bigger than 3 x 3. Moreover, also try to visualize the number of occurrences of such overlaps when we have image sizes of say, 1000 x 1000 (instead of the toy example of 6 x 6 that we have here). In practical, real life scenarios, this repetition of work actually costs us a lot of computation time! Clearly, we need something more efficient, and this is where the concept of an integral image comes to the rescue!

Now we know that the integral image is an efficient way to compute the intensity sums inside rectangular regions. But, what is the meaning of an integral image and what does the integral sum image contain? Simply put, for every pixel (x, y) in the input image, the integral image will contain the sum of all pixel values in the region (sub-image) starting from the upper-left corner (usually designated as location $(0, 0)$–the origin) to the pixel (x, y). Let us clarify this with a couple of examples. Assume that the image is the 6 x 6 grid of intensity values as shown. Take the pixels in the third row (from the top) and fifth column (from the left). This is the pixel with the intensity value of 0, marked in red in the image shown on the left-hand side of the figure that will be shown in a short while. Corresponding to this location, the integral image will store a value that is the sum of all the pixels in the rectangular region that has been demarcated. Note that this rectangular region extends from the top-left of the image till the pixel in question. The value stored by the integral image is:

$$(8 + 8 + 3 + 4 + 5 + 8 + 8 + 3 + 4 + 5 + 7 + 7 + 6 + 1 + 0) = 77$$

Similarly, you can verify the same for the image shown on the right for the pixel in the fourth row and fourth column (intensity value of 7).

If you are looking for a more mathematically rigorous definition of the integral image, here is a formulation of the same:

$$I(x, y) = \sum_{\substack{x' \leq x \\ y' \leq y}} i(x', y')$$

I and *i* represent the integral and the original image, respectively. As you can see, while computing the integral image at any pixel location *(x, y)*, we take a sum of pixels at all locations *(x', y')*, which are less than *(x, y)*. As per our standard framework of taking the origin in the top-left corner of the image and the X and the Y axes extending along the rows and columns, respectively, it is not difficult to visualize that the preceding expression computes the sum of the pixels in the rectangular grid extending from the origin to the pixel at *(x, y)*. The figure shows an example input image on the left and the corresponding integral image drawn to the right. Note that the integral image has been padded with an extra row and a column of zeros. You can ignore this–those are only helpful during the computation that constructs the integral image, and is not of our concern for our present discourse.

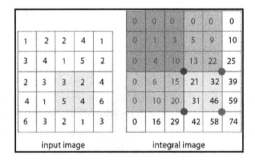

input image   integral image

Having stated what the integral image is, we turn our attention to how it helps us speed up computation. Recall that our motivation behind using such a representation as the integral image is to be able to compute the sums over arbitrary rectangular regions. Thinking about how the integral image directly helps us in our objective is not that straightforward and involves a fair amount of visualization and I would urge you to read the following section carefully (and multiple times, if need be!) to get the hang of how exactly the task is accomplished.

Consider the toy example of a 6 x 6 image that we had been working with so far. Instead of the intensity values, we represent each pixel location by indexing the rows and columns, as shown in the following figure:

i (0, 0)	i (0, 1)	i (0, 2)	i (0, 3)	i (0, 4)	i (0, 5)
i (1, 0)	i (1, 1)	i (1, 2)	i (1, 3)	i (1, 4)	i (1, 5)
i (2, 0)	i (2, 1)	i (2, 2)	i (2, 3)	i (2, 4)	i (2, 5)
i (3, 0)	i (3, 1)	i (3, 2)	i (3, 3)	i (3, 4)	i (3, 5)
i (4, 0)	i (4, 1)	i (4, 2)	i (4, 3)	i (4, 4)	i (4, 5)
i (05, 0)	i (4, 1)	i (5, 2)	i (5, 3)	i (5, 4)	i (5, 5)

Now, let us say that we wish to compute the sum of pixel values within the rectangular region that has been demarcated by the black (solid) rectangle. That is, our aim is to compute the sum:

S=i(1,2)+i(1,3)+i(1,4)+i(2,2)+i(2,3)+i(2,4)

We are going to show you how to achieve this using an integral image. First, consider, what the integral image will hold for the location *(2, 4)*, in other words, what is the value stored in *I(2,4)*? Well, according to the definition of an integral, *I(2,4)* will be the sum of all pixel values from the top-left corner to *(2, 4)*. This implies that:

I(2,4)=i(0,0)+...+i(0,4)+i(1,0)+...+i(1,4)+i(2,0)+...+i(2,4)

Visually, this is represented by the sum of the elements that lie within the rectangular region demarcated in red. You can clearly see that we have summed up a lot of extra elements other than what we need for our target sum, *S*. So, naturally, the next step is an attempt to remove all of them.

First, we'll try to remove some extra elements from the top. For that, consider what *I(0,4)* stands for:

I(0,4)=i(0,0)+i(0,1)+i(0,2)+i(0,3)+i(0,4)

It's pretty evident that if we subtract I(0,4) from the previously obtained, I(2,4), we will be able to rid ourselves from at least some of the extra elements that were bothering us–specifically the extra elements that are surrounded by the green rectangle. But, is that all? Clearly, no because we see that there are a bunch of elements that lie on the left-hand side of the rectangular region of interest that would still remain after we subtract the green from the red. Let's handle them now. Consider I(2,1):

I(2,1)=i(0,0)+i(0,1)+i(1,0)+i(1,1)+i(2,0)+i(2,1)

Just like the extra elements inside the green rectangle, I(2,1) here represents the extras in the blue rectangle. At this point, you might be tempted to subtract both the blue and the green from the red, and then think that the job is done! But herein lies the tricky part! If you observe carefully, there are a bunch of elements that are part of both the green and the blue rectangles! Which means that if you subtract both the green and the blue from the red, those common elements will get subtracted twice, whereas we would want them to be removed only once. Then, what is the solution to this? The immediate (and the most obvious) solution that comes to mind is to add them back if they have been unduly subtracted twice. And that is exactly what we are going to do.

Astute readers might have noticed that we are attempting to formulate the target sum, S, explicitly in terms of the integral image, I. So, naturally, we would also like to express the sum of these *unfortunate elements* (that have been subtracted twice) in terms of *I* as well. And luckily, such a representation does indeed exist! What does I(0,1) stand for? It is not at all difficult to see that I(0,1) is nothing but the sum of the elements that need to be added back to the sum (the *unfortunate elements*)! Doesn't that work out perfectly?

So, in conclusion, this is how we represent the target sum, S, in terms of the integral image I:

$$S(1,2,2,4) = I(2,4) - I(0,4) - I(2,1) + I(0,1)$$

The preceding equation states that the sum of elements in the rectangular region spanning between the coordinates (1, 2) to (2, 4), represented by S (1, 2, 2, 4) is computed by:

1. Summing up the elements in the red rectangle $I(2,4)$.

2. Subtracting out the extra elements from the green $I(0,4)$ and blue $I(2,1)$ rectangles.

3. Adding back the sum of the rectangles that got subtracted twice $I(0,1)$.

To help you visualize this better, and also to help you remember, you can keep the following mental schematic figure in mind:

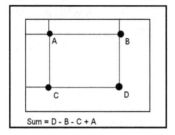

Having learnt about how an integral image helps us compute the sum of intensities in any arbitrary rectangular region, let's take a moment to appreciate how helpful this is while we calculate the Haar features. We saw in the last section that computing Haar features essentially involves summing over intensity values in adjacent rectangular regions and then taking a difference of that sum. Consider two adjacent equal-sized rectangular regions having dimensions 20 x 30. For computing the sum over all pixels for each rectangle using our naive method, we would have needed *20 x 30 = 600* references to our image for each rectangle. This makes it a total of *600 x 2 = 1200* references for computing a single Haar feature at a single location in the image! Now, we compare the number of references using the integral image. The assumption here is that we have the integral image already computed and ready for us before we attempt to calculate the Haar features. We saw that for computing the sum of intensity values inside a rectangular region, we required four references (to the integral image, and not our original image). Then, we should need a total of *4 x 2 = 8* references, right? Not exactly, because when we are computing rectangle-sums for Haar features, the two rectangles always share a common edge (or two vertices). This means that the total number of references required for a single Haar feature at a single location is *4 + 4 − 2 = 6*.

A couple of things are noteworthy here. First, there is a drastic reduction in the number of references that are required. Also, in the naive case, the number of references is dependent on the size of the rectangular sub-section, but it is not so for the integral image method. Second, the integral image is only calculated once and can be re-used for the entire computation cycle. There is no need to re-compute the integral image for every location of the Haar features. Combining both the preceding points, it is not at all difficult to see why using integral images brings so much efficiency into our system. When we start talking about good quality implementations of algorithms, scale becomes a very important issue. And small optimizations such as these go a very long way! The simplicity of Haar features, combined with the concept of integral images provides the Viola-Jones face detector with efficiency of computation.

Integral image in OpenCV

The integral image has turned out to be an important concept that is used outside face detection as well. In fact, OpenCV provides us with a function that allows computing the integral image, for any given image as input. I thought of sharing a small code snippet that demonstrates this. As you read through the code, you will notice that it doesn't really warrant any explanation:

```cpp
#include <iostream>
#include <opencv2/core/core.hpp>
#include <opencv2/imgproc/imgproc.hpp>
#include <opencv2/highgui/highgui.hpp>

using namespace std;
using namespace cv;

int main() {
    Mat input_image = imread("/home/samyak/Pictures/lena.jpg",
IMREAD_GRAYSCALE);
    Mat integral_image;
    integral(input_image, integral_image, CV_32F);
}
```

All the work here is done by the integral() function, which takes the input image, output image, and the type of the output image as its arguments.

AdaBoost learning

In the section, *Haar features*, we stated that there are 180,000 rectangle (Haar) features associated with each image sub-window. Even though each feature can be computed very efficiently with the help of an integral image, using this complete set is prohibitively expensive. In order to circumvent this predicament, a neat little trick was applied. It is reasonable to expect that not all of the 18,000 theoretically possible features within each sub-window are equally important. What if we could sample this huge set of features that we have, and for each sub-window, select a reasonably small subset of features that can help us with our classification task? If we do that, we would have a very small number of these features combined to form an effective classifier.

This is the main idea behind the technique known as AdaBoost learning. In fact, AdaBoost goes a step further and learns multiple such classifiers–each of which learn on a subset of the features. These classifiers are termed "weak classifiers". After learning these *weak classifiers*, AdaBoost combines them (a linear combination) into the final *strong classifier*. In this manner, the training of each of the weak classifiers is not computationally heavy (since they work with only a subset of the features), and we take into account all the features by combining the weak classifiers into a final strong classifier.

So, while the concept of integral image helped us compute the Haar features in an efficient manner, the AdaBoost strategy optimizes the way in which we may use these Haar features for our classification purposes.

Cascaded classifiers

We now come to the final piece in our understanding of the Viola-Jones face detection framework. Before we move on to our discussions on cascaded classifiers, which researchers believe is the single most important contribution of the Viola-Jones framework, let us take a moment to recap where we stand in our understanding of the inner-workings of face detection.

Let's say we are given an input image (of a reasonable size) and asked to detect faces in it. Common sense will tell us that:

1. Faces may be present in any of the spatial locations within the image.
2. The actual size of the face would be a fraction of the total image size (in most cases).

So, we start with a fixed-size sub-window at one of the corners of our image. This sub-window will define the region that we are investigating at any moment for the presence/absence of faces. In the spirit of preceding *point 1*, we would ideally want to slide this window across the entire image (just like a filter is moved during the correlation operation), all the while searching for the presence of images in each of the spatial locations that the window visits. And what do we do inside the window at each spatial location? Well, we compute Haar features (using integral images, of course) and try to find the right-feature set (among the thousands that are possible) using AdaBoost learning so that we may build a classifier out of them (or combine multiple weak ones to form a strong classifier). This classifier then tells us whether the sub-window is a face image or not.

Having talked about the optimizations that are done both during the computation of the Haar features (integral image) and for AdaBoost learning, the process that we just described still seems like a lot of work. Why is that so? Because this sliding of a window across the entire image doesn't happen just once. The face(s) may occur in different sizes (in computer vision parlance, we call this multiple scales) in the image (see preceding *point 2*). Which means that once a scan of a particular window size is done across the entire image, we move the window back to its original position, resize it so that it is slightly bigger, and then continue the process all over again.

Now, what if we could make the detection process at a particular spatial location within our input image very efficient. From what we have just described, such an optimization would no doubt help in speeding up the entire computation a great deal. And this is exactly where cascaded classifiers enter into the picture!

The main idea behind the concept of cascaded classifiers is something along the lines of "Look, I may not be able to tell you whether this sub-window contains a face fast enough, but I can tell you if it doesn't contain one pretty fast!" What this means is that the set of classifiers that we trained using AdaBoost are arranged in the form of a cascade (to be applied one after the other). The sub-window goes through the first cascade, if it is accepted by the first classifier (which means that the first classifier thinks that there might be a face in this window), it is passed on to the next one in the cascade. However, if the very first classifier rejects the window, the window moves on to the next spatial location. In fact, if at any point a window at a location is rejected at a particular stage in the cascade, we move on to the next location. It is also important to note that the classifiers at the initial stages are very simple ones, and they get progressively more complex in the deeper layers of the cascade. The following diagram has been taken from the paper by Viola and Jones and is a schematic representation of what we have just talked about. **T** refers to the sub-window being accepted by one of the cascaded classifiers, whereas **F** denotes a reject:

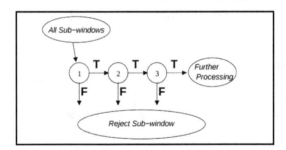

Well, this brings us to the end of the discussion on the theory behind face detectors. From the next section onwards, we are going to learn how to work with face detectors in OpenCV.

Face detection in OpenCV

After a lot of theory, we finally arrive at a point where we are now ready to do face detection using OpenCV. As always, we will straightaway dive into code.

First, we include the required header files. Here, you'll note the appearance of a new header–objdetect.hpp. This file contains all the function declarations that we'll use for our face detection:

```
#include <iostream>
#include <opencv2/core/core.hpp>
#include <opencv2/highgui/highgui.hpp>
#include <opencv2/objdetect/objdetect.hpp>
#include <opencv2/imgproc/imgproc.hpp>

using namespace std;
using namespace cv;
```

Here, we declare the path to what we call the cascade classifier. Let us take a moment to understand what this file contains and why we need it in our code. During our explanation of the Viola-Jones framework, we saw that given some Haar features computed from within the sub-window, a classifier (arranged within a cascade) must then return whether the features correspond to a face-region or not. Also, while talking about image classification systems, we saw that these classifiers are nothing but a set of rules. But in our discussions, we never bothered to ponder where these rules come from? Well, we already mentioned in the very beginning that these rules are *learnt* by the classifiers when we *train* them by showing them examples of what they are supposed to learn (distinguishing faces, in our case). To put it simply, when we attempt to *train* these classifiers, what we essentially tell them is: "Hey! Here's are a bunch of examples of both faces and non-face images, have a good, long, and careful look at each one of them and try to construct some of your own cryptic rules that differentiate a face from a non-face!" Now, once the classifier has learnt the rules that differentiate faces from non-faces, we then apply this *learned* classifier in the cascades that we talked about in the previous section. So now, when it gets some Haar features, it looks at them and goes: "Well, I have seen a lot of faces and non-faces, and carefully constructed my own bunch of rules from my experience, you don't look like a feature that might have come from a face in an image (or you do indeed look like a face to me!)" But in our explanation of the Viola-Jones framework, where did the training phase go?

So, when we talked about the Haar features being computed inside the sliding sub-window, and various classifiers being applied to the features in a cascaded fashion, we assumed that these classifiers had already learnt their set of rules. In practice, we need to provide them with the *training* (examples of faces and non-faces). Well, does that mean that every time we need to run a face detector, we would have to train these classifiers from scratch? That would indeed be a bummer. This is precisely where the cascade classifier file comes into the picture. You can imagine this file to hold the set of rules that bring our cascaded classifiers to life!

OpenCV has provided us with a bunch of such files. They are available for download from the official GitHub repository. You can visit the following link: `https://github.com/openc v/opencv/tree/master/data/haarcascades` where you'll see a bunch of XML files. Each of the files contains these learnt set of *rules* for classifiers. We'll use one particular file for our work here: `haarcascade_frontalface_alt.xml`. This file contains the *rules* for the classifier that has been trained to detect faces (more specifically, frontal faces or faces that are looking to the front). If you go through the other files in the link, you'll find classifiers that have been trained to detect other objects such as eyes, nose, mouth, and so on.

You can either download the file from the link to the GitHub repository that we just shared, or use the file that comes along with the chapter. Make sure you save the file in a place where it is accessible. It is generally a good idea to create a separate folder named data (inside the same directory which houses your source code) and also keep the XML file inside it. Wherever you choose to place the trained XML classifier, make sure you provide the correct path for it in the succeeding line, otherwise the remainder of your code will throw an exception:

```
String face_cascade_file = "data/haarcascade_frontalface_alt.xml";

int main()
{

    Mat input_image = imread("/home/samyak/Pictures/lena.jpg");
```

We declare an object of the `CascadeClassifier` class. This object will be responsible for carrying out the execution of all the heavy-weight stuff that we described in the Viola-Jones framework. The first thing we do is call the `load()` function and load the trained XML file:

```
    CascadeClassifier face_cascade;
    face_cascade.load(face_cascade_file);
```

The `detectMultiScale()` function triggers the algorithm that detects faces in the image for us. Remember, multi-scale here refers to the fact that the algorithm has the capability to detect faces of different sizes (scales) within the image. All the detected faces are returned in a vector of `Rect` objects (which we pass to the function as one of the arguments). Each `Rect` object stores a detected face in the form of what we call a bounding box around the face. A bounding box is nothing but a rectangular box that demarcates each detected face. Each bounding box (`Rect` object) has four components:

1. The *x* coordinate of the upper-left hand corner of the rectangle.
2. The *y* coordinate of the upper-left hand corner of the rectangle.
3. The width of the rectangle.
4. The height of the rectangle:

```
vector<Rect> faces;
face_cascade.detectMultiScale(
    input_image,
    faces,
    1.1,
    2,
    0|CASCADE_SCALE_IMAGE,
    Size(30, 30)
);
```

After the detection is done, we draw the bounding boxes over the input image and display the following:

```
cout << faces.size() << " faces detected...\n";
for (int i = 0; i < faces.size(); ++i) {
    Rect detected_face = faces[i];
    rectangle(input_image, detected_face, Scalar(255, 0, 0), 2);
}

imshow("Faces", input_image);
waitKey(0);
return 0;
}
```

That's it! The entire theory behind the famous Viola-Jones framework has been compressed to a single line of code (at least for programmers using OpenCV)–the call to the detectMultiScale()! As you can see, there are a fair amount of parameters to the detectMultiScale() function. What follows is a brief explanation of this:

- **Image**: Matrix of the type CV_8U containing an image where objects are to be detected.
- Vector of rectangles where each rectangle contains the detected object (in the form of a bounding box).
- **scaleFactor**: Parameter specifying how much the image size is reduced at each image scale.
- **minNeighbors**: Parameter specifying how many neighbors each candidate rectangle should have to retain it. A more detailed explanation of this follows in the *Controlling the quality of detected faces* section.
- **Flags**: Parameter with the same meaning for an old cascade as in the function cvHaarDetectObjects. It is not used for a new cascade.
- **minSize** Minimum possible object size. Objects smaller than that are ignored.
- **maxSize**: Maximum possible object size. Objects larger than that are ignored.

Let's run the preceding code and check the output:

As you can see, detectMultiScale() has been able to successfully detect the presence of a face and has drawn a rectangular bounding box around it. What would happen if there are multiple faces in a picture? Well, let's try that out with the following as an input image!

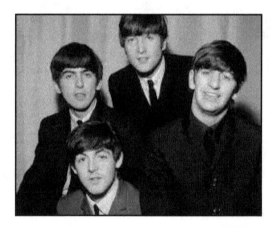

As you can see, the function can also very easily detect the presence of multiple faces and draw rectangles around each one of them!

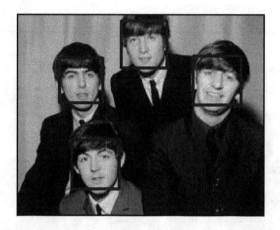

Controlling the quality of detected faces

We learnt how to write a program in OpenCV that detects faces and draws rectangles around the detections. In this section, we are going to talk about the `minNeighbors` parameter to the `detectMultiScale()` function. We are going to get a feel of what the parameter means and see the effects of varying the parameter on the quality of face detection.

Simply put, the `minNeighbors` parameter is related to the confidence with which the system can say that a given sub-window represents a face. Higher values of the parameter puts very strict conditions on what the algorithm can pass off as a face, whereas the opposite is true for lower values.

For example, consider the following image, where `detectMultiScale()` has been called with `minNeighbors` set as **1**. You may say that the algorithm has done a fairly decent job in detecting most of the faces in the image:

minNeighbors = 1.

Now, consider what would happen if we increase the value to **2**. As we stated, the criteria becomes tougher. So, you may expect that fewer of the faces are detected, which is indeed the case, as is evident from the following image:

minNeighbors = 2.

Continuing this trend, we find that as the value of `minNeighbors` is increased to higher and higher numbers, the count of detected faces diminishes:

minNeighbors = 5.

In the extreme case where we have selected the parameter value as **10**, we find that it hardly detects any faces at all:

minNeighbors = 10

A couple of definitions are in order at this point:

- **True positives**: A detection is said to be a true positive if it is indeed a correctly detected face in the image
- **False positive**: A false positive detection would refer to a scenario where the algorithm believes that there is a face, but in reality, no such face exists.

Having said that, we can define the role of the `minNeighbors` parameter as controlling the rate of false positive detections in a given input image. The higher the value of the parameter, the lesser are the number as well as chances of false positive detections.

Gender classification

We have learnt, in great detail, about detecting faces in images. We saw that face detection in itself is a rather complicated thing to accomplish. But, we wish to go a step further! If you look at it from a commercial point of view, simply saying that a face exists in an image is not that exciting. The real questions that one might be interested in come into the picture after the face has been detected. These are questions such as "Whom does the face belong to?", "Is it a male or a female?" or "Is the person happy or sad?" We can have more directed questions, such as "Is the person in the picture wearing a hat?" or "What is the color of their clothing?"

As part of this book, we will show you how to build a system that answers one of the preceding questions, "Is it a male or a female?" Over the next few chapters, we will show you, step-by-step, how to build a computer vision system that recognizes the gender of a person just from the image of his/her face.

During the course of the book so far, we have implemented several small, practical projects. Right at the outset, we implemented a bunch of cool image manipulation techniques (using grayscale transformations) along with some fairly advanced ones such as Vignetting. We also saw how to detect and quantify the amount of blur present in images. All the aforementioned projects involved a single (or a very small number of) computer vision / image processing concept(s) and hence they could be restricted to a single chapter. The task of gender classification that we are going to tackle right now is much more involved than any of these projects. In fact, unless you are not a beginner and have some prior experience in computer vision, it will be the most ambitious project that you will have undertaken till now!

Having said that, it is natural to assume that the explanation of the solution to the problem will span multiple chapters. In fact, all of the remaining chapters will focus on some aspect of the solution so that by the end of the book, we would have developed our system that classifies face images as male or female. I will allow a little amount of foreshadowing and tell you that the solution for the gender classification problem that we are going to develop will follow the same principles of image classification systems that we outlined at the beginning of the chapter. That is, we are going to extract some features that help a classifier learn to distinguish between faces of male and female subjects. But before doing that, we also need to learn something else. To motivate you, here is a sample of what we are aiming to build:

You can see that for any given input image that contains a face, our algorithm should recognize and return the appropriate gender.

Working with real datasets

When we said that the solution will follow the basic framework of an image classification system, it was an indirect way of saying that we need to accomplish the following tasks:

1. Decide upon and extract a suitable set of features from images.
2. *Train* a classifier so that it learns a set of rules that discriminate between male and female faces.

We have also discussed the fact that *point 2* requires us to have a set of images at hand that we can *show* to the classifier for the purpose of learning rules. These sets of images are what is known as the *dataset*. Every image classification task that we wish to accomplish needs a dataset that is tailored to its needs. So, for our gender classification project, we would need a set of images that contain faces of both male and female subjects.

Don't worry, you won't have to download these images. Along with the chapter, we provide you with a set of images that will serve as our dataset. Now that we have the dataset, can we directly take a plunge into the feature extraction in the preceding *point 1*? Not so soon! Before we do that, we have to pre-process and align these face images. What does pre-processing entail and what do you mean by aligning faces images? The answer to this, and many more questions, awaits you in the next chapter.

Summary

In this chapter, we saw how a computer can detect faces in an image. One of the primary strengths of using a powerful library such as OpenCV is the ease with which such seemingly complicated tasks can be compressed to a few lines of C++ code. We saw that by fine-tuning the parameters of our function, we can make our OpenCV/C++ code perform face detection.

As we have stated in this chapter, face detection is often the first step in building a sophisticated computer vision system. In the subsequent chapters of the book, we will build upon the face detection code to perform some interesting forms of analysis on the faces that we detect. In this chapter, we have already taken the first steps towards that goal.

7
Affine Transformations and Face Alignment

We started with the problem of face detection in the previous chapter. Also, towards the end, we mentioned that merely detecting faces in images, although not a trivial problem, isn't the end in itself. Once faces have been detected, endless possibilities open up in front of us–we could identify whom the face belongs to, predict the gender of the person, or maybe even try to guess the age! As part of this book, we are going to tackle one of these issues–gender detection from facial images.

This chapter is a natural continuation of the previous one. Our main focus will shift from explaining the usage of OpenCV functions (which has been the theme of the book so far) to demonstrating how OpenCV can help us in designing and implementing solutions to complex problems such as facial gender classification. This is not to say that you won't be seeing any more new algorithms and functions in OpenCV. In fact, this chapter will introduce a whole bunch of new techniques, called Affine Transformations, which will help us in performing operations such as rotation, scaling, cropping, and so on. We will use all these operations in aligning our face images and getting them ready for a subsequent feature extraction stage (next chapter).

In Chapter 6, *Face Detection Using OpenCV*, we introduced the notion of datasets (albeit briefly), as a resource for classifiers to *train* themselves. We will start this current chapter by looking at and working with a real dataset which will be shared with the readers in upcoming sections. Now, when we are working with datasets, there is a marked departure in our approach of writing code. The programs that we have written up to this point have been run on a handful of images. When you attempt to scale up your code so that it can work with datasets (which typically contain up to the order of 100s, or sometimes 1000s of images), there are some issues which might crop up. This chapter will also share some of the best practices in dealing with such issues.

Given the dual objective of our discourse, here is a brief outline of what you can expect in this chapter:

- Introduction and a short tour of the facial image dataset that we will be working with.
- An exercise as well as an illustrative example on dealing with large datasets–we will run the face detector from `Chapter 6`, *Face Detection Using OpenCV* on the images from our dataset.
- A quick introduction to face alignment and its motivation–why is such an operation necessary when we are dealing with faces?
- A glimpse of the basic steps in the face alignment pipeline that we are going to implement.
- Code samples showing the implementations of the various phases of the face alignment pipeline that we discussed.

As I said before, in this chapter, you will also be learning how to design and implement solutions to problems such as gender detection. Often times, as we involve ourselves with the lower-level implementation details of the problems that we are trying to solve, we lose sight of the big picture. To combat that, we will motivate each of the steps in the solutions that we will discuss in this chapter in the context of the bigger picture. In other words, whenever you precede one step ahead in the solution pipeline, you must pause to ponder how this fits into the overall solution that we are striving for.

Exploring the dataset

In the previous chapter, we talked about the role of a dataset in image classification systems. We saw that any classifier needs to *see* some examples of the images that it wants to classify so that it can use the domain knowledge to learn its own set of *rules*. These *rules* would eventually help the classifier to make predictions for the *new* images during its course of operation. We also shared a small dataset comprising of 200 images in the previous chapter. Let's now take a closer look at the contents.

As mentioned, the dataset contains 200 images–100 images of male and 100 of female faces. Since our goal here is to recognize the gender of faces, our dataset must have representations from both the gender categories. All the facial images belong to celebrities (politicians, actors, sportspersons, and so on). Here is a list of celebrity names (categorized according to their genders) whose faces appear in the dataset that we have curated for our project:

Male	Female
Hugh Grant	Steffi Graf
Muhammad Ali	Catherine Zeta-Jones
Andre Agassi	Mariah Carey
Arnold Schwarzenegger	Jennifer Aniston
Denzel Washington	Hillary Clinton
Zinedine Zidane	Cameron Diaz
Michael Phelps	Martha Stewart
Woody Allen	Emma Watson
Sourav Ganguly	Venus Williams
Elton John	Pamela Anderson
Steven Spielberg	Kalpana Chawla
Atal Bihari Vajpayee	Gwyneth Paltrow
Paul McCartney	Jennifer Lopez
Keanu Reeves	Naomi Watts
Tom Cruise	Laura Bush
Justin Timberlake	Yoko Ono
Richard Gere	Sarah Jessica Parker
Martin Scorsese	Anna Kournikova
George W. Bush	Madonna
Ian Thorpe	JK Rowling

Here are some of the images present in our dataset. The top row consists of female facial images (Emma Watson, Jennifer Aniston, JK Rowling, and Kalpana Chawla), whereas the bottom row shows some male faces in our dataset (George W. Bush, Paul McCartney, Saurav Ganguly, and Tom Cruise).

Running face detection on the dataset

Before we begin with the face alignment process, let us play around with the dataset a little bit more. The intention of doing that is to demonstrate some *best practices* that you should follow while dealing with images that are part of a dataset. Till now, all the programs that you have written in OpenCV operated on a single image (demonstrating some or the other image processing/computer vision algorithm), or at the most a handful of images (for example, to check the impact of parameters on the working of the algorithm). What we'll be getting on to very soon is running our code on the entire datasets of images. You'll discover (in this section, as well as the throughout the course of this chapter) that working with datasets presents a unique set of challenges. Identifying and addressing those challenges will be a major focus of this chapter.

What we are going to do in this section is run the face detection code from the last chapter on the eight images that we showed as examples in the last section. Now, this might seem a little trivial to you at this moment. Since we have already seen how to run the code for a single image, all we need to do is change the path in the argument to the `imread()` function, and we can obtain the results for as many images as we like. Sure, that seems to be a perfectly reasonable strategy. However, as we mentioned just now, the aim of this section is to teach you a smarter way to accomplish things. Let's say that instead of manually entering the file paths in the source code, we create a file called `fileNames.txt`. Each line of the file will contain a string that is the path of a source image. What do we accomplish with such a setting? We can read the file from our C++ code, extract each line (file path), then load the image whose path we just read and run the face detection on the same! Just think about the amount of hassles that this saves us. Earlier, we needed to change the source code and recompile every time that we wanted to try out a new image. Now, instead of that, the code compiles just once and is able to run the face detection on the entire dataset by reading subsequent lines off from a file!

The code for this is shown as follows:

```
#include <iostream>
#include <opencv2/core/core.hpp>
#include <opencv2/highgui/highgui.hpp>
#include <opencv2/objdetect/objdetect.hpp>
#include <opencv2/imgproc/imgproc.hpp>

using namespace std;
using namespace cv;

String face_cascade_file = "data/haarcascade_frontalface_alt.xml";

int main(int argc, char** argv)
{
    CascadeClassifier face_cascade;
    face_cascade.load(face_cascade_file);
```

The name of the file which stores the paths of the 20 images that we would like to process is read in the form of a command-line argument. For a detailed discussion on the usage of command-line arguments, check the Appendix, *Command-line Arguments in C++*. For now, readers can assume that the variable (array element) `argv[1]` stores the name of the file. Also, you should run this program by invoking the following command: `./programName fileNames.txt`

```
    char* file_name = argv[1];
    ifstream fin(file_name);
```

In the `for` loop as shown, we are reading each line (image path) from the file, loading the image that the path points to and running our face detection code on top of the image:

```
for(string image_path; getline(fin, image_path);) {
    Mat input_image = imread(image_path);
    vector<Rect> faces;
    face_cascade.detectMultiScale(
        input_image, faces,
        1.1,
        2,
        0|CASCADE_SCALE_IMAGE,
        Size(30, 30)
    );
    for (int i = 0; i < faces.size(); ++i) {
        Rect detected_face = faces[i];
        rectangle(input_image, detected_face, Scalar(255, 0, 0), 2);
    }
```

Instead of displaying the image as we have done previously on numerous occasions, we use the OpenCV's `imwrite()` function to actually save the images to disk. The first argument is the path where the image has to be saved and the second argument is the Mat object, which stores the image that we want to save. You can see that the code saves the image with the same name, but inside a folder named `detectedFaces`:

```
imwrite("detectedFaces/" + image_path, input_image);


}
```

As we shift our focus and move towards more advanced problems in computer vision, we will rely on the aforementioned method of reading from and writing to files/disk. One of the main reasons is that as the problems become more complex, so do the solutions. More often than not, you would be required to write/implement different programs that share data to solve the problem (remember, we talked about the solutions to problems as *pipelines*?) and performing the read/write operations on files helps us *preserve* the output even after the program has finished its execution. The data that we generate as output for a particular program (say face detection) may be the input to our next program in the pipeline.

Before we conclude this section, I want to introduce one more of the *best practices* that you might find useful. We are sequentially running our code on a series of 20 images. Have you wondered what would happen if something goes wrong in between (when some image is being processed)? If the code encounters some error, it would exit and you would lose the data that had been processed so far (correctly) and the data that remained to be processed would never get a chance to come into execution. Wouldn't it be great if we had a mechanism wherein if the code encounters an error during one particular iteration (processing of an image), it can drop an error message, skip the computations for that particular image and move on with the rest of the images! The `try...catch` block is used to accomplish such behavior. Here is a sample of this:

```
try {
    input_image = imread("images/Dataset/" + image_path);
} catch(Exception& e) {
    const char* err_msg = e.what();
    cout << "exception caught: " << err_msg << "\n";
}
```

Just replace the call to the `imread()` function (inside the `for` loop that reads each line from the file) in the preceding code with this code snippet. To test this, you can make random modifications to the `fileNames.txt` file and execute your program on the modified (corrupted) file. Your code should complete execution and not stop by throwing an error in between.

In the following image, you'll find the output of the face detection code on the sample images from the dataset:

We have run the code and shown the output for a small subset of eight images. Readers are strongly advised to repeat the same experiment for the entire dataset of 200 images. For this, all you need to change is the file that holds the paths to the images. You would need a bigger file with more–one for each of the 200 images. This file has been provided for you as part of the dataset.

Face alignment – the first step in facial analysis

So, we have taken our first steps in getting to know the dataset and also getting a feel of how to operate upon it. At this point, we know that all the images in our dataset contain faces (that can be detected by the cascaded classifier from Chapter 6, *Face Detection Using OpenCV*). Although, you might feel that this is an unnecessary step because we have already told you that the dataset contains facial images of celebrities belonging to both the gender categories. However, along the way, we picked up important skills that are going to help us in the course of our work. For example, if you are working with some other bigger dataset that has noise, then the preceding step can act as a filter to remove the images where the faces can't be detected so that they do not pose problems in the subsequent stages of our solution pipeline. Now, it's time to analyze faces!

When we are working with faces, the first step in any analysis pipeline is face alignment. Face alignment is not the name of any single algorithm, but it refers to a set of techniques that fall under the same umbrella. When we say that a group of faces are aligned, it means the following:

1. All the facial images are of the same size.
2. All the faces are oriented in approximately the same direction. There are no cases where the heads are tilted (either to the left or right) by an extreme degree.
3. Although this condition is not mandatory, ideally we would also like to include only the facial region of the image and ignore all the background clutter.

The set of all operations that bring about changes to facial images such that they satisfy the preceding criteria fall under the domain of face alignment. The remainder of this chapter will be devoted to the study of some of these very techniques.

Simply put, face alignment improves the accuracies of the subsequent processing systems. You will soon realize that when we try to extract features from aligned images, we make certain assumptions based on the spatial locality of the different regions of the images (this is even more so in the domain of facial images). What we mean by this is that the feature extraction step relies on spatial information such as "in the region in and around pixel (20, 20), all faces will have their left eye and somewhere around (100, 150), one can expect to find the nose regions and so on". Note that these pixel location values are just for illustration purposes and have been selected arbitrarily. So, how does this information help us? Now that we know that all images are aligned so that similar facial features fall in similar spatial regions in all images, we can design simple and efficient feature extraction algorithms to operate on our set of aligned images. Maybe you'll appreciate this more after we have completed `Chapter 8`, *Feature Descriptors in OpenCV*. We will briefly return to this point later.

Now that you know what face alignment refers to and why we need such a step, let us talk about the specifics of what we are going to do with the set of faces we have in our dataset. The succeeding flowchart illustrates the different steps in our *face alignment pipeline*:

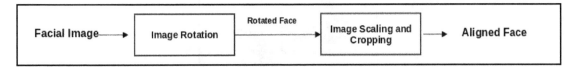

Basically, we have a couple of major steps. The purpose of each of the steps is self explanatory (from their names):

1. **Image Rotation**: This step ensures that the condition (2) is satisfied.
2. **Image Scaling and Cropping**: This fulfils conditions (1) and (3).

We will tackle each of the two steps in the subsequent sections independently at first. After that, we'll demonstrate how they come together to compete our alignment pipeline.

Rotating faces

Let us start with image rotation. As mentioned a while back, the aim of rotating faces is to ensure that all the images have faces that are approximately straight (not tilted to the left or right). If you look at the sample images, you will notice that the face of George W. Bush is tilted slightly to the (the viewer's) left.

On the other hand, Tom Cruise's face has a tilt in the opposite direction–to the right:

We would ideally want all faces to be absolutely straight–as is the case with Kalpana Chawla:

How do we go about doing that? Keep in mind; we need a system that should accomplish the following:

1. If the face is tilted, rotate it so that the tilt is nullified.
2. For faces that are already straight, the system should leave that as it is.

Since our aim is to reach a state where the face has zero-tilt, let's try to *emulate* some properties that such a face possesses so that, given any facial image, we can devise a procedure to reach there. The mechanism that we propose goes something like this. Imagine that you know about the coordinates of both the eyes. Then, what can you say about the slope of the line (more specifically, the angle made by the line with the X-axis) joining the two eye coordinates? It is going to be zero! Another way to put this is to say that the line joining the eye centers will be perfectly horizontal. So, now we have a reference to work with. We can calculate the angle that we discussed just now using the following formula:

$$\theta = tan^{-1}\left(\frac{y_{right} - y_{left}}{x_{right} - x_{left}}\right)$$

Where (x_{left}, y_{left}) and (x_{right}, y_{right}) are the coordinates of the left and the right eye in the frame of the image. Then, we can proceed to rotate the image by an equal amount in the opposite direction of the tilt (note that the sign of the slope gives us an indication of the direction of tilt) in order to nullify it. This method will have the added advantage in cases where there is no tilt to begin with as the angle theta will come out to be zero and a rotation of zero degrees amounts to no change in the image at all.

The rotation of an image requires two different parameters:

1. The angle of rotation.
2. The anchor point, or the point about which the rotation is to be performed.

For simplicity, we take the left-eye coordinate as the anchor point. So, to summarize, we calculate the angle between the eye centers and rotate the image about the left eye in the opposite direction of the tilt in order to nullify it.

For each image in the dataset, we have also provided you with the coordinates specifying the location of the two eye coordinates. If you are wondering about the source of this information, there are a lot of libraries (some of them are built on top of OpenCV itself) which are used to compute the location of facial *landmark points* such as corners and centers of the eyes, tip of the nose, points along the curvature of the lips and so on. One such example is the STASM library which implements the Active Shapes Model (an algorithm for finding the location of key-points within faces) by Tim Cootes. Since we are interested in developing a system for analyzing face images, we do not discuss the details of the STASM library here. Interested readers are encouraged to go through its details.

The file contains three lines per image. The first line will give you the name of the image, and the next two lines will contain the integer coordinates for the left and the right eyes, respectively. The coordinates are specified in the form of space separated integers. If you want to check the correctness/validity of the eye coordinate data that has been provided to you, it is quite simple. You just read the text file respecting the format that we have just shared, extract the eye coordinate points, load the corresponding face image, plot the coordinates on to the image, and check whether they really correspond to the eye centers or not. We share a C++ program that does exactly that. Since the code has been structured along similar lines as the face detection program, there is very little to explain:

```cpp
#include <iostream>
#include <string>
#include <sstream>
#include <fstream>

#include <opencv2/core/core.hpp>
#include <opencv2/highgui/highgui.hpp>
#include <opencv2/imgproc/imgproc.hpp>

using namespace std;
using namespace cv;
```

This function accepts a line read from the text file containing two space separated integers and returns an OpenCV `Point` object corresponding to the coordinate:

```cpp
Point getCoordinates(const string& str) {
    stringstream ss(str);
    string item;
    vector<int> coordinates;
    while(getline(ss, item, ' '))
        coordinates.push_back( atoi(item.c_str()) );

    Point coordinatePt(coordinates[0], coordinates[1]);
    return coordinatePt;
}
```

Data structures to save the left and right eye coordinates along with the image names that are being read from the file:

```cpp
vector<string> imagePaths;
vector<Point> leftEyeCoordinates;
vector<Point> rightEyeCoordinates;
```

The function which reads the input from the text file (whose path is supplied to it as an argument) and saves the information in the data-structures previously defined:

```cpp
void readInput(char* filePath) {
```

```
    ifstream fin;
    fin.open(filePath);
```

You will notice that the `counter` variable allows us to read the text file in the format that was specified–three lines per image:

```
    string line;
    int counter = 0;
    while(getline(fin, line)) {
        counter = (counter + 1) % 3;
        if (counter == 1)
            imagePaths.push_back(line);
        else if (counter == 2) {
            Point leftEyeLoc = getCoordinates(line);
            leftEyeCoordinates.push_back(leftEyeLoc);
        }
        else {
            Point rightEyeLoc = getCoordinates(line);
            rightEyeCoordinates.push_back(rightEyeLoc);
        }
    }

    fin.close();
}
```

After the data for all the images has been read from the text file and saved into the data structures, we traverse those data structures and display the information (mark the eye coordinates on the image):

```
void showMarkedFaces() {
    for (int i = 0; i < imagePaths.size(); ++i) {

        string imagePath = imagePaths[i];
        Mat image = imread("images/Dataset/" + imagePath);

        Point leftEye = leftEyeCoordinates[i];
        Point rightEye = rightEyeCoordinates[i];

        circle(image, leftEye, 2, Scalar(255, 0, 0), -1);
        circle(image, rightEye, 2, Scalar(255, 0, 0), -1);

        imshow("Eyes", image);
        waitKey(0);
    }

}
```

Here is the `main()` function that puts everything together. You can see that the text file is named as `eyeLocations.txt`:

```
int main()
{
    readInput("eyeLocations.txt");

    CV_Assert(imagePaths.size() == leftEyeCoordinates.size());
    CV_Assert(leftEyeCoordinates.size() == rightEyeCoordinates.size());

    showMarkedFaces();

    return 0;
}
```

We have shown the output of running the preceding code on the eight-image subset. You can see (qualitatively) that the eye locations that have been provided to you are indeed accurate!

We finally have all the information that we need to dive into the actual image rotation code. The theory behind the concept of rotation images involves some mathematics. We are going to provide a glimpse of it here.

In your coordinate geometry classes, you might have learnt about what happens to the X and Y coordinates of a point when it is rotated by an angle of θ. The following figure might be of help if you wish to recap the derivation and the formula:

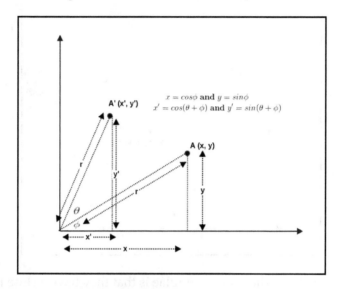

And the derivation of the results look something like this:

$$x' = cos(\theta + \phi) \text{ and } y' = sin(\theta + \phi)$$
$$\Rightarrow x' = cos\theta cos\phi - sin\theta sin\phi \text{ and } y' = sin\theta cos\phi + cos\theta sin\phi$$
$$\Rightarrow x' = x cos\theta - y sin\theta \text{ and } y' = x sin\theta + y cos\theta]$$
$$\Rightarrow \begin{bmatrix} x' \\ y' \end{bmatrix} = \begin{bmatrix} cos\theta & -sin\theta \\ sin\theta & cos\theta \end{bmatrix} \begin{bmatrix} x \\ y \end{bmatrix}$$

For readers who are facing trouble with the derivation, you need not worry. Your main take-away from this should be that the rotation of a point can very succinctly be expressed in the form of a matrix multiplication. In the preceding formulation, (x',y') and (x,y) refer to the coordinates of the new and the original point, respectively.

Similar to image rotation, we also have the much simpler case of translation of a point that is diagrammatically shown:

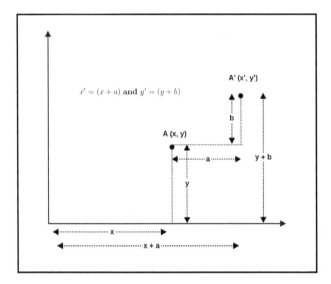

The reason for showing these diagrams/formulae is that they have a close relation with what we are going to do now. Remember that an image is nothing but a collection of points. So, rotating an image is tantamount to rotating all its constituent points individually. We specifically focus on the matrix/vector formulations because that is how we are going to provide the rotation parameters to OpenCV through our C++ code!

Now, another neat thing about working with matrices and vectors is that it allows you to combine multiple, successive operations into a single matrix representation. Imagine that I want to rotate an image by an angle θ, followed by a translation along the X and the Y axes by a and b amounts, respectively. The way to write that in matrix notation would be:

$$\begin{bmatrix} x' \\ y' \end{bmatrix} = \begin{bmatrix} cos\theta & -sin\theta & a \\ sin\theta & cos\theta & b \end{bmatrix} \begin{bmatrix} x \\ y \\ 1 \end{bmatrix}$$

You can evaluate the matrix expressions yourselves to confirm this! Now, one reasonable question to put forth at this point would be, "We understand the rotation part, but why do we need to translate the image?" The answer to that can be explained through the following visualization:

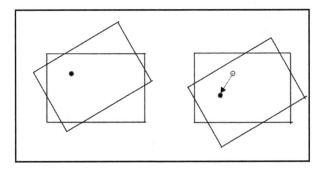

The left-hand side of the preceding figure shows the result of simply rotating the image around the anchor point (shown as a bold dot), whereas the image on the right is the result of a rotation followed by a tiny amount of translation. Intuitively, the latter provides us with a more *centered* output. If it's not clear to you at this point, don't worry, we are going to show the output of our rotation code on the sample images from the dataset. Hopefully, you'll be able to enjoy a better understanding then.

Now that we have a geometric intuition behind the rotation and translation process, we finally get to write some code to achieve what we have just discussed.

Given two points (coordinates of the left and the right eye), this function calculates the angle (slope) of the line joining the two:

```
float getAngleInRad(Point A, Point B) {
    float A_x = A.x;
    float A_y = A.y;
    float B_x = B.x;
    float B_y = B.y;

    float slope = ((B_y - A_y) / (B_x - A_x));
    return (-1 * atan(slope));
}
```

This function computes and returns the 2 x 3 matrix (affine transformation matrix) that we described in the theory. If you follow through the code carefully, you will be able to recognize all the parameters that we have discussed–for both rotation and translation:

```
Mat getAffineTransformationMatrix(float rotation_angle, Point
center_rotation) {
    float cos_rotation_angle = cos(rotation_angle);
    float sin_rotation_angle = sin(rotation_angle);

    float A = cos_rotation_angle;
    float B = sin_rotation_angle;
    float C = center_rotation.x - (center_rotation.x*A) -
```

```
(center_rotation.y*B);
    float D = -1 * sin_rotation_angle;
    float E = cos_rotation_angle;
    float F = center_rotation.y - (center_rotation.x*D) -
(center_rotation.y*E);

    Mat affine_transformation_matrix = Mat(2, 3, CV_32FC1);
    affine_transformation_matrix.at<float>(0, 0) = A;
    affine_transformation_matrix.at<float>(0, 1) = B;
    affine_transformation_matrix.at<float>(0, 2) = C;
    affine_transformation_matrix.at<float>(1, 0) = D;
    affine_transformation_matrix.at<float>(1, 1) = E;
    affine_transformation_matrix.at<float>(1, 2) = F;

    return affine_transformation_matrix;

}
```

This function performs the actual rotation of the facial image. It accomplishes this by calling the `warpAffine()` function, which takes four parameters:

- Input image
- Output image
- The affine transformation matrix
- Size of the output image

```
void rotateFace(Mat original_face, Point left_eye, Point right_eye) {
    float angle_line_joining_eyes = getAngleInRad(left_eye, right_eye);
    float rotation_angle = (-1 * angle_line_joining_eyes);
    Mat affine_transformation_matrix =
getAffineTransformationMatrix(rotation_angle, left_eye);

    Mat rotated_face;
    warpAffine(original_face, rotated_face, affine_Transformation_matrix,
original_face.size());

    imshow("Original_Image", original_face);
    imshow("Rotated_Image", rotated_face);
    waitKey(0);
}
```

Finally, we show the output of running our rotation code on the eight images from the dataset. You can clearly see that we have achieved what we set out to accomplish–rotating images so that the line joining the center of their eyes becomes horizontal!

You can also get the same results using the `getRotationMatrix2D()` function. It takes three arguments:

- Center of rotation as a `Point` object
- Rotation angle (in degrees) as a floating point (or double precision) value
- A scale factor

It returns the 2 x 3 transformation matrix for us. In our case, the function call would look something like this:

```
getRotationMatrix2D(left_eye, rotation_angle, 1.0);
```

You can easily see that the images, on account of being rotated, have developed some *dark regions* around the borders at the corners. Do not worry about these corners of the pictures for now. In the next step, we are going to crop a portion from approximately the center of the rotated image. This will ensure that we retain only the relevant portions of the face and ignore everything else.

Image cropping — basics

For now, we have rotated each face image so that the eyes are horizontally aligned. In this section, we will introduce the next step in the alignment pipeline. We are going to talk about an operation that is very common and ubiquitous with images–cropping. Each one of you, at some point in time, must have used the image cropping feature in one or the other image processing software (Paint, Photoshop, and so on). We are going to show how cropping works in OpenCV.

The cropping operation that we define here is for rectangular image regions. Before we dive into the details, let's try to think for ourselves how such an operation might be defined within the framework of whatever we know about OpenCV. Let's say that you are given an image that you want to crop. If you are using your favorite GUI-based cropping tool, how would you proceed? The natural thing to do would be to take the mouse pointer and place it at one of the points near the region that you want to crop. After that, you drag it across the width and height of that region so that you trace a rectangle that demarcates the area you are interested in. And that's it, you hit *crop* and the software does the rest for you!

Now, let us take a deeper look at what we did from the point of view of images. Essentially, we demarcated the boundary of the region within the image that we wish to retain after the cropping is done. In image processing lingo, this is known as the region of interest, or ROI for short. We are going to stick to the nomenclature of ROI throughout the remainder of the section. And how exactly did we specify this region? Well, without our explicit knowledge, we gave a couple of crucial pieces of information to the software that helped it to programmatically (in terms of code) define the ROI:

1. When we placed the mouse pointer at a location (one of the corners) of the ROI, we defined an *x* and a *y* coordinate of a point, which acts as sort of the *reference* or the *base* point for the ROI. I like to call it the *anchor point*.
2. Next, when we *dragged* the mouse pointer across the ROI to demarcate its boundary, we told the software program about the width and the height of the ROI that we wish to crop out.

Using just these two pieces of information, you can define any arbitrary rectangular ROI within the original image. Now, this might have started ringing a bell! We have already worked with data structured in such a format earlier–a pair of coordinates and width and height. Recall the `Rect` object that we discussed in `Chapter 1`, *Laying the Foundation*. There, the `Rect` object was used to store the result of face detection. Right now, we are going to use this to save arbitrary ROIs within the image that we want to crop. If you think about it, faces demarcated by rectangular regions are also one form of ROIs.

So, the path ahead is somewhat clear now. We are going to define our ROI and then pass it on to the piece of code that does the actual image cropping (we'll come to that soon!). Let's focus on the ROI part a bit more. Let's say that what we want to do is, given an anchor point, we wish to crop out a centrally aligned region from the image. Look at the illustration shown as follows:

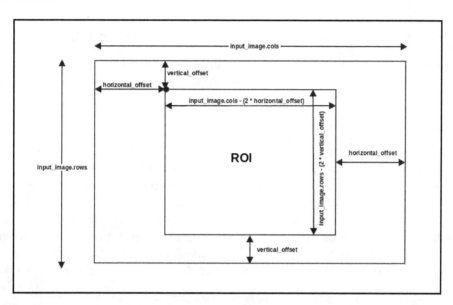

It is quite easy to see that by restricting the ROI to being centrally aligned, we are automatically fixing the width and height of the ROI. For those of you who are not convinced, here is the explanation. The anchor point (shown with a blue dot–the top-left corner of the ROI) is defined by the variables horizontal_offset and vertical_offset. They measure the distance of the ROI-corner from the top-left corner of the image. In fact, the coordinates of the anchor point is given by–horizontal_offset, vertical_offset. Now, if you observe the diagram carefully, we are leaving the same amount of space on either side of the ROI–left and right–and this distance is equal to the horizontal offset. Similarly, the same distance of vertical offset is left from the top and bottom edges of the ROI. This symmetry in the spaces outside the ROI is what makes it centrally aligned. Having said that, it takes basic mathematics to deduce the width and height of the ROI and once you do that, you will notice that the width and height depend only on the parameters: horizontal_offset and vertical_offset.

We have made life quite simple for ourselves! In order to perform the cropping, we only need to specify the coordinates of the anchor point–the horizontal and the vertical offset. By virtue of being centrally aligned, the width and height of the ROI is automatically decided. Before moving on further, let's see how this looks in code:

```
int main(int argc, char** argv)
{
    Mat input_image = imread("/home/samyak/Pictures/lena.jpg");
```

We have already stated that the only input parameters we need to specify the ROI are the horizontal and vertical offset. We take both these values as command-line inputs (`argv[1]` and `argv[2]`):

```
int horizontal_offset = atoi(argv[1]);
int vertical_offset = atoi(argv[2]);
```

Now that we are accepting input from the outside world, it is always a good idea to check what are known as **boundary conditions** before we send the input for further processing. One possible form of checks that you might want to apply here is to see if the horizontal and vertical offsets are non-negative integers. Negative offsets do not make any sense (although a zero offset is perfectly fine!) and can lead to complications in the working of our code. The approach that we have taken here is to check if either of the input values is negative and if so, drop an appropriate message and exit the program with a −1 status code:

```
if (horizontal_offset < 0 || vertical_offset < 0) {
    cout << "The offsets must be non-negative integers!\n";
    return -1;
}
```

The next few lines of code perform the ROI parameter calculations that we discussed a while back:

```
Rect roi;
roi.x = horizontal_offset;
roi.y = vertical_offset;
roi.width = (input_image.cols - (2 * horizontal_offset));
roi.height = (input_image.rows - (2 * vertical_offset));
```

This is followed by another set of checks that makes sure that the offsets that we have provided lead to a ROI that is feasible (with positive width and height). It is easy to visualize from the previous illustration that a sufficiently large value of offsets have the potential to make the dimensions of the ROI zero, or worse, negative:

```
if ( (roi.width <= 0) || (roi.height <= 0) ) {
    cout << "Please provide reasonable-sized cropping parameters!\n";
    return -1;
```

```
    }
```

Due to the rigorous nature of the checks we have performed, we can be confident that the cropping process that is to follow suit will run smoothly. Having declared the ROI as a `Rect` object, we now move on to the section of code which actually does the cropping. You might be expecting a dedicated function call in OpenCV to accomplish the cropping, but interestingly, there isn't any such function available. In fact, the way to crop an image in OpenCV is in the following manner:

```
Mat cropped_image =input_image(roi);
```

The preceding line of code will extract the required ROI from `input_image` and save it as a separate Mat object (both header and data matrix):

```
imshow("Cropped_Image", cropped_image);
waitKey(0);

return 0;
}
```

For the purpose of illustration, I have run the preceding code sample on Lena's image with progressively increasing values of the horizontal and vertical offset (both the offsets are equal, in all cases). You can see that with an increase in the offset values, the ROI becomes progressively smaller:

Also, it is not necessary to have the same values for the horizontal and vertical offsets. You can play around with different scenarios and see the results for yourselves. You will find the following output for a couple of cases as shown:

1. *horizontal_offset < vertical_offse*t
2. *vertical_offset < horizontal_offset*

It'll be an interesting exercise for you to figure out which is which!

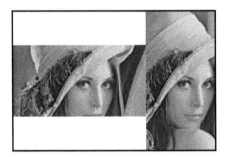

So, in this section, we have seen that cropping an image is as easy as passing an ROI to an already existing image Mat object. The real challenge is defining the ROI. After all, what portions of an image gets retained in the cropped image is dependent on the ROI. In the preceding example, we defined the region of interest in terms of a couple of parameters–the horizontal and the vertical offset. Now that you have an idea of how cropping operates in OpenCV/C++, the next question that we might want to think about is–how do we translate such a *parameterized* cropping module into our face alignment pipeline? More specifically, how do we "define" our ROI? What would be the values of our horizontal and vertical offsets? We attempt to answer such questions in the next section.

Image cropping for face alignment

Having learnt about cropping, we would now want to continue our discourse on face alignment. The cropping is to happen on the rotated images that we generated in one of our previous sections. So, ideally the implementation for image rotation and cropping are part of the same code snippet/function/module. However, for the purpose of illustrating and focusing on scaling/cropping separately in this section, we will first demonstrate the working of the same independent to the image rotation code. Then, in the next section, we integrate them together so that you get an idea of how these two operations can be coupled together to complete our facial alignment pipeline.

The main problem that we are going to deal with in this section is how to come up with suitable parameters that help us define our ROI. Note that in contrast to the previous section, we have a definite goal for the ROI in mind. We are cropping images so that the unnecessary background distractions can be ignored and we only focus on the facial portion of the image. This will no doubt help us in the subsequent steps when we do processing on top of these rotated and cropped (aligned) facial images. Thus, we cannot afford to crop a centrally aligned rectangle and hope that it contains all the features of the face. We need to carefully select the parameters of our ROI.

Let's see what information we have with us at the moment. We know:

1. The coordinate of the left eye.
2. The coordinate of the right eye.
3. The size (width and height) of our original image.

In addition to that, we define a couple of other parameters:

1. **Crop size**: The size of the image after the cropping has been done.
2. **Offset ratio**: This parameter defines the amount of space that is to remain towards the left and above the eyes in the final cropped image. This parameter is specified in terms of the fraction of the cropping size. See the following image for further clarity on what this parameter is about:

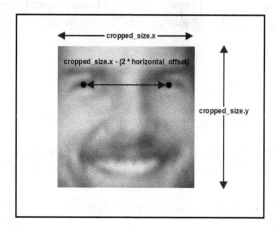

Having defined some additional parameters that we will need, let's dive into the code!

This is just a small helper function that helps us calculate the Euclidean distance between two points whose coordinates are passed to it as arguments in the form of OpenCV `Point` objects:

```
float getEuclideanDistance(Point A, Point B) {
    return sqrt( (A.x - B.x) * (A.x - B.x) + (A.y - B.y) * (A.y - B.y) );
}
```

We declare the variables that hold our parameters–`crop_size` and `offsetratio`. The `crop_size` is specified in the form of a `Point` object to reinforce the fact that we can have different sizes along the width and the height dimension. However, for our current requirements, we have fixed them to be the same at `120` pixels:

```
Point cropping_size(120, 120);
float offset_ratio = 0.23;
```

Since the `offset_ratio` parameter is given in the form of a fraction, we convert it into absolute distances by multiplying with the target cropped width and height to get the horizontal and vertical offset:

```
int horizontal_offset = int(floor(offset_ratio * cropping_size.x));
int vertical_offset = int(floor(offset_ratio * cropping_size.y));
```

If you look closely at the definition of the `offset_ratio` parameter, it is easy to deduce that the horizontal (and the vertical) offset(s) is (are) the distance(s) of the left eye from the left (top) of the cropping boundary. Again, study the preceding image carefully for clarifications:

```
int main()
{
    // Assume left_eye and right_eye have appropriate values
```

In the succeeding lines, we calculate the following two quantities:

1. The distance between the left and right eye coordinates in the current image–given that we know the coordinates, this becomes a simple Euclidean distance computation.
2. The same distance in the final (target) image. For details of the calculation, see the previous image.

Having calculated the preceding two quantities, we define a scale factor as the ratio between the two. It basically gives you the ratio by which we would want to scale the original image so that the lengths (dimensions) and distances are in sync (with what we would expect by looking at the eye-distance as a reference point):

```
float eye_sep_original = getEuclideanDistance(left_eye, right_eye);
float eye_sep_cropped = cropping_size.x - (2 * horizontal_offset);
float scale_factor = (eye_sep_original / eye_sep_cropped);
```

In the subsequent lines, we define the parameters of our ROI. You might complain that these aren't in accordance with what we have discussed. First, we decided on the crop-size to be 120 pixels, but now we are defining it to be the scaled version on 120 (with the scaling parameter calculated precedingly). Similarly, the horizontal distance between the left eye and the left edge of the cropping image was supposed to be equal to the `horizontal_offset`. Since the edges of the cropped image are defined by the anchor point, another way to put this is that the X-coordinate of the anchor point was supposed to lie at a distance of `horizontal_offset` from the X-coordinate of the left-eye (similar reasoning for the Y-coordinate):

```
int crop_anchor_x = left_eye.x - (scale_factor * horizontal_offset);
int crop_anchor_y = left_eye.y - (scale_factor * vertical_offset);
int crop_width = int(cropping_size.x * scale_factor);
int crop_height = int(cropping_size.y * scale_factor);
Rect ROI(crop_anchor_x, crop_anchor_y, crop_width, crop_height);
Mat rotated_face = rotateFace(face_image, left_eye, right_eye);

Mat cropped_face = rotated_face(ROI);
Mat aligned_face;
resize(cropped_face, aligned_face, cropping_size);
imshow("Aligned_Face", aligned_face);
waitKey(0);
return 0;
}
```

Face alignment – the complete pipeline

Now that we have defined all the components of our pipeline, let us put everything together into one single piece of code that performs the face alignment from end-to-end:

```
#include <iostream>
#include <cmath>

#include <opencv2/core/core.hpp>
#include <opencv2/highgui/highgui.hpp>
```

```
#include <opencv2/imgproc/imgproc.hpp>

using namespace std;
using namespace cv;

#define PI 3.14159265

float getAngleInRad(Point A, Point B) {
    float A_x = A.x;
    float A_y = A.y;
    float B_x = B.x;
    float B_y = B.y;

    float slope = ((B_y - A_y) / (B_x - A_x));
    return (-1 * atan(slope));
}

float getEuclideanDistance(Point A, Point B) {
    return sqrt( (A.x - B.x) * (A.x - B.x) + (A.y - B.y) * (A.y - B.y) );
}

Mat getAffineTransformationMatrix(float rotation_angle, Point
center_rotation) {
    float cos_rotation_angle = cos(rotation_angle);
    float sin_rotation_angle = sin(rotation_angle);

    float A = cos_rotation_angle;
    float B = sin_rotation_angle;
    float C = center_rotation.x - (center_rotation.x*A) -
(center_rotation.y*B);
    float D = -1 * sin_rotation_angle;
    float E = cos_rotation_angle;
    float F = center_rotation.y - (center_rotation.x*D) -
(center_rotation.y*E);

    Mat affine_transformation_matrix = Mat(2, 3, CV_32FC1);
    affine_transformation_matrix.at<float>(0, 0) = A;
    affine_transformation_matrix.at<float>(0, 1) = B;
    affine_transformation_matrix.at<float>(0, 2) = C;
    affine_transformation_matrix.at<float>(1, 0) = D;
    affine_transformation_matrix.at<float>(1, 1) = E;
    affine_transformation_matrix.at<float>(1, 2) = F;

    return affine_transformation_matrix;

}

Mat rotateFace(Mat original_face, Point left_eye, Point right_eye) {
```

```cpp
    float angle_line_joining_eyes = getAngleInRad(left_eye, right_eye);
    float rotation_angle = (-1 * angle_line_joining_eyes);
    Mat affine_transformation_matrix =
getAffineTransformationMatrix(rotation_angle, left_eye);

    Mat rotated_face;
    warpAffine(original_face, rotated_face, affine_transformation_matrix,
original_face.size());

    return rotated_face;
}

Point cropping_size(120, 120);
float offset_ratio = 0.23;
int horizontal_offset = int(floor(offset_ratio * cropping_size.x));
int vertical__offset = int(floor(offset_ratio * cropping_size.y));

int main()
{
    Mat face_image = imread("images/Dataset/Tom_Cruise_0006.jpg",
IMREAD_GRAYSCALE);
    Point left_eye(105, 107);
    Point right_eye(149, 115);

    float eye_sep_original = getEuclideanDistance(left_eye, right_eye);
    float eye_sep_cropped = cropping_size.x - (2 * horizontal_offset);
    float scale_factor = (eye_sep_original / eye_sep_cropped);

    int crop_anchor_x = left_eye.x - (scale_factor * horizontal_offset);
    int crop_anchor_y = left_eye.y - (scale_factor * vertical__offset);
    int crop_width = int(cropping_size.x * scale_factor);
    int crop_height = int(cropping_size.y * scale_factor);
    Rect ROI(crop_anchor_x, crop_anchor_y, crop_width, crop_height);
    Mat rotated_face = rotateFace(face_image, left_eye, right_eye);

    Mat cropped_face = rotated_face(ROI);
    Mat aligned_face;
    resize(cropped_face, aligned_face, cropping_size);
    cout << cropped_face.rows << " x" << cropped_face.cols << "\n";
    imshow("Aligned_Face", cropped_face);
    waitKey(0);
    return 0;
}
```

And finally, here are the outputs of the face alignment pipeline on the eight sample images from our dataset. The readers are urged to run the preceding code for all 200 images and save the results using `imwrite()` in a separate folder. This is because we will be operating on the pre-processed and aligned set of images from now on for all the subsequent steps!

So, finally we have it! All faces have undergone rotation, translation, scaling, and cropping to generate the set of aligned images. Although the set of aligned images shown are nowhere as visually pleasing to the human eye as the dataset images we started out with, believe me when I say that we have managed to make them all the more attractive for a machine learning algorithm! As we will see in the remaining couple of chapters of this book, feature extractors and image classifiers absolutely love images that are properly aligned.

Summary

In this chapter, we saw several algorithms that perform face alignment. Right at the outset, we stated the importance of such alignment steps in a processing pipeline. Especially when we are working with faces, aligning them leads to significant enhancements in overall accuracies.

We started off by running the face detection code from the previous chapter on the face images in our dataset. After that, we used affine transformations to scale, crop, and rotate our face images. By the end of the sequence of operations, we had transformed our set of faces into a form that we claim to be very useful for our subsequent step–feature extraction.

Throughout the chapter, we also showed some qualitative results of running the various algorithms on images taken from the dataset. By now, you should have developed an intuitive sense of what each affine transformation accomplishes and how these changes manifest in the output images.

In the next chapter, we will be working with the transformed and aligned images that we generated here. We will see how to convert each of the images into a vector of values. We will call this vector the feature descriptor for the image. The feature descriptors will go into our machine learning systems in `Chapter 9`, *Machine Learning with OpenCV!*

8
Feature Descriptors in OpenCV

We have spent a good amount of time working with faces. Over the course of the last couple of chapters, we have learnt how to detect faces in a given image and how to align a set of faces so that they are of the same size and none of the faces have a head-tilt either to the right or to the left. We also mentioned that such a pre-processing step is necessary to enhance the performance of machine learning algorithms. We did a very brief discourse on image classification systems when we were discussing face detectors in Chapter 6, *Face Detection Using OpenCV*. We introduced the notion of *features* (specifically, Haar features). This chapter, along with the next, is going to be an in-depth analysis of these concepts.

When we introduced the concept of digital images right at the beginning of the very first chapter, we said that an image is represented by its set of pixel values. During the formative chapters, we played around with these pixel values to perform a bunch of interesting operations on images. Since, Chapter 6, *Face Detection Using OpenCV* we have been migrating towards more advanced analysis of images. For example, we have been discussing the idea of detecting objects such as faces from images. As we move on to even more advanced forms of analysis, mere pixel values are no longer adequate representations of our 2D images. We need values which provide us with information that is well-suited to the task at hand. We had a brief glimpse of this when we saw how Haar features can help us detect the presence or absence of faces (or face-like regions) in a given area within an image. The Haar features, although quite simplistic themselves, are much better than raw pixel intensity values in capturing the typical variations that one might expect in face regions. Any technique or framework that allows us to compute such values to represent our image are termed as feature descriptors. In essence, these features help capture the semantic information lying hidden in images, as opposed to low-level details such as pixel intensities or even gradients and edges.

We will see an interesting features descriptor in this chapter–**local binary patterns** (**LBP**). Not only will we study the details of what the LBP captures in an image and how this descriptor is evaluated, we will also see some variations of the traditional LBP and how these variations will help us in our problem of detecting the gender of a person from his/her facial image.

Here is a brief overview of what's in store for the readers in this chapter:

- Some basics on image descriptors
- Introduction to the local binary pattern (LBP) as a feature descriptor and its implementation
- Introducing some variants of the traditional LBP operator
- Applying the LBP operator to the set of aligned facial images from Chapter 7, *Affine Transformations and Face Alignment*

Introduction to the local binary pattern

The local binary pattern is easy, intuitive, and quite simple to compute. These are some very rare qualities of a feature descriptor! Let's first see what local binary pattern means and how it is computed (on paper, we will come to the implementation soon). After we are done explaining the LBP operator using code samples, we will also try to develop an intuition regarding the type of information that it captures from images. Such an understanding would be crucial when you want to decide whether to use LBP features for a particular problem or not.

At the most basic level, the LBP operator assigns a number between 0 to 255 (inclusive) to every pixel in the input image. After this assignment is made, we construct a histogram out of the values having 256 bins–one for each possible value.

First, let's get into the details of how a number is assigned to every pixel. For a given pixel in the input image, we consider a 3 x 3 neighborhood of that pixel location. Consider the following diagram. The grid on the left-hand side shows such a neighborhood for the pixel in the input image having an intensity value of **5**:

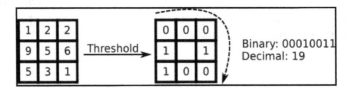

Since we are working with a 3 x 3 neighborhood, there will be eight neighbors for the central pixel. We consider each of these eight neighbors one by one. As you can see in the second grid, we have assigned a value (of either 0 or 1) to each of these eight neighbors. And how do we do that? Well, if the value of the neighboring pixel is greater than (or equal to) the value of the central pixel, it gets assigned a **1** bit, otherwise, we assign a **0** bit. You can check the two grids and see that the assignment of bits (**0** and **1**) follows the rule that we have just described.

Now, after we have done this assignment, we have a sequence of 8 bits corresponding to the central pixel. As a final step, we treat this sequence of 8 bits as a decimal number. It is a well-known fact that a sequence of n bits in binary can represent any decimal number between 0 to $2^n - 1$. It's easy to verify this with $n = 2$ bits, we can represent the decimal numbers 0 (*00*), 1 (*01*), 2 (*10*), and 3 (*11*). Similarly, with $n = 3$ bits, we can represent numbers starting from 0 (*000*), and all the way to $2^3 - 1 = 7$ (*111*). In our case, we have $n = 8$ bits (one bit corresponding to each of the eight neighbors). Hence, these 8 bits are able to represent any integer between 0 to 255–and this is precisely how we associate the 8 bits to a decimal number. For example, as shown in the preceding diagram, the sequence of bits (the sequence is constructed in a clockwise fashion starting from the bit in the upper-left corner of the image) represents the decimal number 19, which gets associated with the central pixel. In fact, 19 is said to be the *LBP code* corresponding to the central pixel. Well, strictly speaking, the 8 binary bits combined form the actual LBP code, but since we have shown that the bit sequence and the decimal number are equivalent, we can assume the number 19 to be the LBP code.

Now, a natural question that might come up at this stage is regarding the order of selecting the bits to form a decimal number. The choice of starting from the top-left corner and moving clockwise seems rather arbitrary. In fact, had we chosen to start from the bottom-left and move counter-clockwise, we would have ended up with a sequence of 10010001, which corresponds to the decimal 145 (which is remarkably different the 19 we got earlier). Then how do we decide on the order? Well, as it turns out, it doesn't matter as long as the same order is followed for every pixel! The explanation as to why this happens is in the next section.

So, till now we have seen that we assign an (8-bit) LBP code (an integer between 0 to 255) to each pixel value of the image, comparing its intensity with its 8 neighbors. As a final step, we construct a histogram out of the LBP codes for all the pixels in the image. This is known as the LBP histogram. As mentioned earlier, the histogram has 256 bins–one for each of the possible 256 LBP codes. So, in effect, the histogram tells us how many pixels in the image have a given value as their LBP code. This vector of 256 values is what represents our image.

A basic implementation of LBP

This section provides you with a very basic implementation of the LBP operator that we just described. The function LBP () takes two arguments–the source image and the output image. The output image is a Mat object that stores the corresponding LBP code for each pixel in the input image. We could have made the function return the output Mat object, but such a design (where both the input and the output are passed as arguments to the function) is also possible:

```
void LBP(const Mat& src, Mat& dst) {
    dst = Mat::zeros(src.rows-2, src.cols-2, CV_8UC1);
    for(int i=1;i<src.rows-1;i++) {
        for(int j=1;j<src.cols-1;j++) {
            uchar center = src.at<_Tp>(i,j);
            unsigned char code = 0;
            code |= (src.at<uchar>(i-1,j-1) > center) << 7;
            code |= (src.at<uchar>(i-1,j) > center) << 6;
            code |= (src.at<uchar>(i-1,j+1) > center) << 5;
            code |= (src.at<uchar>(i,j+1) > center) << 4;
            code |= (src.at<uchar>(i+1,j+1) > center) << 3;
            code |= (src.at<uchar>(i+1,j) > center) << 2;
            code |= (src.at<uchar>(i+1,j-1) > center) << 1;
            code |= (src.at<uchar>(i,j-1) > center) << 0;
            dst.at<unsigned char>(i-1,j-1) = code;
        }
    }
}
```

As you can see, the code uses some clever bit-manipulation techniques to construct the LBP code for a given pixel location (remember that the | operator stands for the bitwise, whereas the << operator allows us to shift the bits to the left by a specified amount).

Let's try to apply the preceding code to the set of facial images that we generated in the last chapter. If you recall, the end product of the last chapter was a set of cropped and aligned facial images. We will take those images and generate the corresponding LBP images using the preceding code.

Let's consider the set of female face images as shown:

The corresponding four images are the LBP images:

Similar to the four female face images, here are the four cropped and aligned male facial images:

And here are the corresponding LBP images:

At this point, you might be wondering "How, on earth are these weird looking images going to help us with detecting the gender?" We will come back to this point shortly when we discuss what exactly these LBP images capture. But before that, let's look at some variants of the LBP operator.

Variants of LBP

In this section, we are going to discuss some variants of the traditional LBP operator that we have been discussing so far. We are going to look at the variants with respect to:

1. How the neighboring points are sampled.
2. How the binary codes (and equivalently, the corresponding decimal numbers) are used to construct the histogram.

Let's look at some variations with respect to criterion *1*. The LBP codes that we have described in the previous sections used a 3 x 3 *local* neighborhood and compared it with eight neighbors. All the neighbors were at a distance of *1 pixel* from the central pixel. This situation is described in the leftmost figure in the following diagram. In terms of notation, this is described as $LBP_{8,1}$. The *8* here stands for the number of neighbors, whereas the *1* refers to the distance of each neighbor from the central pixel.

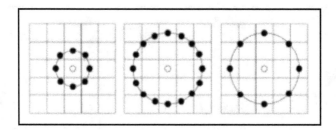

We can take larger neighborhoods and compare them with more than eight neighbors. Such a situation is shown in the figure in the middle. Note that we sample 16 neighbors (instead of eight), and each neighbor is at a distance of 2 pixels (instead of 1 pixel) from the center. This is denoted by the notation $LBP_{16,2}$. However, by using 16 neighbors, we are essentially generating 16-bit LBP codes. This can become a little computationally cumbersome. So, an alternative would be to sample eight points, instead of all 16, as shown in the figure on the extreme right. This would give us $LBP_{8,1}$ codes. For the sake of simplicity, we will stick to the vanilla $LBP_{8,2}$ operator. In fact, most applications (commercial as well as research) use the simplest version of LBP.

Now we come to the second category of variants. As we had stated, 8-bit codes lead to 256 possible decimal values, and hence 256 different bins in the LBP histogram. Now, are these 256 different values equally important? As it turns out, no! It has been proven (by research) that only certain binary codes, which are called **uniform pattern** binary codes, are important when it comes to constructing a histogram for LBP. Now, what are uniform pattern binary codes?

Consider any 8-bit code, say 11001000. Now, we start with the first (left-most bit) and keep moving towards the right, one bit at a time. As we move, we count the number of bit transitions. Bit transitions can be of two types–either from 0 to 1, or vice-versa from 1 to 0. So, in our example, we have the following bit transitions:

1. Second bit to third bit (1 to 0).
2. Fourth bit to fifth bit (0 to 1).
3. Fifth to sixth bit (1 to 0).
4. Eight to first bit (0 to 1).

Notice how we also counted the transition from the last (eighth) bit to the first bit? While counting transitions over the entire bit vector, it is customary to treat the bits in the form of a circular pattern so that the transition between the last and the first bit is also taken into account.

So, we counted a total of four bit transitions in our 8-bit code 11001000. Now, let's come back to our definition of *uniform pattern* binary codes. Uniform pattern codes are those binary codes which have at most 2-bit transitions (with the transitions being counted as we described). So, clearly 11001000 is not a uniform pattern code. While considering the binary codes (and equivalently, the corresponding decimal numbers) for constructing the LBP histogram of an image, we consider only the uniform pattern codes.

One natural question to ponder upon is, "How many 8-bit uniform pattern codes are there?" Well, let's find out! We will write a simple C++ program that computes the total number of 8-bit uniform pattern bit codes. If you wish to, you can modify the program so that it also enumerates the required bit patterns:

```cpp
#include <iostream>
#include <vector>
#include <algorithm>

using namespace std;

vector<int> convertToBinary(int x) {
    vector<int> result(8, 0);
    int idx = 0;
```

```
        while(x != 0) {
            result[idx] = x % 2;
            ++idx;
            x /= 2;
        }

        reverse(result.begin(), result.end());
        return result;
    }

int countTransitions(vector<int> x) {
    int result = 0;
    for(int i = 0; i < 8; ++i)
        result += (x[i] != x[(i+1) % 8]);
    return result;
}

int main() {

    int uniform_pattern_cnt = 0;
    for (int i = 0; i < 256; ++i) {
        vector<int> bin_i = convertToBinary(i);
        int num_transitions = countTransitions(bin_i);
        if (num_transitions <= 2)
            uniform_pattern_cnt += 1;
    }

    cout << "There are " << uniform_pattern_cnt << " 8-bit uniform
patterns\n";

    return 0;
}
```

If you run the preceding code, you will get your answer as 58–there are 58 uniform-pattern, 8-bit binary codes. This means that the histogram that we compute after this will have just 58 bins, as compared to the 256 bins that we were working with originally. This leads to a much more efficient and compact representation. Also, the 58-bin histogram is known as the uniform pattern LBP histogram.

What does LBP capture?

We have described *how* the LBP operator is applied to images, and we have also discussed some variants of it. Now obviously, if we are studying LBP in such great detail, we would definitely be applying it somewhere! We are going to use the LBP operator on the (cropped and aligned) facial images that we obtained in the last chapter. But before we jump in and start running the LBP code on our face images, let's take a step back and ponder upon a very important question, "What does the LBP capture?"

We have already gone through the mechanics of calculating the LBP code for a pixel, and we have seen that the end result is a 256 (or a 58) dimensional histogram. But, what does that histogram tell us about the image? Well, you can say that histograms give us frequency counts and you would be right. It was easy to visualize this in the case of the image histograms from `Chapter 4`, *Image Histograms* where the histogram bins were the grayscale values. Hence, it was easy to intuitively say that the histogram tells us how frequently (or how much) a particular grayscale value occurred in the image. But, here we are constructing a histogram out of LBP codes. So, in order to unlock the mystery of what the LBP histogram represents, we need to understand what the LBP code of a pixel captures.

The binary code (what we call the LBP code) captures the pixel patterns around a small, local (3 x 3) neighborhood. If I say that the LBP code for a given pixel in the image is 65, you can quickly deduce the bit pattern, which is 01000001. And what does this bit vector tell you? It gives you an idea of how the pixel intensity values are *distributed* around the central pixel (whose LBP code we are dealing with). Note that the LBP code can never tell you the exact intensity values in the neighborhood of a pixel. The bits only encode the information pertaining to the relative magnitude (whether the neighbor's grayscale intensity is greater or less than the central pixel). In short, the LBP code for a pixel will give you an idea of the (relative) distribution of intensity values around a small, local neighborhood.

Now, since we are also computing a histogram out of the LBP codes, the final LBP histogram tells us about the frequency of these *distributions* that we talked about just now. Here's another way to think about it. If I say that that the frequency for LBP code 56 is 100. We can then conclude that there are 100 pixel locations in our input image that have a similar distribution of pixel intensities in their local 3 x 3 neighborhood.

Having said that, the concept of these *intensity distributions* still seems quite vague. Let's put this into the context of face images. I want you to consider the face shown as follows:

You can clearly observe the presence of some wrinkles on the face–along the corner of the eyes/eyebrows as well as the edges of the mouth. Now, think of the pixels that are located along the edge of such wrinkles. The wrinkles seem to cover a very small area of the face, but at the granularity level of pixels, there are hundreds of them! Each of these pixels will have a specific distribution of intensities around its local neighborhood. For example, the pixels located on the side of the wrinkle may be darker than those on the other. Now, contrast this with a patch belonging to a relatively smoother section of the face–let's say the nose region. The intensity distribution that a pixel would experience here would be very different from that of a pixel that lies in and around a much more coarse facial region such as a wrinkle. This in turn means that the LBP codes for the two pixels in question would also be quite different. When we think in terms of histograms, all the pixels that are experiencing a coarse facial feature (such as a crease or a wrinkle) will add up to a particular set of histogram bins whereas those belonging to a much smoother area fall into another distinct set of bins.

We have seen how the LBP codes capture the variations within a single face. Now, also have a look at the following face. How does it differ from the face that we discussed just now? The second face is much *smoother* (probably due to excessive make-up) than our previous one. How is this difference encoded in their corresponding LBP histograms?

As you can see, most of the pixels in the facial image have very uniform and smooth neighborhoods. This means that the LBP histogram would have very high frequencies of the codes that correspond to these uniform local neighborhoods.

Note that we have explicitly dealt with facial images throughout our explanation. This does not mean that the LBP feature extractor only works for facial images. LBP has been shown to be effective for a very wide range of image types. In fact, the spatial distribution of intensity that the LBP tries to capture is given a special name in the image processing parlance–image texture.

Applying LBP to aligned facial images

Now that we have an intuition as to what the LBP captures in our image, let's try to apply this to the facial images that we have been working with. But, we aren't simply going to create the histogram of the (uniform pattern) LBP codes like we have been doing so far. We are going to make use of the spatial information that is inherent in faces.

What does exploiting spatial information in faces really mean? When you look at the image of a face, you expect to see some facial features at some distinct locations of the face. For example, the nose will almost be at the center, with the eyes on either side, the chin would cover the lower part of the face image, and so on. Now, when you create a histogram (of the LBP codes) out of the entire face image, you lose such spatial information. And how exactly are we losing spatial information? Consider two pixels–one of which is present near the left eye and the other near the center of the lower lip. If they have similar LBP codes, they would both fall into the same bin in the LBP histogram. Once they have been mapped to the same bin, there is absolutely no way to distinguish between the two pixels. Another way to look at it is like this. After we construct the histogram, let's say I look up the frequency corresponding to a particular LBP code, for example, 243. The count that we get is the total number of pixels in the entire image–across all possible spatial locations that have an LBP code of 243. There is no way to make any further claims such as "Out of all the pixels in this bin, these many are from the left eye region, and so on."

So, is there any way to preserve this spatial information that we have been talking about? The answer is of course, yes! The solution to our problem lies in what is known as **spatial histograms**. Conceptually, spatial histograms are a simple extension over the concept of a normal histogram. So, let's see how we construct a spatial histogram.

We divide our image into a pre-decided number of equal-sized sub-images. For example, we will divide our cropped and aligned face image into 3 x 3 = 9 equal-sized sub-images. Now, for each of these sub-images, calculate the LBP histogram independently. Then, concatenate all the nine histograms into one single, big histogram. This has been represented in the form of a schematic diagram, as follows:

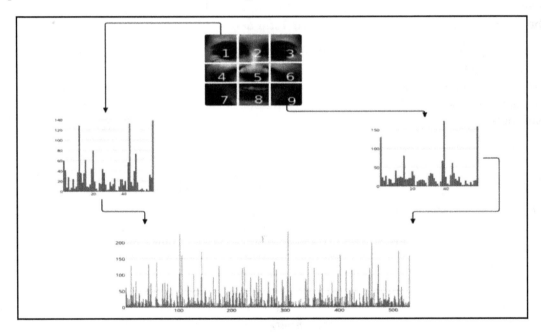

So, how does this solve our problem of incorporating spatial information? If you observe closely, each of the nine sub-images covers only a relatively small region of the facial image. So, the histograms that we generate for the sub-images will contain the intensity (texture) distributions of that particular portion of the face. On top of that, we are concatenating all the nine histograms into one single histogram, as shown in the diagram. It is easy to visualize that this also helps in preserving the spatial information.

So, now the path ahead is clear to us. Here is an outline of the steps that we need to follow:

1. Divide our face image into nine sub-images.
2. Compute the uniform pattern histogram, independently for each of the nine sub-images.
3. Concatenate the nine histograms into one single histogram, which we will call the spatially enhanced, uniform pattern LBP histogram.

In the next section, we are going to start working on implementing this in OpenCV/C++.

A complete implementation of LBP

In the section on LBP, we have already developed the code for computing the LBP code for each pixel, given the input image, and have also seen some basic operations to detect uniform pattern bit vectors. We are now going to focus specifically on building a spatially enhanced histogram.

The following function constructs the uniform pattern histogram of a sub-image given to it as input. Instead of completely ignoring the non-uniform patterns from our analysis, we instead group them together into a single bin towards the end:

```
Mat uniformPatternHistogram(const Mat& src, int numPatterns) {
    Mat hist;

    hist = Mat::zeros(1, (numPatterns + 1), CV_32SC1);
    for(int i = 0; i < numPatterns; ++i) {
        if(countTransitions(convertToBinary(i)) > 2)
            hist.at<int>(0, i) = -1;
    }

    for(int i = 0; i < src.rows; i++) {
        for(int j = 0; j < src.cols; j++) {
            int bin = src.at<_Tp>(i,j);
            if(hist.at<int>(0, bin) == -1)
                hist.at<int>(0, numPatterns) += 1;
            else
```

```
                     hist.at<int>(0,bin) += 1;
            }
      }
      return hist;
}
```

Now that we have the code for constructing a histogram from a given sub-image, let's move on to the code that divides our image into equal-sized sub-images and calls the aforementioned `uniformPatternHistogram()` function before concatenating all the histograms into the spatially enhanced histogram:

```
void uniformPatternSpatialHistogram(const Mat& src, Mat& hist, int
numPatterns, const Size& window, int overlap) {
      int width = src.cols;
      int height = src.rows;
      vector<Mat> histograms;
      for(int x=0; x <= (width - window.width); x+=(window.width-overlap)) {
            for(int y=0; y <= (height-window.height); y+=(window.height-
overlap)) {
                  Mat cell = Mat(src, Rect(x,y,window.width, window.height));
                  histograms.push_back(uniformPatternHistogram(cell,
numPatterns));
            }
      }
      hist.create(1, histograms.size()*(numPatterns+1), CV_32SC1);
            for(int histIdx=0; histIdx < histograms.size(); histIdx++) {
                  for(int valIdx = 0; valIdx < (numPatterns+1); valIdx++) {
                        int y = (histIdx * (numPatterns+1)) + valIdx;
                        hist.at<int>(0,y) = histograms[histIdx].at<int>(valIdx);
                  }
            }
}
```

Putting it all together – the main() function

Over the course of this chapter, we have implemented for different components of our LBP feature extraction system:

1. Computing the LBP code for each pixel.
2. Checking whether a given LBP code corresponds to a uniform pattern code.
3. Computing the spatially enhanced LBP histogram.

The code that we share in this section brings everything together and assembles it under the umbrella of a main() function:

```cpp
#include <iostream>

#include "opencv2/highgui/highgui.hpp"
#include "opencv2/core/core.hpp"

using namespace std;
using namespace cv;

int main(int argc, char** argv)
{
```

This is to remind users that a command-line argument is expected:

```cpp
if(argc != 2)
{
    cout << "USAGE: ./lbp_image [IMAGE]\n";
    return 1;
}
const string imagepath = argv[1];
Mat src = imread(imagepath, CV_LOAD_IMAGE_GRAYSCALE);
```

The next three lines of code call the LBP() function to compute and display the LBP codes for all pixels (the LBP image):

```cpp
Mat lbp_img = LBP(src);
imshow("lbp", lbp_img);
waitKey(0);
```

Next, we call the function that computes the spatially enhanced histogram and ask it to divide our image into 3 x 3 = 9 sub-images:

```cpp
Mat spatial_hist = uniformPatternSpatialHistogram(lbp_img, 256, 3, 3,
0);
```

Finally, we save and display the feature vector, the spatially enhanced histogram that was computed by the previous function call:

```cpp
vector<int> feature_vector;
for(int j = 0; j < spatial_hist.cols; ++j)
{
    if(spatial_hist.at<int>(0, j) != -1)
        feature_vector.push_back(spatial_hist.at<int>(0, j));
}

for(int i = 0; i < feature_vector.size(); ++i)
```

```
    {
        if(i != (feature_vector.size() - 1))
            cout << feature_vector[i] << " ";
        else
            cout << feature_vector[i];
    }
    cout << "\n";

    return 0;
}
```

Summary

In this chapter, we learnt how to convert our image into a feature vector, or a sequence of values. Specifically, we looked at one particular feature descriptor: the local binary pattern (or, LBP) operator. Apart from the traditional LBP formulation, we also saw some common variants that are used. An important takeaway from this chapter is that the LBP captures the "texture" of the input image. We also looked at how such texture information can help us capture the subtle variations present in facial images.

Local binary pattern is just one of the many possible feature descriptors that have been proposed in Computer Vision literature. Some other examples include **Histogram of Oriented Gradients** (**HoG**), SIFT and SURF. HoG uses the concept of image derivatives whereas SIFT and SURF are much more sophisticated feature descriptors (they are patented algorithms as well). In fact, similar in spirit to LBP, we have yet another feature descriptor called **local ternary patterns** (**LTP**). Instead of assigning 0s and 1s to the neighboring pixels depending on their relative intensity magnitudes, in LTP, we assign a code using three *symbols*: *-1, 0* and *1*. Interested readers are encouraged to go through the details of some of these other feature descriptors. In fact, the implementations of HoG, SIFT and SURF are available in OpenCV.

We selected LBP as our subject of discourse in this chapter because it is simple, intuitive, easy to understand and at the same time gives good results for a wide range of Computer Vision problems one of which we'll witness soon.

In the next chapter (Chapter 9, *Machine Learning Using OpenCV*), we will learn how we can build intelligent systems that take these LBP feature vectors as input and make predictions based on the data, such as what is the gender of the person and whose face is in the image!

Machine Learning with OpenCV

9

We are now at the last leg of our journey. We started off with the very basics of images, pixels and their traversals, and gradually moved on to our very first image processing algorithms: image filtering box filter as well as Gaussian smoothing). Gradually, we paved our way up to the more sophisticated image processing and computer vision algorithms such as image histograms, thresholding and edge detectors. To understand and grasp the true power of the OpenCV library, we demonstrated how seemingly complex algorithms, such as those for detecting faces in images, can be so effortlessly run by a single line of OpenCV / C++ code!

After having covered the major parts of the OpenCV toolkit, it was time to dig into a real-world project. Using the example of gender classification from facial images, we demonstrated the concept of feature detectors, especially digging deeper into the nuances of the uniform pattern LBP histograms. This chapter will witness a culmination of the same. You are going to learn how to teach machines to learn from our images and then go on to make intelligent guesses (such as, "What is the gender of this person?") on an image that it has never seen before. In short, we are going to impart human-like capabilities to our algorithms.

This chapter in no way covers the entirety of machine learning literature. The world of ML is so huge that many books have been written on the subject itself. We have made an attempt to present the basics of the field. After reading this chapter, you should feel comfortable with the terminologies and jargons to understand the academic text belonging to the vast corpus of ML literature scattered throughout the web and become confident enough to use ML while building your own independent projects.

Here is a list of the topics that will be covered in this chapter:

- An introduction to machine learning, followed by a description of its two variants: supervised and unsupervised learning.

- An example each from both the supervised and unsupervised learning paradigms. For unsupervised learning, we will discuss k-means clustering–an algorithm that automatically groups together your data into meaningful clusters–and in the supervised paradigm, we will talk about the k-nearest neighbors classification algorithm that has the ability to classify our data into classes.
- Next, we will introduce one of the most popular and widely used classification frameworks–the support vector machines (or SVMs).
- We will take a brief look at overfitting and cross-validation (and the associated concepts of training, validation, and test sets).
- Finally, we will talk about some common metrics that we can use to evaluate the performance of our classification algorithm, with special emphasis on the results that we get from the task of gender prediction that we have been working on.

What is machine learning

Most programs that we have worked with as part of this book followed a specific pattern. We gave the computer detailed instructions on how to operate on input data (mostly images in our case), and our algorithm diligently followed our instructions to generate the output (which could have been an image or a sequence of values as in the case of a histogram). For example, let's consider image filtering covered in Chapter 2, *Image Filtering*. We call the OpenCV function, filter2D(), with the appropriate parameters. The implementation of filter2D() holds the detailed instructions to perform image filtering, that is, it consists of the logic to traverse through all the pixels in the image and perform the correlation operation at each pixel location. Everything, including the input image and the filter parameters, is provided to the algorithm. It simply follows the instructions and generates the output image.

In fact, this is how programs were written for a long time. The general paradigm was to explicitly tell the computer what is to be done, and the only way the machine could make our lives easier was by crunching numbers (the actual computation) at breakneck speeds. But then, humans have always been on the lookout for pushing the frontiers of computation. As a result, scientists then began to ponder on a very important question. Can we impart human-like intelligence to computers?

Before we attempt to impart such qualities, we need to ask ourselves, "What does possessing *human-like* abilities really mean?" Human beings have an innate ability that computers do not possess: the ability to learn from examples. In fact, this is so natural that we have been relying on this ability since our very formative years. Think about how infants learn to recognize the faces of people around them? Do we instruct them to follow a predefined sequence of steps to achieve this? Most certainly not (an infant is definitely not capable of following any instruction given to it). What essentially happens is that the brain sees (through the eyes) thousands of instances of faces every waking second of the day. This allows the brain to *learn* these faces so that it *remembers* the next time they come around.

The basic framework within which these *human-like* learning processes operate is the same. A system sees a lot of examples of whatever it's trying to learn or predict, and it creates a sort of model that helps it to make predictions in the near future. More often than not, these *models* that are constructed will not be glaringly obvious to you. In fact, understanding and interpreting these models will be one of the core focus areas of this chapter.

Here is another analogy that would help you understand how this paradigm works. When you attend a class in school or university, a professor explains the theory in class and provides you with some examples to further illustrate the concept. As a student, you would ideally go through all the sample problems and examples, try to connect whatever you have learnt as part of theory with the questions, and attempt to create a strong mental model. Now, when you are given assignments, you are expected to use the aforementioned mental model that you have created in order to figure out the solutions. Remember that the problems that you solve in your assignments may not be the same as the ones that the professor had discussed in class, yet you are able to figure out a way to get to the solution of problems that you have never seen before!

Since *learning* this set of rules is a key component of these algorithms, we often call them *learning algorithms*. Also, since our aim is to impart such a behavior to a computer system (or a machine), they are also termed as machine learning algorithms. In this chapter (and also throughout the computer science literature), the two terms, *learning* and *machine learning* are used interchangeably. Usually, the phase when our system is seeing these examples with the aim of learning a set of rules is termed as the training or the learning phase (again, these two terms are interchangeable).

Supervised and unsupervised learning

Now that we know what machine learning involves–learning a set of rules (or building a model) by looking at examples and then using these rules to work out answers for previously unseen data–let's dig a little deeper. In this section, we will discuss two major categories of learning algorithms–supervised and unsupervised learning. These two categories differ in the nature and type of data being presented to the learning algorithm.

Instead of working with formal definitions, let's go with examples. Let's say that we are interested in building a machine learning system that can differentiate between the images of cats and dogs. That is, given an image, our algorithm should tell us whether the picture is that of a cat or a dog. Following the general guidelines that we laid out in the previous section, we have to present our system with a set of example images from where the learning will take place. For such a problem, we present to our system, what are known as *labeled data*. What this essentially means is that for each of the example images, we also specify whether it is a cat or a dog (the label) so that the algorithm knows what it's looking at. In other words, our system deals with *labeled data* during the training phase. Some texts prefer seeing the data and label as being the input and output of the system (the image goes as input and the label that is *cat* or *dog* is what we would want our system to output). Under such a nomenclature, we can also define the supervised learning setup as a scenario where the input and the (expected) output are given to our algorithm during the training phase.

While the supervised learning setup we just described might seem to be the only logical way of doing things (during the training phase, our system should know what it's looking at, right?), there is yet another learning paradigm: the unsupervised setting! In contrast to its supervised counterpart, there is no information about any sort of labels or expected output provided along with the example images. Sounds strange, right? However, the unsupervised approach is quite common in the machine learning setup. This is because, at times, labels for data (images) are not readily available. Think about this in supervised learning: for each example image, we also told our system whether it was a cat or a dog. Where do you think these labels came from? Someone (or a group of people) would have looked at each image and annotated it with the appropriate label. That is, getting labeled data requires a significant amount of manual labor in most cases. Wouldn't it be cool to have a class of machine learning algorithms that can figure out a way to work with data even if labels were not provided? That is one of the reasons why the unsupervised machine learning tools were developed! We will be looking at one of the representative algorithms that fall under this domain in one of the upcoming sections.

Revisiting the image classification framework

Right at the outset of `Chapter 6`, *Face Detection Using OpenCV*, we had a brief discourse on image classification systems. Let's revisit that once again and put it in the context of what we have learnt about machine learning so far.

For convenience, we reproduce the figure representing a typical image classification framework that we introduced in `Chapter 6`, *Face Detection Using OpenCV*:

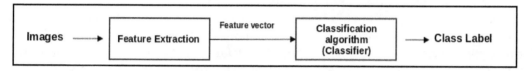

This schematic is, in fact, incomplete! While this perfectly describes what happens once our algorithm has already seen the training data and created its model, it does not depict what goes on during the training phase. In order to incorporate that information, let's revise the preceding diagram as follows:

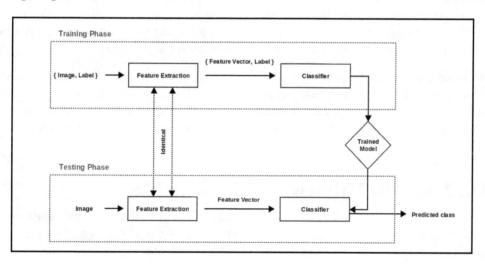

As you can see, during the *training phase*, we provide both the image and the associated label as inputs (assume that we are dealing with a supervised machine learning setup for now). The first step is to extract relevant features from the input image. We have seen a few examples of feature descriptors throughout the course of this book–Haar features (Chapter 6, *Face Detection Using OpenCV*) and LBP histograms (Chapter 8, *Feature Descriptors in OpenCV*). You might recall that these features transform the image into a sequence of numeric values. Also, in the figure, note that the feature extraction module does not need labels (they are simply passed as is to the classification module). Once our image has been converted into a feature vector (for example, we generated a 531-dimensional vector when we used spatially-enhanced, uniform-pattern LBP histograms), we pass that to the classifier module (along with the corresponding image label). Now, the behavior of the classifier is different in the training and testing phases. As we mentioned earlier, during the training phase, the classifier is responsible for creating a model by looking at the data, whereas during testing, it classifies new and unseen data by taking help from the model built during training. However, note that the feature extraction step remains identical for both the training and testing phases. Also, the testing phase, by definition, does not use any form of labels. In fact, the goal of the testing phase is to classify unseen examples (images for which no label is available).

Now that we have a basic idea of how image classification systems (and also ML-based systems, in general) operate on image data, it is time for us to get familiar with some actual machine learning algorithms. We will be discussing a few representative algorithms from the domain of both supervised and unsupervised learning algorithms.

Keep in mind that the techniques we will discuss in this chapter are in no way exhaustive. Entire books have been devoted to the exposition of machine learning. We are just going to give you a glimpse of some important terminologies and techniques so that you do not feel overwhelmed while taking up any project that involves machine learning in future.

k-means clustering – the basics

We are going to start with an unsupervised learning algorithm that goes by the name of k-means clustering. As the name suggests, k-means clustering is a type of a more generic class of clustering algorithms. So, what do we understand by clustering?

Clustering does what you would expect it to do–group together similar objects (similar in meaning to what the English word *clustering* implies). What do you mean by *similar* objects and how exactly does it perform the grouping? We will answer these questions in detail in this and the following sections.

Like before, we will motivate the basic concept behind k-means clustering by showing examples of what kind of data it operates on and what it does. Let's say that we have a sufficiently large class of students. We want to divide them into three separate groups for the purpose of some academic activity. We want the group division to happen on the basis of the marks that they obtained in the most recent exams. For each student, we have a record of their marks for two subjects, say, English and Maths. Each of the groups will be exposed to a particular type of curriculum that has been optimized with respect to their academic performance. So, it is natural to expect the students to be segregated in such a manner that all members of a particular group are of the same academic capability. Essentially, we want to know how such a group division would look like. Or in other words, which students will belong to which group.

Now, in such a setting, students can be represented with the help of two numbers–their marks in English and Mathematics. Conceptually, this is very similar to the case where we represented an image using 531 numbers in Chapter 8, *Feature Descriptors in OpenCV*. In fact, we will call these two numbers (the English and Mathematics marks) as features for each student! Since there are just two features, we can very easily put them on a Cartesian plane and visualize how our dataset looks. Note that, we did not have this luxury when we were dealing with LBP histogram features in Chapter 8, *Feature Descriptors in OpenCV* because in that case, our feature vector was 531-dimensional. It is difficult to visualize more than three dimensions, let alone 531! Let's say that the scatter plot shown below represents the student data we just described (ignore the color coding for now; we will come to that soon):

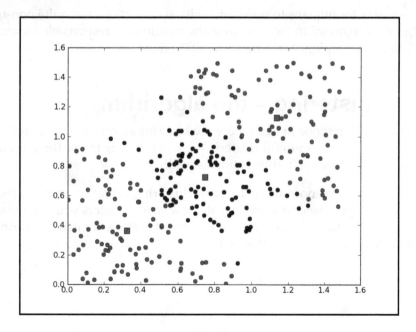

We will introduce another terminology at this point. We have described our data using two numbers. The entire space of all the possible values the features can theoretically take is known as the feature space for the problem. In our case, the entire two-dimensional Cartesian plane is the feature space. If you want to be really particular, you could say that since marks will range between 0 and a maximum (usually 100), the actual feature space is a subspace of the two-dimensional Euclidean plane. This line of reasoning is also correct, but for practical purposes, we assume the entire 2D plane to be the feature space (which is technically not wrong).

One important aspect of our data is worth discussing here. The data we are dealing with is unsupervised. For each data point (student), we only have the feature vector (marks in English and Mathematics) and nothing else. There are no labels, such as student names or the group they should be assigned to, and so on, along with the data. As we mentioned in the beginning of this section, k-means clustering is an example of an unsupervised learning algorithm.

The k-means clustering algorithm operates on the kind of data that we have shown above. Now, recall what our original objective was–using only the information available at hand, we want to divide the students into groups. If you look closely at the data points that we have plotted in the preceding image, you will be able to figure out that the data points form some sort of natural groups in the feature space. To help you visualize better, we have color coded each point as green, blue, or red. All the points possessing the same color visually belong to the same group.

Again, it is very easy for humans to make such visual deductions but quite non-trivial for a computer algorithm to do so! In fact, the k-means algorithm is responsible for exactly this kind of clustering or grouping. Now, how does it do that?

k-means clustering – the algorithm

In this section, we will describe in detail how the k-means algorithm manages to segregate a bunch of data points into meaningful clusters. We will continue to use the preceding example for all our discussions in this section as well.

The first thing you need to know about k-means clustering is that you have to fix a value of k beforehand. That is, you need to know exactly how many clusters you want your data to be divided into. In our example, we stated at the outset that we wanted to distribute the students into three separate groups, that is, $k = 3$.

Once the value of *k* is fixed, the algorithm follows these three key steps:

1. **Initialization**: We randomly initialize *k* cluster centers. Now what role do these cluster centers play? These centers act as the representative points for their respective clusters. We have one cluster center corresponding to each cluster. We will get to know more about their role in the clustering algorithm in the subsequent steps. In the following image, the data points have been drawn as gray squares, whereas the three cluster centers (*k* = 3) are depicted as colored circles. The current state shown in the image is just after random initialization:

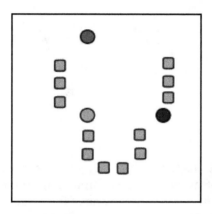

2. **Assignment**: Now we assign each of the data points to one of the *k* cluster centers. For a given data point, how do we decide the center to assign it to? Remember that the assignment of a data point to a cluster center is tantamount to putting that data point in the corresponding cluster. So, we would naturally want to assign the point to the cluster it is most similar to. Now, how do we quantify this similarity? Recall that our data points are in the 2D Euclidean space. One of the most common notions of similarity in such a space is the Euclidean distance (also sometimes known as the L-2 distance)–points separated by a smaller distance in the Euclidian space are considered to be similar. Hence, the reasonable thing to do is to assign each data point to the cluster center that is closer to the point. We follow this process for all the data points that are present in our dataset (which means, in our case, that we do this for all the students). After the assignment step is done, all the data points are now associated with one or the other cluster centers. Speaking in terms of our example, all students have been assigned to one or the other group. The following figure shows such an assignment. Note that each of the squares that represent a particular data point has been colored in accordance with the color of the cluster representative it has been associated with. Also, note that the entire feature space has been divided into some non-overlapping regions with the help of linear (straight line)

boundaries. Each of these regions is known as a **Voronoi cell**. Any data point that falls within, say, the cell marked in red, will belong to the cluster defined by the red cluster center. So, essentially, the Voronoi cells define a non-overlapping division of the feature space, which helps us visualize the membership of a data point in a cluster. So, we have already decided upon the cluster membership for each of our data points. Does that mean our job is done?

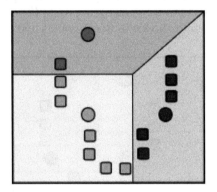

3. **Update**: This brings us to the third step of our algorithm (clearly, we aren't done yet!). We started off with randomly initializing some cluster centers and then we assigned each of our data points to one of the centers. Note that we call these cluster representatives as cluster *centers*. Right now, do you think that they are actually at the center of their respective clusters? Well, no! And that is because, we have initialized them randomly. We will now bring each of the cluster centers to the actual centers of their respective clusters. How do we define the *center* of a cluster? Well, we simply take the arithmetic mean of all the points that have been assigned to the given cluster in the *assignment* step and shift the cluster representative to the mean position. This has been described in the following image. The dotted circles denote the initial positions of the cluster centers (after the assignment step and before running the update operation), whereas the arrows indicate the change in position of the cluster centers as a result of the update step:

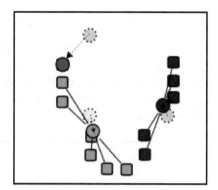

So, eventually we end up in a scenario similar to what is shown in the following image (notice how the Voronoi regions also change with a change in the centroid positions):

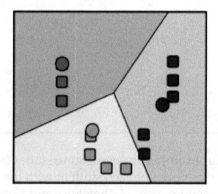

So, now that we have each data point assigned to a cluster and all the cluster representatives at the actual centers of their respective clusters, can we finally say that our job is done? Not yet! After the update step is done, it is expected that each cluster center would have shifted by some amount. Recall that the assignment in step 2 was done on the basis of the distance of each data point from the cluster centers. Now that the centers have changed positions (*update* step), it is reasonable to expect it to affect the cluster memberships as well. Does that mean that we have to start all over again? Well, yes. In fact, once the initialization step is done, the steps for assignment and update have to be alternately repeated again and again over several iterations.

Isn't there any end to this algorithm? How do we know when to stop? There are two options:

1. We go on for a fixed and pre-decided number of iterations.
2. We continue till there is no significant change in the position of the cluster centroids.

When the second condition is met, the k-means algorithm is said to have converged.

Before we close this section, there is one final comment. The k-means algorithm is in no way restricted to the two-dimensional data setup. It can be generalized to any arbitrary number of dimensions. The number of dimensions depends on the size of the feature vector used as a representative for our data. As an example, the following image shows the plot of some data points in the three-dimensional space:

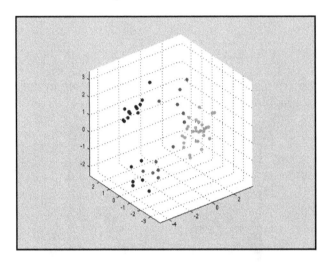

Working along the lines of our example on segregating students into groups, such a data plot would arise if we decide to represent each student with the marks obtained by them in three subjects instead of two, say English, Mathematics and Computer Science.

k-means clustering in OpenCV

Having discussed the details of k-means clustering, let's now see a sample program that performs the same on some randomly generated datasets. As always, we start with some header file and namespace declarations:

```
#include <iostream>
#include <opencv2/core/core.hpp>

using namespace std;
using namespace cv;

int main()
{
```

In our chapter on OpenCV basics (Chapter 1, *Laying the Foundation*), we stated that the Mat object can serve numerous other purposes apart from being containers that hold images. Here, we will use the Mat object to store our training data. In fact, all of the ML functions that we will discuss in this chapter accept data (and labels) in the form of Mat objects:

```
Mat_<float> data(10, 2);
data <<   0, 0,
              0.5, 0,
              0.5, 0.25,
              1, 1.25,
              1, 1.5,
              1, 1,
              0.5, 1.5,
              0.25, 1,
              2, 1.5,
              2, 2.5;
```

Let's take a closer look at how the data is arranged inside Mat. You can see that the data has 10 rows and 2 columns. Each row corresponds to a training data point and each column holds a feature value. This means that there are 10 training data points, and each point is represented by a feature vector of size 2.

Having defined our data, we now focus on setting up the parameters of the k-means clustering algorithm and calling the appropriate OpenCV function that runs the same. The very first thing that we need to do is fix a value of k. As you can see, we have set it to 2 (you can try out different values and compare the output. In fact, a good idea would be to accept the value of K as a command-line argument). We also define some criteria. As we discussed in the theory, the criteria object determines when to stop running the k-means clustering algorithm. As per our definitions in the next code, the code will stop when either of the following two things happens (whichever happens the earliest):

1. A maximum limit of 10 iterations is crossed.
2. None of the cluster centers change their positions by an amount which is greater than epsilon (0.000001).

Check out the following code:

```
int K = 2;
TermCriteria criteria(TermCriteria::EPS+TermCriteria::MAX_ITER, 10,
0.0001);
```

Having defined the data as well as the parameters that the algorithm needs to operate, we now move on to the function that does the actual computation:

```
Mat labels, centers;
kmeans(data, K, labels, criteria, 1, KMEANS_RANDOM_CENTERS, centers);
cout << labels << "\n";
cout << centers << "\n";
```

You will notice that we store results in a couple of different Mat objects: labels and centers. The labels Mat returns the cluster label for each data point in our dataset, whereas the centers object holds the cluster centers:

```
    return 0;
}
```

k-nearest neighbors classifier – introduction

We have covered an unsupervised learning algorithm: k-means clustering. It is time we move on to the supervised counterparts. We are going to discuss a machine learning algorithm that goes by the name of k-nearest neighbors classifier, often abbreviated as the **kNN** classifier. Although the names of both (k-means and kNN) sound similar, they are, in fact, somewhat different in their working, the most glaring difference being the fact that k-means clustering is an unsupervised technique used to divide the data points into meaningful clusters, while the kNN algorithm is a classifier that associates a class label with each data point.

As always, let's use an example to motivate the main concepts behind the kNN classification algorithm. In the previous example, we had information about the marks of every student in a couple of subjects. Based on this information, our goal was to divide them into some meaningful groups so that each group can then be subjected to a personalized curriculum. We saw how the k-means clustering algorithm helped us in our objective. Now, assume that this exercise was carried out in the school last year. The students were divided into groups as the algorithm deemed fit, and each group was made to undergo a personalized training program. At the end of the training program, the students were made to fill in a questionnaire where, among other things, they were asked whether they actually benefited from the training or not (a simple yes-no answer). Based on the feedback, the administration decided to record this information for each student. So this year round, the school has even more information available. Along with the students' marks in Mathematics and English, the school also has information about whether the training program last year was helpful for them. Also, note that since it was a simple yes-no question, the school administration decided to save this information using a binary label. That is, if the student answered with a *Yes*, then they saved a *1* alongside their name. On the other hand, if the answer was a *No*, then they put a *0* in place.

Great! But why go through all this hassle? Because the school is facing a new challenge this year. They want to repeat this experiment again for their new batch of students. Note that they already have the information about marks for the new batch. The question that they want to answer goes something like this:

> Given the marks in English and Mathematics for any student of our current batch this year, can we draw some inferences from our training program experience last year and predict whether the program this year would be beneficial to the concerned student or not?

Assume that you have been hired as a data scientist, or an ML engineer for the school. How would you proceed? We know what problem we are dealing with; let's try to translate the problem statement into a more technical framework and see how it fits into our machine learning paradigm.

The first question that you should answer is: is this data supervised or unsupervised. To address this question, let's try to figure out whether we have a label for each data point. Well yes! We have saved the information about whether the training program was beneficial to the students last year, and that serves as our label. This also means that all the student information from last year (along with the labels) becomes our training set and the student information from the current (which only has the features, or marks, and no labels) will become the test set. We will then try to employ a classifier on the training set, which will learn from the training data, and try to classify the data points in the test data set. That is, from the marks obtained by a student in the current batch (features in the test set), it will try to figure out whether the training would be useful for him/her this year round (the *0 – 1* label). To do so, it would use some rules that it learnt by looking at the marks and the labels from the training set. This seems to be the perfect example for our supervised machine learning setup.

Now that we have everything figured out, let's dive into the details of the algorithm.

k-nearest neighbors classifier – algorithm

In this section, we will discuss how the kNN classifier operates. Keep in mind the objective we are trying to solve. Given the features (marks) of a student, we wish to predict whether the school's program will benefit them. We have last year's data to assist us in making this prediction.

The techniques that we'll use to visualize our data points in the feature space will be very similar to k-means clustering. At the very outset, we plot each point belonging to the training data set in the 2D feature space. Recall that when we initially plotted the data points for k-means clustering, we represented all points using a gray colored box (that is, all points were identical to begin with). However, in the case of kNN, our data is supervised. This means that there is a label (*0* or *1*, in our case) associated with each data point. In order to visualize the position of both the data point in the feature space and the class it belongs to, we represent the points using different shapes and colors as shown:

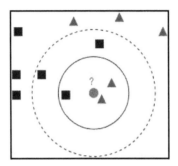

Ignore the dotted circles and the green colored point for now; we will come to that soon. You can assume that the blue squares represent the students belonging to class '1', that is, those who benefited from the academic training program, and the red triangles represent the students who felt the program wasn't beneficial (class '0'). This is what our training data looks like.

Having said that, let's come to the main issue. Now, suppose we have the marks for a student belonging to this year's batch. If we know his marks, it means we know the position of the corresponding data point in the feature space (we call it the test or the query point). Let's represent that using a green colored circle as shown in the preceding diagram. We want to predict the label for this query point. In other words, we want to know whether the student would belong to class *0* or class *1*, that is, whether he is likely to benefit from a similar program by the school. How does the kNN go about doing that?

If the same question is put to a layman, what do you think their answer would be? Well, one of the obvious things you could do is to take a quick look around and see what class(es) the immediate neighbors of the test point belong to. Based on that information, you could make an educated guess on the class label of the test point. This is exactly the intuition behind the operation of the kNN classifier.

Let's put this more formally. Given a query point, the kNN classifier looks at the k-nearest neighbors in the feature space. The class assigned to the query point will be the one that has a majority among the k-neighbors. So, in the preceding example, let's say that $k = 3$. So, we look at the three points that are closest to our query point in green. These are enclosed by the (solid) circle. Among those three points, we see that two of them belong to class *0* (red triangles) whereas one belongs to class *1* (blue circle). This means that class *0* has a majority here, and hence, our query point gets classified under class *0*.

What k to use

Now, what would happen if we select the value of k to be 5 instead of 3? Well, the function of the algorithm remains exactly the same. Now, we will look at the five nearest points. These are enclosed by the dotted circle in the preceding diagram. It will be a good exercise to work the solution out for yourself! You will notice that changing the value of k changes the prediction for the given query point. Clearly, the output for any given test data point depends on the value of k that we use. So then, how do we decide on the appropriate value of k?

The value of k in a kNN classifier is what what we call a **hyperparameter**. In simple words, they are parameters that affect the working of the algorithm. Proper selection of hyperparameters is a crucial step in most machine learning solutions. Before we share some tips on how to optimize for a particular value of k, let's get an idea of what problems we would run into if we select the wrong k value.

Let's take two extremes. What would happen if we set k to 1? This would mean that the prediction for any query point would happen by looking at the class of only the nearest data point. Can you think of any scenarios where this might not be a good idea? What do you think will happen in the scenario in the following diagram:

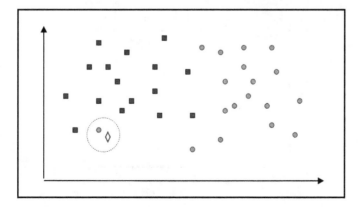

The query point (the data point that is shaped in the form of a diamond) gets classified as belonging to the *green* class. Do you think that this is a good prediction? By visually inspecting the preceding diagram, it is not difficult to see that the region of the feature space where the query point falls is more suited to the *red* class. The solitary data point belonging to the *green* class that has found its way into the *red* region of the feature space is termed as an outlier. When you deal with real-world data, you will come across such outliers on a regular basis. The takeaway from this discussion is that selecting an extremely small value of k (such as 1) can make our prediction system sensitive to outliers. As a side note, the kNN classifier with $k = 1$ is termed as the nearest neighbor classifier.

How about the opposite scenario? What if we set k to be equal to the number of data points in our training set? It is quite apparent that this is a foolish thing to do. Setting k to the size of the training set is tantamount to saying that we will take the vote of all the points in our data set for determining the label of any query point. Now, since the class labels for the points in our training set are fixed, the outcome of the majority vote will be the same for every single query point. That is not an intelligent classifier at all!

So, now that we know the importance of selecting an appropriate value for k, how do we go about doing that? There is no universal answer to the question. It depends on the training data that you have. A good practice is to test the accuracy of your system for a handful of k values and select the one that gives you the best results. Such a technique for hyperparameter optimization is known as **grid-search**. The term *grid-search* comes from the fact that if there are multiple hyperparameters that we need to optimize (instead of a single k as in the case here), then this method essentially iterates over all possible combinations of the values of both the parameters and then selects the best ones, based on an accuracy metric. We will return to grid-search when we discuss it in the context of support vector machines (a supervised classification algorithm that we will discuss in the upcoming sections of the chapter):

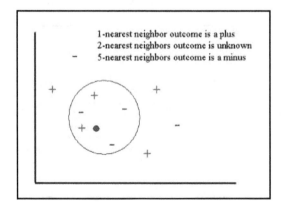

k-nearest neighbors classifier in OpenCV

In this section, we will look at the implementation of the kNN algorithm in OpenCV. The definitions for all the ML-related functions reside in the *ml* module of OpenCV. From now on, whatever code we write will be including the following header file among the declarations in the beginning of the code:

```
#include <opencv2/ml/ml.hpp>
```

So, we start off with the following set of declarations:

```
#include <iostream>
#include <opencv2/core/core.hpp>
#include <opencv2/ml/ml.hpp>

using namespace std;
using namespace cv;

int main()
{
```

Before we can start running the kNN classification algorithm, we need to declare a kNN model that will be responsible for performing all the kNN classification related operations:

```
Ptr<ml::KNearest> knn(ml::KNearest::create());
```

Now that we have initialized our model, the next step is to prepare the training data. Since, we are working within the realm of OpenCV, it is no surprise that the training data will be supplied to kNN in the form of a Mat object:

```
Mat_<float> trainingData(10, 2);
trainingData <<  0, 0,
                 0.5, 0,
                 0.5, 0.25,
                 1, 1.25,
                 1, 1.5,
                 1, 1,
                 0.5, 1.5,
                 0.25, 1,
                 2, 1.5,
                 2, 2.5;
```

The preceding lines of code declare a Mat object that stores the training data.

We have established that kNN is a supervised learning algorithm. This means that each data point that we just defined needs to have a label as well. We will store these labels in a separate Mat object, as follows:

```
Mat_<int> trainingLabels(1, 10);
trainingLabels << 0, 0, 0, 1, 1, 1, 0, 1, 1, 1;
```

Note that the trainingLabels matrix holding the label values has 1 row and 10 columns. This means that all the labels are stored in the same row and the number of columns is equal to the number of training data points that we have defined earlier, that is, 10.

We have all the information we need to train our kNN model. So, the next line of code uses the kNN model object we had declared right at the outset in order to call the train() function and pass the relevant parameters:

```
knn->train(trainingData, ml::ROW_SAMPLE, trainingLabels);
```

As you can see, we have passed the two Mat objects holding our training data and class labels for each of the training data points to the train() function. In addition to that, we have also passed another flag: ml::ROW_SAMPLE. This basically tells the train() function that we have stored our training data in the row major format, that is, one data point per row.

Now, that our model has seen (and learned from) all the training data, it is time to test our classifier with some test data points. Similar in spirit to the manner in which we handled our training data, we will use Mat objects to store our test data and send it to the classifier for prediction:

```
Mat_<float> testFeatures(1, 2);
testFeatures << 2.5, 2.5;

int K = 4;
Mat nearestNeighbors, distances;
knn->findNearest(testFeatures, K, noArray(), nearestNeighbors,
distances);
    cout << nearestNeighbors << "\n";
    cout << distances    << "\n";
```

In the preceding code snippet, we set the value of K to be 4. You will notice that we have used a couple of Mat objects, nearestNeighbors and distances, to save and display the results. The former stores the class labels of the k-nearest neighbors of the query point. Since we have a single query (test) data point, the nearestNeighbors Mat will have just 1 row. The number of columns is equal to K (it is easy to reason why). Similarly, the distances Mat object (also having the same dimensions as nearestNeighbors) stores the distances of the k-nearest neighbors from the query point.

Some problems with kNN

We have gone over the idea behind the kNN classification algorithm in great detail and also looked at the code that runs the kNN classifier on some data using OpenCV/C++. Before we close the section on kNN, let's look at some problems with such a classifier. No algorithm or system that you would build using machine learning will be perfect. It is no surprise that all the machine learning algorithms have their own set of pros and cons. It's exactly due to this reason that ML is a continuously evolving field. So, what are some situations where using a kNN classifier might not be the best idea?

One of the situations where kNN might fail to perform is a skewed dataset with a highly unbalanced distribution of classes. Again, let's use our example to understand this situation better. Let's suppose that our training data had 1,000 data points. This means that the school had managed to collect a record of 1,000 students along with the label. Say, out of those 1,000 students, 950 of them had responded favorably when asked about the utility of the training program. This means that our training data set has 950 examples of class *1* and a mere 50 examples belonging to class *0*. So, how does this affect the operation of our algorithm? If the data is dominated by examples belonging to class *1*, then it is highly likely that the k-neighborhood of any random query point will also have a majority of examples from class *1*. This means that more often than not, our query points end up being classified into the class that dominates our training data. Note that this is not a problem of the algorithm per se. It is still doing a logical operation: looking at the neighbors of the query point in order to make an educated guess about its class membership. Rather, our data is at fault. If we do not *show* the kNN algorithm enough examples of both classes, *0* and *1*, it is never going to be able to perform well on the test data. In this scenario, it hasn't seen enough examples of students who didn't like the training program. So, it's not surprising when it classifies most of the query points under class *1*.

There is one more scenario where kNN is known to give subpar results–the presence of irrelevant features in our training set. Let's see what that means. In our example, we considered the marks of just a couple of subjects, English and Mathematics, as features. Did you ever wonder about the choice of subjects? Why only these two? Well, it may have been because the training program was based on the student's' knowledge of these two subjects alone. What if we had completely ignored this fact and taken the marks of the students in five subjects as our features. What kind of an effect do you think it would have had on the kNN classifier performance? You may think that after all, the more features we have for our students, the more informative and richer is our representation in the feature space! However, that is not always the case with machine learning! In fact this counter-intuitive phenomena is a very common pitfall for early ML enthusiasts.

It is easy to see that using extra (irrelevant features) has a detrimental effect on the classifier. Imagine two students with the following profiles:

```
Student_1 = {Mathematics=90, English=85, Science=95, Social_Science=91,
Music=83}
Student_2 = {Mathematics=88, English=87, Science=65, Social_Science=71,
Music=98}
```

You can see that they have quite similar profiles when it comes to English and Maths. However, there is a huge difference in marks when it comes to the other three subjects. As a consequence of this discrepancy in the non-relevant subjects, the data points corresponding to Student_1 and Student_2 will be separated in the feature space by a huge margin when they should have been placed in close proximity to each other.

Some enhancements to kNN

We have seen cases where kNN might fail to give reasonably good results. In this section, let's briefly discuss some enhancements to the classifier, which aim to improve its classification performance.

First, we have used the Euclidean distance as a measure of similarity between data points in the feature space. The Euclidean distance between two d-dimensional vectors x and y is given by the following relation:

$$d(x, y) = \sqrt{\sum_{i=1}^{d}(x_i - y_i)^2}$$

In fact, the Euclidean distance (also known as the Euclidean norm) is a special type of distance that belongs to a family of norms that goes by the name L_p norm. The general formula for calculating the L_p norm between two vectors is given by the following equation:

$$L_p(x, y) = \left(\sum_{i=1}^{d} |x_i - y_i|^p\right)^{\frac{1}{p}}$$

You can easily check that putting $p = 2$ in the preceding equation leads us to the formula for Euclidean distance. Hence, the Euclidean distance is also known as the L2 norm. Another very commonly used norm is the L1 norm that is given by the following equation:

$$L_1\left(x, y\right) = \sum_{i=1}^{d} \left|x_i - y_i\right|)$$

This is also known as the Manhattan distance. In fact, it is often used in place of the Euclidean distance for some ML applications.

Apart from using different variants of the distance metric as shown here, there is one more noteworthy way in which the kNN classifier can be modified. The variant that we will talk about right now offsets one of the issues with kNN that we discussed a while back–imbalanced class distribution.

Imagine that we have decided on a particular value for k, and for a given query point, we are looking at the k-nearest neighbors of that point. These k data points (the nearest neighbors) will each get to *vote* and decide the class label for the query point (that's one way to look at it). Now, the way kNN operates is that the vote cast by each of the neighbors has equal importance. However, that is not a very good idea because a data point situated far away from the query (but within the radius of k-neighbors) should have a lesser influence on deciding the label for the query than a point which is relatively nearer. To capture this idea, a new variant called the **weighted kNN** algorithm was proposed. What weighted kNN does is that it assigns a weight to each of the k-nearest neighbors, which is inversely proportional to the distance of that neighbor from the query point. These weights play their roles during the voting process by giving importance to each neighbor in accordance with its distance from the query point.

Support vector machines (SVMs) – introduction

Right at the outset of this chapter, we defined the modus operandi of machine learning algorithms. If you recall, we had said that an ML system is presented with training data. It then makes its *own set of rules or builds a model*, which it uses to further make predictions on unseen (test) data. By revisiting this definition, I want to focus on the two key things that an ML algorithm can do with the training data:

1. Formulate a set of rules.

2. Build a model.

We have covered the basics of the k-nearest neighbor classifier in great detail. Let's try to place the operation of the kNN algorithm in the context of the two points we have listed above. Given the training data and a query point to classify, the kNN looks at the neighboring points and decides the class of the query point based on a majority vote. Clearly, this is a case of an ML algorithm that applies a set of rules based on the training data it has been presented with for the purpose of classifying a given query point, the rules here being to take a majority vote among the neighboring points in the training data set.

So, now we are going to look at yet another classification algorithm that falls under the supervised learning paradigm. In contrast to the kNN classifier, this technique is known to construct a *model* by looking at the examples in the training data set, which means that it operates under the context of point (2) that we just listed. The classifier is known as **support vector machine**, often abbreviated as **SVM**.

Intuition into the workings of SVMs

Before we get into the nitty-gritty of any ML algorithm, it is very important to have a good grasp of its intuitions. So, as always, we shall start with the same. For motivating SVMs, we shall operate in the same problem space of binary classification. That is, given a query, we have to predict a *0* or *1* label for the same. Often, the *0 – 1* labels are replaced by *-1 – +1*. The idea is the same–assigning a numeric label to each of the two possible classes.

Again, consider the two-dimensional feature space. The data points plotted in the following diagram (ignore the jumble of straight lines that you see for the time being) should be familiar to you by now. Let's say that the squares represent the points belonging to class *-1* and that the circles belong to class *+1*. Note that we are not adhering to any specific examples (such as our students and training program), but we are operating within the general domain of data, features, and classes. By this point of time, I guess you should be comfortable enough with the related concepts to understand the discussions without resorting to the specifics of examples:

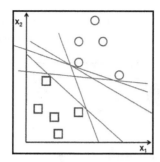

So, given the training data, how does the SVM classifier classify unseen data? What it tries to do is astonishingly simple. The SVM classifier tries to come up with a line that it thinks best separates the two groups of points. Speaking in terms of ML jargon, the idea of "coming up" with a line is referred to by the term, *fitting a line*. So, in other words, it tries to fit a line that it feels best separates the two classes of data.

But there is still a problem. Look at the preceding figure. You can see a lot of lines (in green) drawn in the feature space. All of the lines do the job of segregating the points belonging to the two classes, which means that all of them are viable solutions as per the SVM classifier. So, does it use all of them? One of them? If it selects just one of them, which one?

The answer is that it indeed selects just one among them. The basis on which it makes that selection warrants a nuanced discussion. Let's say that the classifier decided to select the green line that is almost touching the two red squares in the preceding diagram as we have noted that this is a valid separation of our training data. However, do you think that it is a good separation? Clearly no! This is due to a reason very similar to the one we encountered during our discussions on the drawbacks of kNN–sensitivity to outliers. Let me explain this in detail.

If our separating boundary passes very close to a cluster of data points, then we have a problem. Imagine that, during test time, we encounter another data point belonging to class '-1' (a red square), which, although lying reasonably close to the other red squares, unfortunately falls on the other side of the line of separation (on account of the line being so terribly close to our cluster of red squares). In such a scenario, our SVM classifier will classify the point as belonging to the other class (blue circles). However, we know that the query point was better represented as being a red square. The same line of reasoning applies to separating lines which lie close to the cluster of blue circles.

The following diagram is a visual representation of the concept that we just discussed. Imagine this is the distribution of our training data and a separating line fitted by the SVM:

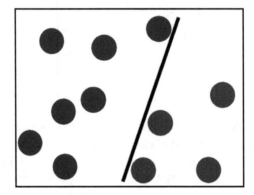

Now, say, we introduce another point which gets misclassified (as per our discussion) on account of the line being too close to the cluster of red points:

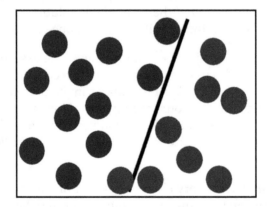

So, what is the solution to this conundrum? You might have started to guess the solutions on your own! Yes, instead of choosing lines which are close to either of the classes, we select lines that lie approximately in the middle. The original creators of the SVM algorithm formalized this intuition into a mathematical optimization problem–they selected a particular line that maximizes the margin between the two classes as the decision boundary (note that the separating line is called the decision boundary). The following diagram should make it clear:

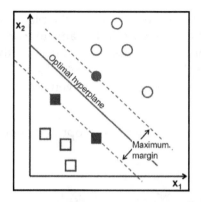

So far, we have been explaining everything in the two dimensional domain. However, the SVM classifier is in no way restricted to the 2D domain (this holds true for the kNN classifier as well). Depending on the problem domain that we are applying the SVM classifier to, we can extract as many features from our data as we want, and consequently, our classification problem then lies in an *n*-dimensional space. So, let's assume that instead of 2D, our data was in the 3D space. Then, how would the SVM classifier operate? Well, the mode of operation would remain exactly the same. Instead of a straight line, the classifier would now fit a plane to segregate the data points. Here is a visualization of this:

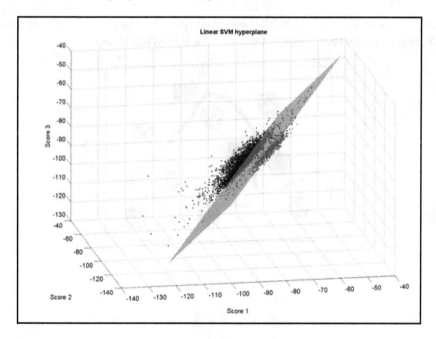

What if we go to even higher dimensions? Just like the plane is a 3D *generalization* of a straight line in 2D, what is the counterpart of the same in 4 or higher dimensional spaces? Well, thankfully, we have a terminology that is used irrespective of the number of dimensions. We call it a **hyperplane**. So, when we say *hyperplane* in 2D, we mean a straight line, whereas in 3D, it would refer to a plane. For even higher dimensions, it represents the respective counterparts.

So, now we can say that an SVM classifier fits an optimal hyperplane that maximizes the margin of separation between classes.

Non-linear SVMs

If you have been following the discussion on SVMs closely, you will have noticed a fundamental limitation in the way an SVM operates. We have discussed how the SVM classifier fits a hyperplane to our data such that the margin of separation between the classes is maximized. Now, doing that involves a very strong assumption. It assumes that our data is linearly separable. This is another fancy way of saying that we can separate the data using geometrical structures such as straight lines or planes (hyperplanes, in general). What would happen if our data is non-linearly separable.

For example, try as hard as you would, there is simply no way that you can fit a straight line that can separate the two classes of data in the following image:

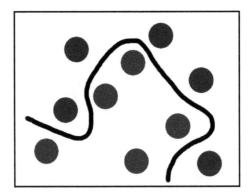

As you can see, the decision boundary here is highly non-linear. So, how does an SVM classifier overcome this? The answer is known as the *kernel trick*.

The basic idea behind the kernel trick is that even if our data is not linearly separable in the input space, we can *transform* the input vectors to another feature space where the data would be linearly separable. Check the following image for an illustration of the concept:

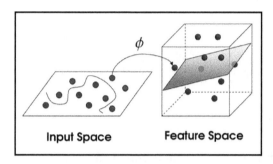

Kernels are mathematical operators that aid us in this transformation process. Well, this is not entirely accurate (and you would find ML purists cringing if you tell them this definition), but our aim here is to get an intuitive understanding of the working of various ML systems without going into the mathematical intricacies. For this purpose, the intuition that we have provided here for kernels would suffice. Note that each data point in the input space goes through the exact same transformation to end up as another point in the (new) feature space. Again, this transformation is necessary because the data becomes linearly separable in the transformed feature space and the SVM algorithm can proceed with its usual workflow!

So, what are the examples of some popular kernels? There are a lot of different types of kernels that have been proposed, and the creators of OpenCV have made some of them available for our use. Some examples are listed as follows:

- Linear: The linear kernel refers to the case where no mapping is done from the input to the feature space (a simple, vanilla SVM classifier)
- Polynomial
- Radial Basis Function

In the next section, we will see how we can apply different kernels using the APIs that OpenCV has provided for us.

SVM in OpenCV

In this section, we demonstrate a basic implementation that runs the SVM classifier on a dataset (the same dataset that we have been using for k-means and kNN):

```cpp
#include <iostream>
#include <opencv2/core.hpp>
#include <opencv2/ml.hpp>

using namespace std;
using namespace cv;
using namespace cv::ml;

int main()
{
```

The setting up of the training and test data remains the same:

```cpp
Mat_<float> trainingData(10, 2);
trainingData <<   0, 0,
                  0.5, 0,
                  0.5, 0.25,
                  1, 1.25,
                  1, 1.5,
                  1, 1,
                  0.5, 1.5,
                  0.25, 1,
                  2, 1.5,
                  2, 2.5;
Mat_<int> trainingLabels(1, 10);
trainingLabels << 0, 0, 0, 1, 1, 1, 0, 1, 1, 1;
```

Similar to the kNN classifier, we first create an SVM object, and then use it to set some properties of the SVM classifier that we want to train:

```cpp
Ptr<SVM> svm = SVM::create();
svm->setType(SVM::C_SVC);
svm->setKernel(SVM::LINEAR);
svm->setTermCriteria(TermCriteria(TermCriteria::MAX_ITER, 100, 1e-6));

svm->train(trainingData, ROW_SAMPLE, trainingLabels);

Mat_<float> testFeatures(1, 2);
testFeatures << 2.5, 2.5;

Mat res;
svm->predict(testFeatures, res);
```

```
    cout << res << "\n";

    return 0;
}
```

Using an SVM as a gender classifier

Now that we have seen how to implement a generic SVM classifier using OpenCV/C++, in this section, we outline the steps to use SVM for the gender classification project that we have been working on.

If you noticed in the example that we discussed in the last section, the training data that we loaded was 2-dimensional and had 10 data points. In the previous chapter, we discussed the fact that we are going to represent our faces using the 531-dimensional uniform pattern LBP histogram descriptor. This means that each data point (face) will be represented using 531-dimensions. These values (the feature vector corresponding to the representation of a face) are usually read into the source code through text files. This means that we design our program to accept two files as input, one holding the feature vectors of the faces in the training data set and the other for the test data.

So essentially, this means that we want the feature descriptors of all our face images to be written down in text files, one descriptor per line. In addition to that, we also need the label corresponding to each face image. The label will tell us whether the face is male (*0*) or female (*1*). This information can accompany the feature vector as a suffix. What this means is that if we have a 531-dimension feature vector for a female face, the 531 real number values (the feature descriptor) will be followed by a *1* at the end. We will assume this protocol in the text files that we use for the SVM classifier code.

The following code snippet reads the feature vectors (and class labels) from the training and test data files and loads them into appropriate Mat objects:

```
int main(int argc, char** argv)
{
    if(argc != 3)
    {
        cout << "USAGE: ./svm [TRAINING] [TEST]\n";
        return 1;
    }
    const char* training_file = argv[1];
    const char* test_file = argv[2];

    ifstream fin_train, fin_test;
    fin_train.open(training_file);
```

```
fin_test.open(test_file);

Mat training_data(NUM_TRAINING_EXAMPLES, NUM_FEATURES, CV_32FC1);
Mat class_labels(NUM_TRAINING_EXAMPLES, 1, CV_32FC1);
Mat test_data(NUM_TEST_EXAMPLES, NUM_FEATURES, CV_32FC1);
Mat prediction_results(NUM_TEST_EXAMPLES, 1, CV_32FC1);

for(int i = 0; i < NUM_TRAINING_EXAMPLES; ++i)
{
    for(int j = 0; j < (NUM_FEATURES+1); ++j)
    {
        vector<float> example((NUM_FEATURES+1), 0.0f);
        fin_train >> example[j];

        if(j < NUM_FEATURES)
            training_data.at<float>(i, j) = example[j];
        else
            class_labels.at<float>(i, 0) = example[j];
    }
}

vector<float> correct_results(NUM_TEST_EXAMPLES, 0.0f);
for(int i = 0; i < NUM_TEST_EXAMPLES; ++i)
{
    for(int j = 0; j < (NUM_FEATURES+1); ++j)
    {
        if(j < NUM_FEATURES)
            fin_test >> test_data.at<float>(i, j);
        else
            fin_test >> correct_results[i];
    }
}
```

The remainder of the code for actually training the SVM remains the same as the previous example, with slight modifications to the SVM parameters. In the previous example, we worked with linear SVMs, but for this case, we are going to use the **radial basis function (RBF)** kernel. A lot of different kernels were tried out, and the RBF kernel was found to give the best results:

```
Ptr<SVM> svm = SVM::create();
svm->setType(SVM::C_SVC);
svm->setKernel(SVM::RBF);
svm->setC(2);
svm->setGamma(0.0000305176);
svm->setTermCriteria(TermCriteria(TermCriteria::MAX_ITER, 10000, 1e-6));

svm->train(training_data, ROW_SAMPLE, class_labels);
svm->predict(test_data, prediction_results);
```

After the SVM has been trained and the trained model run on our test data, we can display the predicted and the actual class labels side-by-side:

```
for(int i = 0; i < NUM_TEST_EXAMPLES; ++i) {1
        float prediction = prediction_results.at<float>(i, 0);
        cout << prediction << " " << correct_results[i] << "\n";
}
```

With the knowledge of the actual class and the predicted class labels for our test data, we can get quantitative estimates of how good or bad is our classifier's performance. One obvious metric that you might calculate is the overall accuracy–the percentage of correct classifications over the entire test set. In our upcoming section, *Common evaluation metrics*, we discuss a few more informative measures that we can look at.

Overfitting

This completes our discussion on some representative machine learning algorithms. We will now focus on some extremely crucial issues that we need to keep in mind while we apply these ML algorithms in any application domain. First, we will discuss the concept of *overfitting* to our training data.

The whole point of presenting our learning algorithm with training data is that it can, in the future, predict labels for data points that it has never seen. The ability of any learning algorithm to apply its learnt set of rules to completely new and unseen data is known as the **generalization** ability of the algorithm. The aim of training any ML classifier is that it should generalize unseen data well.

Let's briefly go back to an example that we introduced early on in this chapter. When students attend classes, a professor teaches them a concept using some illustrative examples (training data). The students (ML algorithms) are expected to build a mental model out of the information they are exposed to during the lectures so that they can solve similar (but not exactly the same) problems in quizzes and/or exams (the test data set). Now, imagine a student who simply memorizes everything that has been taught in class (without thinking about the why's and how's). When such a student faces a slightly modified version of the classroom problems in the exam, he/she will be at a complete loss and will obviously not perform well in the test. This is a classic example of what happens when a training algorithm starts overfitting the data. They might perform exceptionally well on the training set (due to memorization) but fail to perform in the test set.

To see how this phenomenon looks in real-world machine learning settings, look at the following diagram:

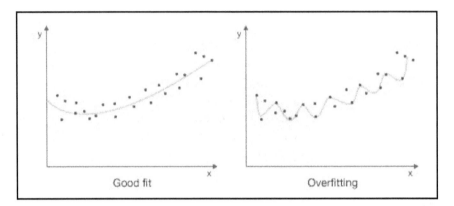

Out of the two curves, which one do you think accurately predicts the distribution of the underlying data? The one on the left. This is because it has successfully managed to capture the variations in the data at a sufficiently abstract level. What this means is that it doesn't try to *over-optimize* on the data by enforcing the curve to pass through each data point. Rather, it has observed the *general trend*. On the other hand, the curve on the right does a rigorous optimization by attempting to make the curve pass through every single point in the training set. It is quite intuitive to see that if you over-optimize on the training set, then you will perform pretty poorly on the test set. You don't know where the test data might come from, so you have to keep some *room* for accommodating the test data points in your model, and that can never happen in a situation similar to the overfitted model on the right.

Cross-validation

Now that we know overfitting is a serious issue in designing and running machine learning-based systems, let's look at a way in which we can mitigate its effects. Remember that we need to ensure that our learning algorithm doesn't start overfitting on the training data; instead, it should maintain a good enough generalization power to predict labels on unseen data.

How can we enforce such a behavior? Let's go back to our classroom example. To make sure that the students are actually understanding the concepts and not merely overfitting by memorizing the classroom problems, the teacher hands over certain assignments. These assignments contain questions that are similar in concept to what has been taught in the classroom but at the same time, also give the students an idea of the type of questions to expect in the actual exam. In machine learning parlance, the assignments are analogous to the validation set. The students are expected to periodically check their level of understanding by solving problems from the assignments. Once they feel confident regarding their performance in the problems laid out in the assignments, they can then proceed to take the examinations (the test data set).

So, we have already come across training and test sets and now we introduce another type of data set called the validation set. To avoid any potential confusion among the three, we will clearly delineate their respective roles.

Whenever we obtain a dataset, our first step is to separate it out into 2 disjointed subsets: the training and the test data set. Usually, an 80-20 split is considered to be good (sometimes people may also go for a 75-25 split). This means that 80% of our data becomes the training data whereas the remaining 20% is the test set. Now, the test set is kept aside, we won't be touching the test data until our model is ready for testing. Now, we take the training data and further segregate it into training and validation data sets (here, a 90-10 split for train-validate is done). The actual training happens on the training data set (this is the data that our ML algorithm will look at). Occasionally, at regular intervals, we pause the training and evaluate our performance on the validation set (to get an idea of how well we are generalizing). The following diagram will make it clearer:

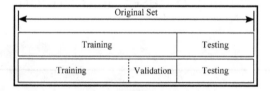

To avoid overfitting, the validation error (that we periodically check) must show a decline. If you notice that with the passage of time (as the model gets trained), the validation error starts to increase, this is a clear indication that our learning model has started to overfit on the training data (thereby causing the error on the (unseen) validation data to increase). Note that, in some sense, the validation data set is another type of test data set. However, it is used as an aide to the training process, whereas the actual test set is used after we are confident that our models have been successfully trained.

The use of validation sets goes well beyond keeping a check for possible overfitting. Remember our discussions on hyperparameters in the section on kNN classifiers? We can use the validation set to choose the optimal hyperparameter(s) for our model! How do we do that? Let's take a very simplistic example and say that we have to select among four different choices of k in kNN: $k = 3, 5, 7,$ and 9. We take each possible value of k and run the kNN classifier on the validation set and record the accuracy. We select a particular value of k that gives us the best accuracy figures. Now, when we want to run our model on the test data, we will use the k that we selected using the validation set.

As an illustration, we show the following two pie-charts, which represent the distribution of classes (**Male** and **Female**) for the LFW dataset that we have been using for our gender classification experiments. The green region represents male faces whereas orange represents female:

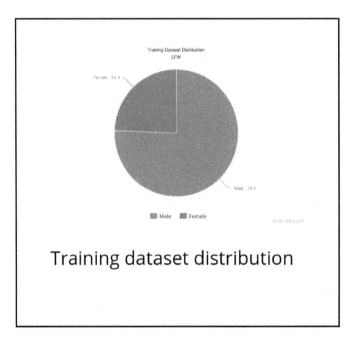

Training dataset distribution

As stated earlier, we do an 80-20 split on the entire dataset to divide it into train and test. The validation set is sampled from within the training set later:

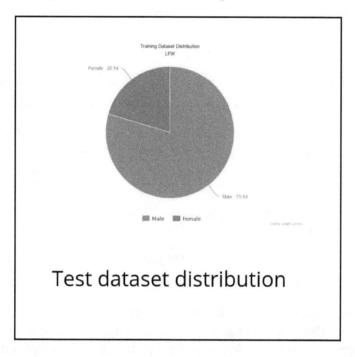

Test dataset distribution

Common evaluation metrics

I hope the previous section gave you a nice insight of how to deal with your dataset while training ML models and also how to avoid some common pitfalls such as overfitting. In this section, we will take a brief look at some evaluation metrics that can help us judge how well our model is performing. For the purpose of all our explanations, we will assume a binary classification framework.

Before we begin, let's introduce some new terminologies. When we are dealing with a binary problem, instead of labelling the classes as *0 – 1*, or even *+1 – -1*, we usually prefer to use the labels, *positive* and *negative*. Which of the two classes is positive is a choice that is left to the designers of the ML algorithm. Now, having said that, each prediction that our algorithm makes on the test data can be classified into the following four categories:

- **True positive** (TP): The data points which actually belong to the positive class, and have indeed been classified as positive by our learning algorithm

- **True negatives (TN)**: The data points which belong to the negative class and have been correctly classified as such
- **False positives (FP)**: The data points which belong to the positive class but have been incorrectly classified by our algorithm
- **False negatives (FN)**: I think you get the drift by now

Here is a table that summarizes all the four categories that we have just described:

		Actual	
		0	1
Predicted	0	True Negative	False Negative
	1	False Positive	True Positive

Now, having stated all the different types of classification scenarios that might emerge from a binary classification task, here are some evaluation metrics that are used quite often

- **Overall accuracy**: This is the most simple and intuitive evaluation metric that everyone is most familiar with. It can computed as $\frac{TP \quad TN}{(TP+TN+FP+FN)}$.
- **Precision**: The precision value tells us the number of examples that actually belong to the positive class out of the total number of examples that have been classified as positive. Mathematically, this can be expressed as $\frac{TP}{(TP+FP)}$.
- **Recall**: This is a metric that tells us the fraction of examples our system was able to classify correctly out of all the positive examples that were present in the test set. This means that the formula for recall turns out to be $\frac{TP}{(TP+FN)}$.

There is a very subtle nuance between precision and recall. We are going to explain the same in the next section. Before that, we present some metrics for the gender classification task. Note that these figures represent the performance of an SVM-based classifier using the uniform pattern LBP histogram features to represent cropped and aligned facial images:

	Precision	Recall
Male	92.11	92

| Female | 70 | 69.5 |

While calculating the precision and recall values for a particular gender category, we assume that category to be the positive class and the other automatically becomes the negative class. It might also interest you to know that the overall accuracy of our system stands at 87.38%. The statistics for the *Female* class are not as good as those of the *Male* class primarily because of the imbalance in the dataset (refer to the dataset statistics pie-charts).

The P-R curve

Why do we need two separate metrics–precision as well as recall? Let's dig a little deeper into their meanings. When we say that a classification system has a high precision, what does it exactly mean? It means that if the system predicts that a particular data point belongs to the positive class, then there is a very high probability that it indeed does so. You can revisit the definition of precision to convince yourself that this is indeed the case. Now, imagine that we have a classification system in place at a pathological laboratory, which, given the necessary medical details of a patient, classifies it as a positive (or a negative) occurrence of cancer. Now, obviously, we would want such a system to have a very high precision. It would be disastrous (mentally, physically, and financially) to tell a healthy patient that they have been diagnosed with cancer.

Now, we would like our cancer classifier to have a high recall. Having a low recall would mean that there are a lot of cancer cases that are not being reported at all! This is equally as disastrous as the previous outcome. In fact, such an expectation is common from all binary classification systems. We would want the precision and recall both to be high. Unfortunately, maximizing both of them at the same time is not possible.

This leads us to what we call **Precision-Recall curves** (or **P-R curves**). As the name suggests, they plot the different combinations of precision and recall values. Now, looking at the P-R curve of a classifier, we can decide on the region of operation. This means that we can select a combination of precision and recall values that best suits our needs and then use the model that operates on that P-R value.

The following image is an example of a P-R curve (positive class = 'Female') for our gender classification problem using an SVM classifier:

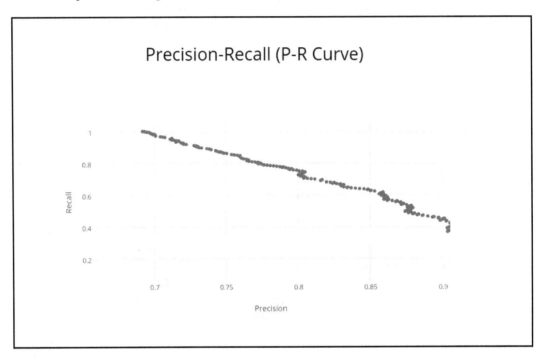

Some qualitative results

So, we have covered a lot of ground in this chapter! Before we close, it would be a good idea to see what all this effort has resulted in. One of the key motivations of doing an image processing computer vision project is that by the end of it, you get to see some really cool results!

The following are some images which have been classified as *Male* by our algorithm! There are some interesting results for Justin Bieber fans:

Female Predictions

In the following image, you can see some *Male* predictions:

Male Predictions

Summary

This brings us to the end of our chapter on machine learning with OpenCV. We started the chapter by introducing the *learning* paradigm of solving problems. Under such a scheme, we saw that if our algorithm is presented with a lot of data, it can learn to detect patterns and develop its own set of rules that the further help to make predictions on new, unseen data.

We touched upon a lot of different aspects of ML, both in the supervised and the unsupervised domain. We discussed in detail about the k-means clustering algorithm (unsupervised), k-nearest neighbors classifier, and support vector machines (both supervised). We also looked at some practical issues that crop up when we are trying to deploy a machine learning algorithm on our data. Also, you must have noticed that employing ML algorithms enables our programs to make much more human-like predictions using the available data.

This completes our journey that we began in Chapter 1, *Laying the Foundation*. The book started with the basics of images, gradually introduced the notion of grayscale transformations and image filtering as algorithms that involve manipulation of intensity values at a pixel-level. Then, from operating at a pixel-level, we moved on to aggregating pixel values into histograms. We also saw some more sophisticated vision algorithms which detected edges in images. Among the more exciting things that we saw in this book, we learnt how to write code that detects faces in images and further performs some basic operations such as cropping and alignment.

Moving ahead, we introduced the notion of image descriptors and learnt about LBP codes. In contrast to the form of image representation that we saw in Chapter 1, *Laying the Foundation*–raw image pixels being stored as a two-dimensional grid of values–the image descriptors that we discussed in Chapter 8, *Feature Descriptors in OpenCV* allow a more compact representation of images that is apt for subsequent processing (the machine learning algorithms that we saw in the current chapter).

Command-line Arguments in C++

When we started running our code on datasets of images, as opposed to a single image (or a handful of them), you learnt a neat trick. We could read the image names (image paths) off a file and then, once the image path is available to us, we could proceed with our usual image processing steps. So, the only thing that was left was to include the name of the file into our code and then pass it to the `open()` function of the `ifstream` class. And how did we do that (pass the filename to the code)? In some of the examples in this chapter, you would have come across something called **command-line arguments** that we used for this purpose. They are nothing but effective techniques used by all the programming languages (this is not something specific to just C++) to pass arguments (such as filenames) to your code. This Appendix section will be an attempt to demystify the same.

Introduction to command-line arguments

Most of the OpenCV programs that we have written so far require explicitly taking some input from the user. For example, it is highly likely that an OpenCV program would require an image (or video) to operate upon, and hence, requires a path to that multimedia file as an input. Alternatively, similar to the case we discussed just now, our code might need to read some text file to obtain the input, and the program needs to know the path of that text file. Most of the image processing and vision algorithms come with a set of parameters that need to be a specified-size of filters used in smoothing, threshold values for image thresholding or edge detectors, pre-trained classifier files for face detection, and so on. These parameter values also need to be passed to our code, and command-line arguments are an effective tool to accomplish that.

We will motivate the need for command-line arguments using a small dummy example. Let's say that we need to write a piece of code that adds two numbers. What do you think such a code will require from the user as input parameters? The two numbers to add, of course. Now, assuming that you haven't heard of command-line arguments, how would you go about accomplishing this task? There are a couple of different techniques that come to mind:

1. We could try hardcoding the values of the parameters in the source code itself (an approach we have been following throughout the major parts of the book).
2. We could have the user type in the value of the parameters in response to a program-generated prompt after the code has begun its execution.

Let's see how both these approaches look for our small example. We'll start with approach (1):

```
#include<iostream>
usingnamespacestd;

int add(int x,int y) {
    return(x + y);
}

int main()
{
intnum1=10,num2=20;
cout<<"Sum = "<< add(num1,num2)<<"\n";
    return0;
}
```

The problem with approach (1) is quite evident. If I want to test this code with 1000 different pairs of integers, I will have to make changes to the source code 1000 times and do as many re-compilations to get the outputs. Clearly, not something that can be scaled to a large data!

Now, moving on to approach (2), here is the same code, modified to take input through runtime prompts:

```
#include<iostream>
usingnamespacestd;

int add(int x,int y) {
    return(x + y);
}

int main()
{
```

```
intnum1,num2;
cout<<"Enter 1st number : ";
cin>>num1;

cout<<"Enter 2nd number : ";
cin>>num2;

cout<<"Sum = "<< add(num1,num2)<<"\n";
    return0;
}
```

Now, the preceding approach obviously counters the drawback in (1)–we no longer need a separate re-compilation every single time. However, there is an added hassle of writing out the prompt messages, which can make your source code quite messy. In fact, there is a bigger reason for not being in support of (2). It doesn't resonate with the *design principles* of developing good, clean, and reusable software code. Imagine what happens when you call, say, the blur() function in OpenCV to smooth an image. Does it throw out messages during the course of its execution urging you to pass the necessary parameter values? No, you quietly pass all that blur() might need in the form of arguments along with the function call. There is an implicit understanding between the user (any entity that calls the blur() function) and the function itself, where the user knows the number and the kind of arguments that the function is expecting. This is the *design principle* that we had been alluding to.

How do we port the same design principle to the case of the source codes that we write? In Linux (or any UNIX-based system), when we want to execute a C++ program, we generally follow this sequence of steps:

1. Compile the source code file by running, g++ addNumbers.cpp -o addNumbers.cpp. I have assumed that the preceding source code has been saved in a file, named addNumbers.cpp. This step should produce an executable file, named addNumbers.

2. Run the executable file generated in the previous step by running the command:./addNumbers.

Now, wouldn't it be nice if we could somehow pass the arguments (parameters) to our source codes while we are running the executable from our command-line. This is exactly what command-line arguments accomplish! When we are using command-line arguments, we would run the executable by writing a command, such as:

```
./addNumbers 1020
```

The `10` and `20` here are the command-line arguments. They offer a much more orderly, compact, and convenient method to supply parameters in comparison to any of the previous techniques. Also, it is quite easy to see that the mechanism of command-line arguments is not conceptually very different from passing arguments to functions in C++.

Parsing command-line arguments

Keep in mind that the job is half-done. We still need to incorporate the logic to parse the command-line arguments in our source code. Here is how it's done:

```cpp
#include<iostream>
#include<cstdlib>

usingnamespacestd;

int add(int x,int y) {
    return(x + y);
}

int main(intargc,char**argv)
{
intnum1=atoi(argv[1]),num2=atoi(argv[2]);
cout<<"Sum = "<< add(num1,num2)<<"\n";
    return0;
}
```

You might be seeing the `argc` and the `argv` variables for the first time. These are the two variables that allow us to access the arguments that were supplied from the command-line (the `10` and the `20`) inside our source code. When we execute our program, the operating system calls the `main()` function and also provides the command-line arguments as parameters to `main()` (remember, `main()` is just like any other C++ function; it can accept parameters and return values).

The `argc` integer variable holds the number of command-line arguments and the `argv` is an array of string (`char*`) values that contain the command-line arguments as strings. Now, there is one more nuance to this. If you try printing the value of `argc` for the preceding piece of code, you will see a value of 3 instead of the 2 that you were expecting. Why does this happen? This is because the operating system treats the program name as one of the arguments as well! Refer to the following illustration:

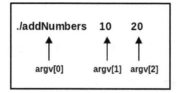

This is the reason that the two numbers have been pulled out from **argv[1]** and **argv[2]** in our code (as shown in the illustration). The **argv[0]**variable is reserved for the program name.

There is another issue with the preceding code. The logic we have implemented assumes that the user will supply two arguments while running the program from the command line. What happens if the arguments are not provided to our code or if only one argument is provided? It is evident that in such a scenario, either **argv[1]**or **argv[2]** (or both) would be undefined, and hence, the preceding code will throw an exception. How do we overcome such a scenario? We will make use of the `argc` argument. Recall that `argc` holds the number of command-line parameters that have actually been passed to the program during execution. So, we check whether `argc` is equal to the number of expected arguments. If not, then we simply display an informative error message and quit! The code for the same has been shown as follows:

```
#include<iostream>
#include<cstdlib>

usingnamespacestd;

int add(int x,int y) {
    return(x + y);
}

int main(intargc,char**argv)
{
if (arg != 2) {
cout<< "The program expects two integer parameters.\n";
        return -1;
  }

intnum1=atoi(argv[1]),num2=atoi(argv[2]);
cout<<"Sum = "<< add(num1,num2)<<"\n";
    return0;
}
```

Summary

In this Appendix, you learnt the basics of command-line arguments in C++ programs. We saw that these arguments are potent tools that allow the users to pass information (such as filenames or values for parameters) to our programs during execution time.

We looked at some alternatives to command-line arguments that reinforced the fact that they are indeed the cleanest and the most effective way to deal with such cases. We also saw how we can exploit the `argc` and `argv` parameters to process the parameters inside our C++ code. Incorporating the practices that are discussed in this chapter will indeed make your code easier to maintain, user-friendly, and professional.

Index

A

AdaBoost learning 184
adaptive thresholding
  about 94, 103, 106
  block size 107
  constant C 108
  maxValue 105
  thresholding type 106
algorithm, k-means clustering
  assignment 253
  initialization 253
  update 254
anchor point 60

B

binary images 92
binary threshold 98
blur detection
  OpenCV, using 167
boundary conditions 218
box filter 59

C

Canny edge detector
  about 159
  double threshold 159
  non-maximum suppression 159
cascaded classifiers 185, 186
cascades
  reference 188
classification system, images 173
color histogram
  in OpenCV 126
command-line arguments
  about 289, 290
  parsing 292

common evaluation metrics
  about 281
  categories 281
  overall accuracy 282
  precision 282
  recall 282
cross-validation 278, 281

D

dataset
  exploring 198
  face detection, running 200, 201, 202
  working with 195
digital image
  about 8
  color channels 11
  color depth 9
  pixel intensities 9
dilation
  about 111, 112, 114
  in OpenCV 112

E

edge detection
  about 137, 153
  and image noise 163
  Laplacian 165
  Sobel derivative filter, using 153
erosion
  about 110, 114
  in OpenCV 112
exponential transformation 46, 47, 49

F

face alignment
  about 204

image, cropping 220
pipeline 223, 226
face detection
  about 175
  detected faces quality, controlling 191, 193
  in OpenCV 189, 191
  running, on dataset 200
faces
  rotating 205, 206, 208, 210, 211, 212, 215
facial analysis
  steps 204
filters
  using, in OpenCV 77, 78

G

Gaussian filtering
  about 68, 70, 71, 73, 74, 75
  in OpenCV 75
Gaussian function 68, 70, 71, 73, 74, 75
Gaussian smoothing 66, 67, 68
gender classification 194
generalization ability 277
global threshold 94
grid-search 262

H

Haar features
  2-rectangle features 175
  3-rectangle features 175
  4-rectangle features 176
  about 175
histogram
  basics 116, 119
  dimensions 118
  in OpenCV 120, 121
  plotting, in OpenCV 121, 124, 125
  range 118
  size 118
hyperparameter 261
hyperplane 272

I

identity transformation 32
image classification framework 249, 250
image derivatives

about 138, 139, 141, 142
  in two dimensions 143, 144, 145
  visualizing, with OpenCV 145, 146, 147
image enhancement 51
image filters 55, 56, 57, 58
image noise
  about 79, 80, 81
  and edge detection 163
  Gaussian noise 80
  Salt and Pepper noise 80
image thresholding
  about 92, 94
  in OpenCV 95
  maximum value 96
  threshold value 96
  thresholding type 96
  types 97
image
  averaging, in OpenCV 54, 55, 59, 62, 64
  blurring, in OpenCV 66
  classification systems 172
  cropping 216, 218, 220
  cropping, for face alignment 220, 221, 222, 223
  enhancements 28
  filtering 52
integral image
  about 177, 179, 183
  in OpenCV 184
inverse-log transformation 46
inverted binary threshold 99
inverted threshold-to-zero 102, 103

K

k-means clustering
  algorithm 252
  basics 250, 252
  in OpenCV 256, 258
k-nearest neighbors classifier (kNN)
  about 258
  algorithm 259, 260, 261
  enhancements 266, 267
  in OpenCV 263, 264
  issues 265
  value of k, selecting 261, 262

L

Laplacian 165
linear transformations
  about 31
  identity transformations 32
  negative transformation 33
local binary patterns (LBP)
  about 230
  applying, to aligned facial images 239
  images, capturing 237, 238
  implementation 232, 241
  variants 234
log transformation 38, 40, 41, 42, 43, 44
logarithmic transformation
  about 38
  exponential transformation 46
  inverse-log transformation 46
  log transformation 38
lookup table (LUT) 30

M

machine learning 246, 247
main() function 242
Mat class
  about 11, 12
  default initialization value 19
  exploring 13
  images, loading 13, 14
  Mat objects, declaring 15
Mat objects
  about 8
  color channels 16
  color depth 16
  data matrix, continuity 23, 24
  declaring 15
  default initialization value 17
  exploring 19, 20, 21
  image size 17
  image traversals 24, 27
  spatial dimensions, of image 15
  traversing 22, 23
morphological operations 92, 108
multidimensional histograms
  in OpenCV 131

N

nearest neighbors classifier (kNN)
  issues 266
negative transformation 33, 34, 35, 36
non-linear support vector machines (SVMs) 272,
  273

O

OpenCV
  about 7
  color histograms 126
  dilation 112
  erosion 112
  face detection 186, 187, 189
  filters, using 77, 78
  Gaussian filtering 75
  histograms 120, 121
  histograms, plotting 121, 124, 125
  image averaging 58
  image thresholding 95
  image, blurring 65
  integral image 184
  k-means clustering 256, 258
  k-nearest neighbors classifier (kNN) 263, 264
  multidimensional histograms 131
  non-linear support vector machines (SVMs) 274
  used, for blur detection 167
  used, for visualizing image derivatives 145
  Vignetting implementation 83
overfitting 277, 278

P

parameters, Canny() function
  edges 160
  image 160
  L2 flag 161
  size of kernel 161
  threshold1 160
  threshold2 160
pixel 52, 53
Precision-Recall curves (P-R curves)
  about 283
  example 284

R

radial basis function (RBF) 276
region of interest (ROI) 19
results 284, 286

S

simple thresholding 94
Sobel derivative filter
  about 149, 150, 152
  using, for edge detection 154, 155, 156, 157
spatial histograms 240
supervised learning 248
supervised learning algorithm 173
support vector machines (SVMs)
  about 267, 268
  in OpenCV 274
  using, as gender classifier 275
  working 268, 269, 270

T

threshold-to-zero 100
truncate 100
types, image thresholding
  about 97

binary threshold 98
inverted binary threshold 99
inverted threshold-to-zero 102
threshold-to-zero 100
truncate 100

U

unsupervised learning 248

V

variants, local binary patterns (LBP) 234
variations, image derivatives
  backward difference 140
  central difference 140
  forward differences 140
Vignette filter 81
Vignette mask 81
Vignetting filter 81
Vignetting
  about 81, 82
  implementing, in OpenCV 83, 85, 86, 87

W

weighted kNN algorithm 267